My Father, My Don

Always

Tony Nap

Copyright © 2008, Tony Napoli

All rights reserved. Printed in the U.S.A.
No part of this publication may be reproduced or transmitted in any form or by any means, electronic or mechanical, including photocopy, recording or any information storage and retrieval system now known or to be invented, without permission in writing from the publisher, except by a reviewer who wishes to quote brief passages in connection with a review written for inclusion in a magazine, newspaper or broadcast.

Published in the United States by
Beckham Publications Group, Inc.
P.O. Box 4066, Silver Spring, MD 20914

ISBN: 978-0-9802380-5-1

Library of Congress Control Number:
2008928864

for Bear

My Father, My Don

A Son's Journey from Organized Crime to Sobriety

Che Bella

Tony Napoli
with
Charles Messina

*Always
Tony Nap*

The Beckham
PUBLICATIONS GROUP, INC.
SILVER SPRING

To My Mother,
Grace Perrotta Napoli

My mother raised me more so than my father. He was hardly ever home. If he wasn't in jail he was traveling. And when he was home and conducting his gambling business in the neighborhood, he would leave the house at 11 a.m. and not come back till 4 a.m. the next morning. Only on Sundays would he stay home in his bathrobe all day. He'd read every word in the newspaper and at 6 p.m. order everyone to be cleanly dressed and sitting at the dinner table.

My mother did all the cooking and I washed and dried the dishes. She helped me with my homework. She scrubbed my scalp with Lifebuoy soap, the same soap she used to rub the dirty clothes over a scrub board. She used a very fine comb to get the bugs out of my hair. We had no washing machine until I was about 10 years old—when my father started to earn big money from his numbers business. He'd go out all dressed up to be with the crew, while my mother stayed with her crew, her children.

It is the woman that helps the successful man to reach his goal. And it is the woman who is the backbone of the family.

CONTENTS

Preface		ix
Chapter 1:	I've Gotta Be Me	1
Chapter 2:	Pipeline, New Jersey	13
Chapter 3:	Precious Cargo	22
Chapter 4:	Leader of Men	32
Chapter 5:	First Prodigal Son	40
Chapter 6:	Lorimer Street Gang	47
Chapter 7:	The Torpedo	55
Chapter 8:	The Other Side of The Family	61
Chapter 9:	Al Capone and The Kiss of Death	75
Chapter 10:	Rise to Power	87
Chapter 11:	A Meeting in The Church	95
Chapte 12:	The Son Is Born	100
Chapter 13:	The Language of Money	107
Chapter 14:	The 'Fix' Is In	118
Chapter 15:	Irreplaceable	132
Chapter 16:	The Road Not Taken	138
Chapter 17:	Crooked Cop	148
Chapter 18:	Welcome To Tucumcari	172
Chapter 19:	Losing My Mother	189
Chapter 20:	Stick-Up	201
Chapter 21:	Prince of Vegas	211
Chapter 22:	Laura	224

Chapter 23:	Trouble with The Cleveland Crew	240
Chapter 24:	A Gambling Empire	249
Chapter 25:	Jimmy Nap Is Made	258
Chapter 26:	Out of Control	262
Chapter 27:	Giuliani Time	267
Chapter 28:	Father Knows Best	276
Chapter 29:	Sentenced to The VA Hospital	284
Chapter 30:	The Road To Sobriety	292
Chapter 31:	Wiseguy Turns Nice Guy	298
Chapter 32:	The Pen Is Mightier Than The Sword	303

PREFACE

My father went to Rome in the early 1970s in search of the Napoli family crest. He went to the Vatican for a one-on-one sit-down with Pope Paul VI. My father told the Pope about the Napoli family history that he had learned from his father. Supposedly we descended from Italian royalty and our ancestors worked in the king's castle. The Pope told my father how to recover the family crest.

After spending one week at the Vatican, being interviewed by the Pope's administrators and executives, and donating $10,000 for the research services, my father returned to the United States with crest in hand.

It had been discovered in the library at the town hall in Salerno, Italy. The coat of arms was striking and colorful, extremely regal in its presentation, with a knight's head and shield symbolizing the royal bloodlines. Along the bottom was the family name, printed on a rippled, flowing banner.

The crest remained in my father's Manhattan townhouse on East 31st Street, hanging prominently on a wall in his den, where he died lying on the floor beneath it in 1992. Three days before he died, my father told me to keep the crest in my home after he was gone. I followed his orders.

That's where the crest—a source of heritage and pride for the Napoli family—hangs today. It is on my living room wall, in the center of a showcase of family pictures. It also adorns the cover of this book.

"Fin dal 1200 si trovo questa Casata stabilita nella provincia di Salerno, derivata da quella Nobile di Benevento e di Brindisi ed ascritta alla Nobilita di Capaccio. E rappresentata dal Signor Vincenzo Napoli, fu Antonio, residente in America."

These words inscribed on the crest are translated roughly as: *This lineage has been in existence since 1200, established in the Province of Salerno, derived from the Nobles of Benevento and of Brindisi and related to the Nobility of Capaccio. And represented by Signor Vincenzo Napoli, formerly Antonio, who now resides in America.*

Whenever I look at the crest, which is just about every day, I am reminded of the importance of family, loyalty, and allegiance. I am reminded of my father and the values he espoused. He believed in honor and the value of a man's word. He also knew the importance of knowing where you come from and where you've been, so you can know exactly where you are going.

Where was I going? I lived more of a life than most men can ever even dream about. I lived nine lives. I was a boxer, a soldier, an enforcer, a casino boss, a fugitive, a hustler and above all, a husband and a father. And a son.

I think a lot about all the beatings I handed out in my day. And all the ones I didn't get in return. The ones I should've gotten. But didn't. Because of my father. *Madone!* I would have been dead a hundred times over if not for that man. For so much of my life, I was no good. If not for him, I wouldn't have lived one life, no less nine.

I was high on life, or on drink. Behind bars. Or teetering on the edge somewhere. And every time I fell, my father would pick me up. Even when he was sick of picking me up, he picked me up.

Chapter 1

I've Gotta Be Me

It was a cold November afternoon in 1993 when, in a feverish burst of fury, I pulled the young punk's pants down to his ankles and cut his balls off with the switchblade that he had stupidly pulled on me.

The students and teacher crowded together in the back of the classroom, their backs against the large map of the world. They were probably scared that they might be next. After all, I must have looked like some mad drunk wildly slashing a student. For what reason? How would they know? They were just part of a freshman biology class at a community college in New York City.

If every man has his moment of clarity, this was mine. As I looked down at the punk—spurting blood from where no man wants to bleed from—I thought about how he had put his filthy hands on my daughter. He was going to pay for what he had done. And he was going to pay for everything that *I* had done to everyone and for everything that had been done to me. He was the sacrificial lamb, the beast of burden who would take the brunt of every terrible memory I stored inside of me. The memories were making one final, violent push to be purged from my system.

Yes, I knew that this was it for me. A lifetime of harming and being harmed was coming to an end. A voice inside me said that this was going to be my last drunken rage. I wasn't going to get away with this one. Strangely, I didn't even want to get away with this one. But I did want to see him suffer.

I stood over him writhing in pain, covered in his own blood, squirming for dear life. I had sliced the punk—calling him a rat bastard repeatedly—at least a dozen times. But there is no reason to continue, a voice inside me said. And then I really felt my insides surge and turn as I watched him bleed.

Sixty years of insanity had come to this. I had gone off the deep end, once and for all, in the most unlikely of places—a community college classroom.

I had come home that morning from another of my 72-hour benders of drinking, gambling, and living the wiseguy lifestyle that I had been living for…well, most of my 59 years on Earth. I would drink so much and for so long that I would almost drink myself sober again. So when I staggered into the house that morning, I was dazed from lack of sleep and from watching day turn into night and back into day. Everything seemed larger, closer and louder to me.

When I walked into the house that morning, it was eerily quiet. I called out to Laura, my wife. No answer. I noticed the crack of my daughter Tanya's bedroom door.

I went to open it. She was on her bed asleep, curled up in a ball. I closed the door and headed to the kitchen. Laura stood over the stove.

My voiced sounded hoarse from my three-day spree. "Why's Tanya still sleeping?"

"You haven't been home in three days. Did you forget yesterday was her birthday?"

"Let me ask you again and maybe I'll get a straight answer this time." My voice went up, "Why is Tanya sleeping? Why isn't she at school? Is she sick?"

Laura turned and walked past me and out of the kitchen. I followed her.

"Are you gonna answer me or what?"

She kept walking in silence, avoiding the question and trying to avoid me. Like the thick-headed Calabrese that I am, I wasn't going to accept no answer. I followed her into the living room.

"What the hell's goin' on?"

Laura avoided eye contact. She knew that engaging a drunk, especially this drunk, was a bad idea. She had lived with me long enough to know that. When some people get drunk, they get jolly, they fall down, they make an ass out of themselves, and it's all in good humor and fun. That wasn't me. I was a nasty drunk. Aggressive and violent, and I wasn't one to let something go.

My oldest daughter, Veronica came into the living room and I blasted her too.

"Is somebody gonna tell me what the hell is goin' on in this house?"

Veronica looked over to Laura, who was still looking away. I moved a little closer to her, thinking that I could push her into saying something. My physical presence might intimidate the words right out of her. I was good at bullying. Of course, it worked. Veronica talked.

"Tanya...had a little problem in school yesterday."

"A problem? What kind of a problem?"

I heard the story only in fits and bursts because my brain had shut down after learning that Tanya had been forced into a bathroom at school by some punk who tried to feel her up. I rushed into Tanya's room.

I tried to control my rage, but I was never any good at that, so why would I think I could start here? I grabbed Tanya by the arm and pulled her from the bed. I didn't realize then that manhandling someone after she's been through that type of a trauma is one of the worst things you can do. But even if I had known it, I probably wouldn't have cared anyway, because drunks are self-serving people who put themselves above everyone else. I was turning this situation, like most situations, into something about me. *I* was mad. *I* was going to avenge what had been done to my daughter. I. I. I. Drunks live in the world of *I*; except when the time comes to accept responsibility for what they've done. Then it's everyone else's fault.

But here I was, not 30 seconds removed from hearing that some scumbag had touched my daughter, on her birthday no less, and what was my first reaction: *I* was going to get revenge.

Tanya was shouting and pulling away from me and crying. Laura and Veronica pleaded with me, but it was no use. I had reached the point where my anger was at the white hot point of no return. The liquor was still pumping through my veins, fueling a freight train that could not be stopped from reaching its final destination.

"You're coming with me and you're pointing him out," I ordered.

"No, Daddy, I don't want to!" she wailed and resisted.

"Tanya, throw somethin' on and let's go. Don't make me raise my voice."

My voice was already raised.

"It's all over. I went to the doctor. I just don't want to see him again. Please."

Seeing her fear and her hurt just made me angrier. Everything that she tried to say to calm me down, to make it better, just made it worse. She was my daughter, my baby, and seeing her like this made me lose all reason, and all control. The bastard who did this was going to hurt ten times—maybe a hundred times more—than she was hurting.

"You don't have to see him. All you gotta do is point in his direction. I'll take it from there."

"What are you going to do?"

"Don't worry about it. I'm just gonna talk to him."

"No, you're not. I know you."

"Don't concern yourself with what I do with him."

"Just promise you won't kill him."

"Tanya..."

"Daddy...promise!"

"Okay, all right, I promise."

I didn't know if I could keep it, but it was a promise that I had to make to get her to come with me.

"He's a big guy, Daddy...a gang leader from Astoria...he carries a knife in his boot."

"Get dressed."

I had one of my guys drive us down to the college that wasn't too far from our apartment in the Williamsburg section of Brooklyn. I took Tanya by the hand and we walked into the school, father and daughter.

The lobby was crowded, so we blended in with the others. Nobody could guess what my mission was. We looked like any father and daughter walking together. Tanya had pulled it together and wasn't crying anymore. Her anxiety over what I might do replaced her sadness or distress over what had happened. No one could see that under my dark tinted sunglasses was a man with fire in his eyes and whose wrath would soon be unleashed.

Walking down a long, busy corridor, Tanya pointed out the punk who had grabbed her.

"That's him. Right there. The tall one."

I nodded and kissed her on the forehead.

"Go 'head, go back to the car," I told her.

She first looked at me, then down the hallway at the punk, who did not see her.

"Go 'head. I'll be right out."

Tanya turned and rushed off.

Students filed into their classrooms, but the punk remained in the hallway, leaning against a wall with one leg tucked up behind him.

I marched down the corridor toward him.

This walk must have taken me ten seconds at most. Yet I could see my whole life flash before my eyes as I took it. I could see my father, who had died a year earlier, and I could hear him tell me, "Don't let the liquid courage rule you." But it always ruled me. To that point in my life, at age 59 it had always won.

I remembered other guys, like this punk, whom I had straightened out over the years. There were a lot of them. Probably too many. I could see all that I was, and I all that I had been. I had been given nine lives to live and had used each one of them up. I could see them all now, right there in front of me, as if they were being reflected in my sunglasses. There I was: a boxer, a soldier, an enforcer, a casino boss, a fugitive, a hustler, a tough guy. A drunk. They were all me.

I could hear the soundtrack of my life too, playing right along with every image, with every misstep, every triumph, every thing, good and bad, mostly bad, that I had ever done. The song was Sammy Davis Jr's "I've Gotta Be Me." That was my song. It could have been written for me.

I'll go it alone, that's how it must be
I can't be right for somebody else
If I'm not right for me
I gotta be free, I just gotta be free
Daring to try, to do it or die
I gotta be me

I could hear the words, playing over and over again in my head. Their meaning, or at least the meaning I gave them, pushed me forward...giving me strength...goading me to take that one, last, long-time-coming step over the edge.

I stopped right in front of the punk.

"Hey punk."

He looked at me for a second and then spoke, with a slight Italian accent: "Who the fuck are you?"

He really was a punk bastard, with a sharp tongue and a chip on his shoulder. Any thought of turning this ship around—not that I had had any such thought anyway—went right out the window when he cursed at me.

"Who am *I*?" I took a breath. I wanted to say something more to him. But words escaped me. My rage had built to a fever pitch. This was not a time for words, it was a time for action. "This is who I am..."

The gates of hell flew open and the hurt was on its way. My life was about to change forever.

I unloaded a right hand on the punk's jaw, knocking him back into the wall. Then I grabbed him by the collar with two hands and spun him around, pushing him up against another wall. Or at least what I *thought* was a wall. Turns out, it was a door.

The door flew open to a biology class in session. The punk fell to the floor. The students and the teacher were scared shitless. The punk reached for his boot. I remembered what Tanya had said about his having a knife in there. I kicked his hand away and pulled the knife from his boot.

That's when the slicing started.

I was possessed, attacking this punk. I wanted to hurt him the way he hurt my daughter. And in the same places. So I sliced both his nipples. I sliced the cheeks of his ass. His blood shot everywhere: on the floor, the walls, on him, on me. I can still hear some of the female students screaming and crying in the back of the room. But I didn't give a shit. I didn't care about them.

Then I got the idea about castrating the fuck—the Italian way of punishing a rapist. I wanted to take away his manhood, humiliate him. I wanted him to feel what he made my little girl feel; but ten times more. So I sliced both his testicles. When it came time for me to cut off his penis and stuff it in his mouth, there was so much blood that I couldn't find the fuckin' thing.

I heard somebody vomit in the room.

Then I got one more idea. Now understand, these weren't well thought-out ideas at this point. These were just happening on the fly, inside the mind of an angry, drunken, violent man. *Me.* I'm just saying I had another *idea* so you will understand the order of events. But every act was happening instinctually, as if I were a lion hopping on its prey. I just wanted to tear him apart. I was going with the flow. Whatever will hurt him more, that's what I was listening for. That's what I wanted The more hurt I could inflict, the better. If you've ever been in any kind of a fight, then you know what I mean. Things happen so fast, yet they slow down. You have to look for your opening, your opportunity. You have to sense what your enemy's weakness is and seize on it. I learned that in the ring; I learned it even better on the street.

So I pulled the knife back over my head and I thought—yes, actually *thought* for the first time since this thing started out in the hallway—that I should plunge the blade right into his fucking heart and end him.

He's a pitiful, bloody mess writhing on the floor, I thought. He doesn't look so tough now. Doesn't look like he's ready to corner a defenseless girl in the bathroom now, does he? I bet now he knows who I am!

Something—a voice, a conscience, God—who knows—told me not to kill him. And the overriding thought was: he's not worth it. I just wanted to teach him a lesson. I think I did that. The commotion from the students, who had been dissecting frogs just before I started dissecting the punk, brought me back to reality.

I dropped the knife on the floor. I didn't look at the students who were screaming and huddled in the back. I walked calmly out of the classroom and back down the corridor toward the exit. My shirt and pants were covered with punk blood.

At the exit, a speechless security guard stared at me. He didn't know what to do. He sure as fuck wasn't going to apprehend me. I asked him for a cigarette. With a shaking hand, he gave me one, then lit it for me.

After I cut that young punk's balls off, I knew it was time to get some help. Somewhere deep inside me, I knew it. Not that he didn't deserve what he got. He did. But one thing I have learned in life is that "deserves" has nothing to do with anything. I don't deserve to be alive. I don't deserve to be happy. I don't even deserve to be telling this story. Not after all the shit I've done in my life. No way. But I'm here still, alive and well, and I'm telling my story—the story of a guy who would be, could be, and probably should be dead, if not for a good woman, a strong constitution, and a big-shot father.

So I stood beside the guard and puffed away on my cigarette. Neither of us spoke.

Then I heard sirens. I think, maybe he called the cops. Good for him. I wasn't running. I was giving myself up. At least for now. It was time to pay the piper. It was time for a change.

The sirens got closer and louder. They were coming for me for sure. And I was going to let them come. But first I was going to finish my cigarette.

Almost instantly, it seems, I was in the police station being questioned—but not about the punk. There was no question about that. I did what I did. They were asking me about other stuff. Bigger stuff. And they weren't regular cops or even detectives. They had brought in the feds. I knew they were the feds because they're a little smarter— Not much, but a little more—than the regular cops.

They had been trying to get me to talk for years about my father, his business and all his associates. And for years I had been telling them the same thing: shove it up your ass. They wanted to flip me. They obviously didn't know me too well.

"You're going away for a long time this time, Tony," one of the agents told me. "Now's your chance to talk. Tell us what we want to know. Tell us all about your friends. About Vincent Gigante and the Genovese crime family. About your association with the Bonannos. The Gambinos. And the other New York crime families. Tell us what we want to know, Tony. And we'll forget what you did to this two-bit punk in the school. We'll have a limo pick your wife up at home right now and it'll take you far away. We'll give you fifty thousand dollars..."

"Fifty thousand dollars?" I interrupted him. "If I ever talked for fifty thousand dollars, my father would come back from the grave to give me a slap."

"This is your last chance, Tony."

"Listen to me, popcorn, don't waste any more of your precious breath. I never talked before, I'm not talking now, and there's nothing you or anybody else can do to make me talk. You could throw away the key on me first."

I went to trial for what I did to the punk. I did my penance. And everything about my life changed from that point. But it changed the way I wanted it to change. My way. Not the way they wanted it to change.

I did my talking eventually, but it wasn't to them. I'm not a rat. My father didn't raise a rat. A rat is the worst thing anybody could be. I did my talking, but it wasn't in a courtroom, or to some salaried G-man, who wanted the names of people I spent my life with; people who were family to me. I was a lot of things in life, but I wasn't a fool, and I wasn't a stool pigeon.

The only talking I ever did and will ever do is here, on these pages, to you. I will tell you the story of a wild man, a son of a capo, at times a son of a bitch, who made life crazy for his father and for everyone else around him. It is the story of a recovering alcoholic who has been through the fires of hell and back again. And it is the story of a man committed to helping veterans get the benefits that this country owes them.

Telling this story was never an easy decision. I was always torn about it. And there were always roadblocks to telling it. My father, my friends, and my own conscience too disapproved of my going public with my story. But now, in my 73rd year of life, I know it must be told. I want to set the record straight. I want to help others. I have to do what I know is right. I've gotta open up because opening up is the best way to heal. *Daring to try, to do it or die.* I've gotta tell my story now. I've gotta be me.

Chapter 2

Pipeline, New Jersey

ON MY 26TH BIRTHDAY IN 1961 I sat in my room in the Napoli family home on Metropolitan Avenue in Brooklyn. In my hand was one of those black-and-white marble composition notebooks that I wrote in from time to time.

At first it was just a diary. After what had I just done to that crooked cop in the parking lot after he tried to shake me down in my Club Ragdoll, I thought it was a good time to get it all out. I started documenting places and people that I would go see and how I felt about those places and people I would go see. I wouldn't put anybody's last name in the notebook. I wasn't that stupid. But I thought the things I was seeing first-hand were worth writing down. I thought maybe someday somebody would give a shit about what and who I saw and maybe want to read about it. Especially if I got life in prison. What the hell did I know? Isn't that what most writers think?

I started to write more and started to like writing. I had nothing but time on my hands since I was on the lam without being on the lam—holed away in my room. I wasn't any good at writing really. My grammar was bad. My spelling was worse. But I was getting it down on paper. That was the key. If I know anything at all about this writing stuff, it was that you had to get it down on paper and you should write about what you know.

So I was getting it all down and I was writing what I knew: the streets and everybody on them. Everybody. Including my father.

It was never my intention to write about my father. I was writing about me. It was my point of view. My experience. Anyway, I never saw it as disloyal. I never thought I was exposing anyone or anything. I wasn't even sure if any other eyes besides mine would ever see it. I wasn't thinking that far ahead. I was figuring I'd be in jail or dead before long, and what the heck. I was just writing.

My father opened my bedroom door without knocking. Correction. He knocked once—a courtesy knock—just as he always did, and then he entered in one, fast motion. In other words, there was no time for me to say "Just a moment..." or "One second, please..." No time for me to respond to his knock, and take the notebook and stick it back in my drawer—buried under t-shirts, underwear, and a jewelry box—where no one would ever look to find it. There was no time for me to hide the notebook and get it out of my father's sight.

So he entered my room, the way he entered every room, with authority and presence. Thinking back now, even if I had said, "Just a second..." to his knock, he wouldn't have listened anyway. Nobody told my father what to do, or how to do it. If he wanted to come in, he would come in, and nothing and no one could stop him. So he came in.

My father, James "Jimmy Nap" Napoli, entered a room like he owned it. And in fact, most rooms he entered, he did own. Or at least he had a "controlling interest in" as people in his business might say. He certainly owned my room and everything in it. Including me. As his son, I was his property to do with as he pleased. That's how he saw it. Even on my 26th birthday. That's just the way it was. He was the king of his castle. He was the man.

And a big man he was too. My father stood six feet tall, just under 200 pounds for most of his life. He was imposing. But who he was and how he carried himself made him appear even bigger. Looking up at my father was like sitting in the front row of a movie theater, gazing up at the screen. He was a movie star. He was larger than life. He was always nattily dressed in dark wool suits and silk ties. He wore big, tinted sunglasses, even indoors, which gave him an air of mystery. The glasses veiled his eyes and made it difficult to read him. His hair was perfectly coifed with Brylcreem. He smelled like a man, too. His scent was unmistakably Brut. To this day, if I smell Brut aftershave or cologne, I think of my father. Jimmy Nap commanded every room with his presence and carried himself with the demeanor that only a man of great stature could possess. One that only a boss could bear.

So there I was, sitting on my bed, as I had been for a while since getting out of jail, with a notebook in my hand, scribbling away. He didn't seem to notice the notebook at first and greeted me with a hearty "Happy Birthday, TN." He always called me by my initials, TN. He was in a good mood, even jovial,. That would soon change. We had been going through a lot. The heat had been turned up high since I broke that crooked cop's ass in the parking lot in Union

City. My father had been trying to make everything right through his connections in the courts. It was a tough time and this was the best mood he'd shown in a while.

Maybe if I had been a little quicker on the draw. Or if I had just set the notebook down beside me in a more nonchalant manner, perhaps I wouldn't have drawn as much attention to it. But my father's eyes went right to the notebook, like a coin to a magnet.

My father had a sixth sense about things like this, sharpened from living in a world of double-crossers, liars and rats for so many years. He was a street guy, with street smarts, but he also had the intellect of a Harvard graduate. You could not get anything by him. There was no point in even trying.

So when his head turned and his attention went to the notebook, I knew he smelled something. What he smelled was the putrid odor of dirt, his dirt, the dirt of his business, thick in the air of my room, and emanating from my notebook.

"What's that?" he asked pointedly, his joviality suddenly gone and replaced with suspicion.

"Oh, it's just some writing I've been doing. It's nothing," I tried to explain it away.

"So you're a writer now?"

"No...No, definitely not...I'm just jotting some things down. That's all."

"Jotting some things down, huh? After what you did to that cop, you got a lot of time on your hands now. Let me see what you're jotting down."

He held out his thick, strong, but well-manicured hand and kept it out for what seemed like 10 minutes. It wasn't even 10 seconds. But it was long enough for him to repeat himself. My father didn't like to repeat himself, and the tone in his voice made that clear.

"Let me see it, TN."

I lifted the notebook, which now felt heavy in my hand. The marble cover felt like real marble, as I placed its dead weight into my father's outstretched hand. This was the proverbial cinder block tied to my ankle and I was about to get tossed into the river.

My father looked down at the pages and stared at them, over the top of his sunglasses. I know he must have been reading, but it didn't look like he was reading. I did not detect any side-to-side movement in his eyes. It was just a dead, lifeless stare. He appeared to be doing more than reading the words. It was as if he were studying them. Memorizing them. Checking them for spelling and grammar maybe? Or else, he was looking right through them and seeing only a son who betrayed him; a son who would tell the world all his secrets; a son who should have known better.

Looking at his eyes, as they peeked out through the top his tinted shades, which were now low on his nose, I could see that there was no blinking in them. No reaction. He was totally focused. He would turn a page, examine it thoroughly and then turn to the next page. With each turn of every new page, my heart beat a little faster in my chest. So many thoughts rushed through my mind at this point. I didn't have to worry about going to jail for life. I'd be dead soon! But the recurring thought that kept screaming out to me was, Run! But I knew I couldn't run. Where would I go?

Then my father reached the last page and he closed the notebook. Now he stood there, staring at the back cover.

He would not look at me. He would not acknowledge my physical presence before him at all. I grabbed my breath and held it, trying not to bring any more attention to myself. I awaited his reaction.

For a moment, I had the crazy, fleeting thought that he was so taken with my writing, so enamored of my guts in daring to put onto paper such details of illicit activity, that maybe he had suddenly developed a newfound appreciation for me, his son.

No such luck. My twenty-sixth birthday would be one to remember, for all the wrong reasons.

Finally, my father looked up from the notebook, which he still gripped tightly between his fingers, and he moved toward me, shouting at the top of his lungs.

"Are you out of your mind, TN?"

I couldn't answer him. I couldn't even look up at him. I was scared. I was ashamed. I kept my head down. If he was going to kill me, I was going to let him. I was expecting to feel, at the very least, his hand on the back of my neck. At the most, I thought I might hear the pop from a .38 caliber and then, quickly and easily, I would be no more. Whatever he was going to do to me, I had it coming. I wasn't going to fight back. I wasn't going to run. I was going to take it like a man. *Go ahead, Daddy-O*, I thought to myself, *whatever you want to do to me, I'm yours!*

Then, suddenly and quite unexpectedly, my father began to... read aloud from the notebook!

Huh? But don't you want to punch me? Hit me with a lead pipe? Shoot me? Leave me for dead for my stupidity? Was I getting off easy?

As he began to read and I heard my words coming out of his mouth, I wished he would punched me, shot me and hit me with a lead pipe. Or leave me to rot in that Union City jail. The mortification was unbearable. I squirmed as I heard my father repeating my words. In fact, they didn't sound much like words at all. They were painful, awful sounds—noise really—that had no business contaminating the universe. They were inner thoughts, observations, descriptions best kept to oneself. They were nails on a blackboard, a jackhammer ripping through concrete, a nun saying the word "fuck." I wanted to put my hands over my ears and wish them away. But I couldn't. All I could do was sit there and listen to them, as my father read them back to me.

"*'Pipeline New Jersey...How we were able to use the Hudson Tubes from New York to New Jersey to run our numbers action across the river...'* Tell me, is there something wrong with you, TN?"

I was telling the story of how we ran the numbers slips from New Jersey to New York by using the Hudson Tubes out of a Hoboken train station. We had a runner from Brooklyn meet with a runner from Hoboken on the train and they switched brown paper bags with the action (number slips) in both bags. My father made the runners dress like construction workers, holding their "lunch" in brown paper bags. It was a brilliant decoy. Also, because of the time of day that they made the switch—3pm in the afternoon—each each runner had time to get back to their own people before the seventh race was over at any of the New York tracks.

"Dad...I can explain..."

I really couldn't explain. Not in that moment, for sure. Maybe not ever. But "I can explain" felt like the right thing to say, so I said it.

"Are you trying to destroy people's lives? Because that's what guys who talk do. They destroy people's lives!"

I could barely open my mouth to defend myself, but somehow these words came out. These were the best I could muster. "Dad...Dad, listen, please..." I pleaded, "The real names won't even be used in the story. The outline was just to guide me along and..." He cut me short. This was not the right thing to say.

"The real names won't be used? That's your excuse? That's your idea of an explanation? Don't you understand, TN, that you're going to get us all killed or put in jail! What's the matter with you? Didn't I raise you smarter than that? You're twenty six years old today, facing life in jail for the stunt you pulled, your mother is sick in the hospital, and what're you doing, going backwards here? You're becoming a writer now?"

He looked at me, offering a brief moment where I was free to add something. I didn't.

"Now you wanna be a writer? Didn't I raise you to be smarter than that?!"

Again, he looked to me, waiting for something to come from me—a defense, a reasonable counter-argument, an apology. But I had nothing.

He held his gaze on me for what felt like forever. I could feel the weight of it, but would not, *could not* look at him. Then he held the notebook out before him. He opened it and began to tear the pages out, one after the other. Then he ripped them in half and let them fall onto the carpeting in my room.

"Dad, no, please..." I begged, "I worked hard on those."

I leaped from the bed onto the floor and tried to collect and salvage the torn pages.

My father reached down, grabbed me by my arm and squeezed tightly.

"You never talk about our business, TN. You never open your mouth about what we do. Never!"

He released his grip on my arm and then ripped the remaining notebook pages to shreds and threw them into the air. They fell to the ground all around me, like tickertape. But this was no celebration.

As he reached the door, he turned back to me.

"Smarten up," he warned, "If you want to be a writer, wait until I'm gone. Then you can tell whatever stories you want. I won't be here to stop you, or protect you. Write what you want then. And get yourself shot."

He slammed the door behind him and left me there, on my knees, scrounging to piece together the scraps of my writing, which were now nothing more than paper fragments strewn about the floor of my room.

I wanted to cry, or scream, or do some other unmanly thing, but then suddenly another feeling washed over me. I felt fortunate. Even with my months of hard work reduced to shreds, I still felt lucky. Lucky that I had gotten off as easily as I did. Lucky that he did not kill me.

What's more, I felt lucky that my father did not disown me. Because in the end, nothing would have been worse than that.

Chapter 3

Precious Cargo

My family came to America, like a lot of families did around the turn of the twentieth century, on a boat. Mind you, they weren't Carnival Cruise ships they came in either. They were freighters, meant for cargo, not passengers. They were banana boats. They called them that because people; human beings, my *family*, and maybe yours too, were crammed onto these boats in hordes like a bunch of bananas. And they were treated about as humanely as a cluster of rotten bananas too.

Even though conditions were rough on these boats, for many—for *most*— were the only way out of an even rougher situation at home: an overcrowded country plagued by low wages and high taxes. And one that offered them little or no financial opportunity or hope.

In the late 1800s, Italy was suffering from a poor economy, particularly in the Southern regions, where due to several natural disasters and soil erosion, the land had betrayed those who had come to depend on it for farming and sustenance. There was no money, no food, the illiteracy rate had skyrocketed, and people were looking for a better way, and a way out. So when an opportunity came to escape hunger, disease and poverty, they took it. That opportunity for my family came unexpectedly, in the middle of the night.

One of the things I have come to hold as a truism in life is this: it's good to know a guy. It's always good to know a guy. No matter what business, what area, what *thing* you are looking for, if you know a guy, a guy on the inside, a guy who can work an angle for you, then things can go much more smoothly. From 1820 to 1920, over four million Italians arrived in the United States, looking for a better way of life. One of them, fortunately, was my grandfather, my namesake, Antonio Napoli. And the reason he was able to get over here to America was because he knew a guy.

Really, he knew a guy who knew a guy, which is just as good as knowing a guy; a guy who knew a captain, of a freighter that was coming to America.

When people are desperate and forced to live *in extremis*, they will do desperate things, like loading their family onto a cargo ship in the middle of the night and heading to another continent. In my grandfather's case, it meant loading his wife, his infant daughter, and himself onto a tanker in the hopes of reaching this new land of opportunity, America.

Some Italians left their homeland with the belief that they would return some day; that they would find work in this new and prosperous America, and save enough money to come back to Italy and help the rest of their family. And some of them did. But many did not, could not. They planted themselves in America and laid down roots. In the case of my grandfather Antonio, my father's father, he knew that he would not and could not ever return to Italy.

Grandpa Antonio was born in Italy in 1870, in the town of Napoli. As a young man, Antonio was knighted a duke and worked in the castle of King Umberto I. His title afforded him a swath of land to grow grapes, for wine, as well as a vegetable garden. Antonio also served in security and maintenance for the king's castle, and as a local tax collector. He would collect the taxes from landowners in cash or in goods (usually produce of some kind from their farms). A certain percentage of the taxes he collected had to be turned over to the king, but he was allowed to keep a small percentage for himself.

The reign of Umberto I was a time of great social upheaval in Italy. Socialist ideas and the ever-growing resistance to the colonialist plans of the Italian government were beginning to swing popular support against the king. Protestors, including a young Benito Mussolini, were growing in number and strength. The king and the royalty were under great pressure. Eventually, as their detractors amassed power and prestige, the king and those in his court were in grave danger. That threat extended to Antonio and his family, as he had been a member of the royals since he was 17 years old.

The royals were under attack. They were robbed of their jewels and homes. Many were executed, some publicly. For Antonio, the time to leave, to flee, had come. Antonio had to get out of the country or face a firing squad. Luckily, he knew that guy.

The way to get yourself and your family on a ship in those days was to get to the captain of the ship. The captain could be persuaded—*bribed*—to sneak people onto the ship. For a fee. Usually money or jewels, or anything else of value would do. For the right price, the captain would see to it that men, women and children were snuck onto a ship, whose final destination was America.

So Antonio took what he had, in tender and treasure, which wasn't all that much, and through his guy, his connection, he offered it to the captain. The captain accepted.

While the overriding reasons to get on one of these ships were freedom and opportunity, the conditions on board could only be described as sub-human. The immigrants were, in essence, stowaways, who had to spend most of their time in steerage, below deck, out of sight and mixed in with the cargo.

That's because the ships were never meant to carry people, and certainly not hundreds of people, thousands of miles across the sea. They were freighters meant to carry only cargo—barrels, steel, metals, cork. Mixed in with these cold, raw materials, in the bowels of these vessels, were mothers, fathers, babies—precious cargo. These freight ships, old and weather-beaten as they were, designed to haul commodities in bulk, and other lifeless tonnage, were now being asked to carry something they never imagined they would carry—lives, hopes, and dreams. And the journey was a long and difficult one.

But it wasn't all freedom and smiles on these boats. The length of the trip, coupled with the conditions made for a bumpy ride in every sense of the word. It was unsanitary, cold; the immigrants were hungry, and often became ill. In some cases, those with infectious diseases, who were contagious and posed a threat to other immigrants, were thrown overboard. Women were raped. Men were murdered. Others died of natural causes—or unnatural causes. Like starvation.

There was no food, so the women packed what they hoped would be enough for the long trip. Sometimes it was, sometimes it wasn't.

Being cramped up and on the ocean for weeks—or even months, in some cases—made people nuts. Not knowing who or what was waiting for them at the other end was a scary proposition, even for the most level-headed of the bunch. So the men kept the women and children close, and they all prayed for the best as they floated toward this mysterious new land.

In the back of their minds was the hope that this place they were going to would offer them a chance to work, to make money, to provide for their families. The adage that the streets of America were "paved with gold" was a sentiment most took figuratively. But not all. Some thought it was literal: that there would be a yellow brick road of gold waiting for them upon their arrival in the U.S.

The more realistic of the immigrants, like Grandpa Antonio, knew what it meant. It meant that there was a booming economy in America that could offer him and others at least the chance to make a living, if not a fortune.

What the mostly agricultural Italian immigrants, like Antonio, did not realize was that when they arrived in America, they would be forced to become mostly urban. They would settle into American cities like New York, Philadelphia, Chicago, Baltimore, and Detroit and find unskilled labor at the bottom of the occupational ladder.

Italian immigrants would work such jobs as shoe shining, rag picking, sewer cleaning, and whatever other hard, dirty, dangerous jobs others didn't want. Even their children would start working at an early age, as they did in Italy, at the unfortunate expense of their formal educations. The Italian immigrants were known for rarely, if ever, accepting charity. Nor would they resort to illegal means for money. They were a proud, strong people who believed in the virtues of hard work and fair play.

In fact, with their willingness to work long hours for low wages, the Italians became the chief rivals to the Irish for much of the unskilled work available in the industrial areas of America. This often led to problems and resentment between the two ethnic groups. By the 1920s over four million Italians and over four million Irish immigrated to the United States. That made for over eight million people, many of whom were vying for the same jobs. And by extension, it made for a lot of problems.

Grandpa Antonio figured with his diverse background working maintenance and security in the king's castle in Italy that he would have no trouble landing a job in America. He was a dedicated, nose-to-the-grindstone kind of a guy who wasn't afraid to put in a hard and honest day's work. In fact, he relished the opportunity. Having escaped what would have been certain death, either at the hands of rebels, or at the hands of poverty, back in Italy, what lay ahead of him had to be better, he thought. But like a lot of things in life, sometimes they get worse before they get better.

My grandfather and my grandmother, Anna, who was an angel of a woman, came to America for a better life.

They brought with them only the clothes on their backs—he in a sharp, black suit and hat, sporting his handlebar mustache; she in her petticoat and bonnet. Of course, they brought their hopes too. And to this new land and to this new city, New York City, they brought with them the last name of the home they had left behind...Napoli.

It's a funny thing. Of the millions of Italians who immigrated to the United States during this period, isn't it ironic that both sides of my family happened to be on the same boat? I could never get over that fact. This one boat carried my father's mother and father, Anna and Antonio Napoli, and their baby daughter, as well as my mother's mother and father, Maria and Giuseppe Perrotta. One boat, two sides of the family. Amazing.

For all of these immigrants, Ellis Island, at the mouth of the New York Harbor, was the first point of contact with the new world. No sooner were these huddled masses greeted by Lady Liberty than they were cattled off through the golden doors of the island's processing center for paperwork checks and physical exams.

Just getting into the center was a major production unto itself, as thousands of other immigrants, not just Italians, but Germans, Irish, Russians—men, women, and children—filed off the docked boats in droves and flooded the island. Once inside the processing center, it took several more hours, as lines were long, and slow moving. The healthy were separated from the ill. The legals from the illegals. If they were cleared for entry, then they were finally set free to fend for themselves in their new land.

Legend has it that the expression wop, as an insult to Italians, began at Ellis Island. Italian immigrants who did not have their papers in order were labeled "Without Papers" or WOPS. Others say that WOP comes from the Neapolitan word "guappo," meaning "thug." The word refers to those who belonged to the Guapperia or "Camorra," a criminal organization similar to the Sicilian Mafia, located mostly in the province of Campania and its capital of Naples. Either way, wop was and is definitely a nasty thing to call an Italian. Sometimes it is even paired with the word *Dago*. As in Dago Wop. Dago seems to have come from the word *"Diego,"* which was used to describe those of Spanish origin. Whites, or Anglo-Americans, used the word liberally and indiscriminately to describe anyone who was different, or darker, than they were. It goes to show you how they made little distinction between ethnic groups. You were either like them or you were not. *Dago.*

Once in America, Italian immigrants clustered into groups relating to their place of origin. Neapolitans and Sicilians settled in various sections of New York, and people from different parts of Italy even settled on different streets. This is how certain areas became almost exclusive Italian enclaves. Over time, these enclaves became known as Little Italys.

However, early on, living conditions for Italian immigrants were not very desirable. They were overcrowded and even filthy in many cases. They moved into tenement buildings in urban areas that were unkempt and sometimes infested with bugs and rodents. This was all they could afford on the low laborer's salaries most of them were bringing home.

Italian immigrant men found themselves working construction jobs. Many became manual laborers. They dug tunnels, laid railroad tracks, constructed bridges and roads, and even erected the first skyscrapers. My grandfather Antonio was no different. He worked as a bricklayer and mason to provide for his family, which was now starting to grow, with the arrival of a new baby.

Antonio and Anna's apartment was a cold flat in New York's Hell's Kitchen. They had a potbelly stove in the kitchen that burned coal, when they had enough money to buy coal to burn. They had five rooms that ran from the front of the building to the rear. Railroad style rooms is what they would call them. There was no dining room and no living room, and little furniture. There was a dining room table, a bunk bed, some chairs. Most of it was either left behind by another tenant or pieced together from street sales.

On November 4, 1911, in the back room of this old, run-down tenement apartment, my father, Vincenzo "James" Napoli was born.

After a long labor, which unnerved an ever stoic, but constantly pacing Antonio, the mid-wife—it was always a mid-wife in those days, no doctors, no hospitals—held the newborn baby in her arms. The baby's cries filled the apartment and awakened little Angela from her bottom bunk. The wailing carried out into the hallway of the building as well, where neighbors celebrated the arrival of the new child with traditional Italian cakes and cookies.

Italian Immigrants were all about family. The birth of a baby signified the growth and extension of the family. It symbolized health, luck and wellbeing. It was reason for joy and celebration. It was a very good thing. Even if the crying awakened people in the middle of the night. Even if it was piercing and shrill. That crying was the sound of life. It was the affirmation of a growing community that was laying down roots in this new land of theirs. It was one more Italian, one more of them, being brought into the world.

"*E un bambino...Un bambino proprio bello!*" the mid-wife proclaimed.

It was a boy, a beautiful baby boy!

"*Che lo chiameremo?*" the mid-wife asked, as she placed the baby in Anna's arms.

A weary Anna cradled the baby boy and looked down at him.

"*Chiamomallo Vincenzo,*" Anna said, after thinking for a long moment, "*Che ne pensi, Antonio? Ti piace quel'nome?*"

She wanted to call him Vincenzo, after Antonio's father. She wanted to know if Antonio liked the name.

Antonio, with tears welling up in his eyes at the sight of his wife holding their newborn child, readily agreed with Anna. "Vincenzo." He repeated the name. "*Si, lo chiamamo Vincenzo.*"

Anna held the baby up to Antonio, who took him in his hands and looked at him, long and hard. The baby stopped crying and settled into Antonio's firm grasp. "Vincenzo Napoli..." Antonio said the name aloud. "*Mi figlio...*" ... my son.

My father.

Chapter 4

Leader of Men

MY GRANDFATHER ANTONIO BROKE HIS ass working as a bricklayer and mason. But he was a tough, sober man who never complained. Antonio was a man free of passion, seemingly unmoved by joy or grief. He submitted without complaint to the unavoidable necessities of life. Like hard work. Even when his back broke, his hands bled, and his knees gave way, he never said a word about it. And he never missed a day's work. Not in 30 years on the job.

Antonio's job didn't have many perks. He had no job security, other than being well-liked and well-respected; no personal days, no expense account, no 401K. He was a man who got up in the morning, before the sun, went to work, and came home after the sun went down. He did this because he had to. Because his family needed him to. And because he had a rock solid sense of what it meant to be, above all else, a man. And he taught his son, Vincenzo, to do the same.

By the age of ten, Antonio was taking my father along with him to his work sites. He wanted to teach young Vincenzo Napoli, or "Jimmy Nap," as everyone would come to know him, what it meant to be a man of the soil. The soil, in this case, being bricks, concrete, and mortar.

My father would lay the bricks as he was instructed to do by his father. He was obedient and hard working and that made Antonio proud. Hard work was the highest virtue to Antonio, and he felt it was the most important thing he could pass along to his young son. It was valued above any other skill or talent, and unfortunately, for many of the old timers like Antonio, it was valued even more than a good, formal education.

My father went to school only to the sixth grade and never continued to grade seven. Antonio insisted that he go to work, to help him support the family. Antonio was a practical, immediate man. One dollar in his pocket today was worth more to him than two in his hand tomorrow. Food on their table, clothes on their backs, and a roof over their heads was priority number one. But what Antonio possessed in work ethic, he lacked in foresight. He did not place a premium on education because it did not produce instant results. Work did.

"Bravo, Vincenzo," Antonio would encourage his husky son, as the boy would set heavy bricks atop a stack of other heavy bricks, all lined in a row. *"Tu sei forte. Forte come quel'mattone."* You are very strong, he would tell my father, almost as strong as that brick itself.

My father was strong, and a big boy for his age. One look at him showed this undeniable outer ruggedness and physical prowess. Invisible to the eye, however, were the other proclivities that lay just beneath the surface of young Jimmy, like his intuitive intelligence and his complex, mathematical mind. These were skills that were not being put to good use—or to any use really—with him laboring as a bricklayer. But still he was a good son. He did as he was told. He did as his father asked.

One day at one of the worksites, Jimmy was doing his job, moving and stacking cinderblocks, when Antonio approached him and asked him a question. "Vincenzo, do you know what we are building?"

"No, Papa", Jimmy responded, "I don't know."

"We are building a bridge." Antonio informed him…in Italian, of course. "A tall bridge that will reach into the heavens and stretch across the water, connecting one part of this city to another. Your hard work is doing that, Vincenzo. You should be very proud."

Jimmy smiled, and he continued to work.

"Hard work is the answer to everything, Vincenzo." Antonio grabbed Jimmy's arm to command his attention. "Don't ever be like some of the others, who come here and choose the wrong path. They want riches, but they want to take short cuts. Do you understand what I am saying to you, son?"

"*Si, Papa, capisco,*" Jimmy reassured him.

"Bravo. And never forget it. Remember, you must be as strong as that brick, Vincenzo. Even stronger, if you are to reach the sky."

Jimmy nodded. He took in what his father was telling him. And he wanted him to know that he was taking it in.

Then they stood there, staring at one another for a long, quiet moment. Father and son.

Jimmy broke the awkward silence. "Can I get back to work now, Papa?"

Antonio smiled. His words were getting through. Jimmy returned to laying the heavy bricks.

Disputes among laborers were a common occurrence in those days. Jobs were hard to come by. Work could be sporadic for some men. There were a lot of guys vying for jobs and only so many jobs to go around. The Irish and the Italians were always at each other's throats over work shortages. But the Italians fought amongst themselves too. This was another unfortunate result of their desperation and lack of organization.

One day on the work site, a laborer approached Antonio. The laborer addressed him with caution, and spoke to him in a timid manner, in their native tongue. "*Scusami* Antonio, but there seems to be a problem down at the Meeting Hall," the portly, polite worker informed him. "Perhaps you can come and see if you can solve it."

"Me?" questioned Antonio, "What can I do?"

If Antonio was anything, he was a strong, silent type. Not the type to make a fuss, to prop himself up, or to stick his thumbs under his armpits. He had never told anyone that he was a duke back in the old country. But some people in the neighborhood knew it. Some people in the neighborhood knew everything. Word had spread. Without him having to say it. People knew. So there was always an unspoken recognition of this fact and a level of reverence with which people addressed Antonio.

"Well, with all due respect, Antonio, back in Napoli you were a man of respect. All of the men know that. They will listen to you. They will follow you. Please, perhaps there is something you can do."

Antonio shot a look over at my father, who had been listening in. "Mind your business, Vincenzo! Get back to work!"

My father looked away and pretended to busy himself with the cement mixing.

"*Per favore,* Antonio," the laborer pleaded.

Antonio thought for a moment, then he gave in. "*Vengo.* I will see what I can do."

"*Grazie, Antonio. Grazie.* The men need you."

When Antonio walked into the meeting hall, he found a group of laborers engaged in a heated argument with another group of laborers. All Italians, all jawing at each other and in each other's faces. They were aggressive and belligerent.

Antonio listened to the verbal dispute from the back of the hall. The laborer who had requested his presence stood by his side.

One laborer, an older, rugged man stood nose to nose with another, younger, but just as tough looking, man. "There is not enough work for us and you son-of-a-bitches come along and steal what little work there is," accused the older worker.

"We have families too. What else can we do? We need to work!" the younger worker shot back.

"Find another job. You're young. Sell fish. Cut hair. But leave our jobs alone."

"There are no other jobs. If we do not do this, we will starve. Our families will starve."

"And if we do not work, so will ours. Should I make my children starve to death so that yours can eat?"

Back and forth they shot their barbs, with their respective groups rooting them on. Tempers soon escalated to the boiling point and a brawl became imminent. Getting physical was the only thing left for them to do.

The peacemaking laborer beside Antonio whispered in his ear, "Antonio, *per favore*, do something. They will listen to you."

Antonio deliberated for a moment and then he stepped forward and intervened. "*Signori! Signori, per favore*, do not fight."

All lips went silent and all eyes went to Antonio. He stepped right in between the two laborers who were about to come to blows. "*Siamo tutti fratelli.* We are all brothers. We come here to this country together. We raise our families together. And we work together. If we look out for each other, there can be work for everyone."

"*Ma come*, Antonio? But how? There is not enough work for everyone," the older worker explained to Antonio, in a far calmer tone than what he had expressed to the younger worker. "The companies will not pay for all of us to work. They will not spend the money."

Without a moment's thought and shooting straight from his gut, Antonio proposed the solution. "If we stand together. If we organize. *Se nessuno di noi lavora a meno che non ci facciano lavorare tutti…*If none of us works, unless all of us works…then they will have no choice then to hire us all."

The laborers fell dead silent.

Then the young worker addressed Antonio. "Will you speak for us, Antonio? Will you be our voice?"

"Oh, I don't know if I can do that."

"*Per favore*, Antonio. You can make it happen. We believe in you!" one laborer shouted.

Another chimed in, "Per favore. *Per le nostre famiglie. Per le nostre vite.* For our families. For our lives."

Antonio contemplated for a moment. "I will do all I can to help you, my brothers."

The laborers cheered him and sang Antonio's praises.

The laborer who had brought Antonio there, whispered in his ear once again. "This is why you were a duke in the old country. *Tu sei un leader degli uomini.* You are a leader of men."

Antonio smiled and nodded in humble acceptance. He sat down with some of the construction bosses on behalf of all the laborers. He insisted that more men were needed on the job, and gently suggested that if all the men weren't put to work, none of the men would work. Coming from another man, this would have sounded like a threat. But coming from Antonio it sounded like diplomacy. Like a genuine way of bridging the gap between the workers and the bosses. It was a way of saying to the bosses, if you give us what we need, we will give you what you need. More men on the job means more work gets done faster. And more work getting done faster meant more jobs completed. He knew the bosses would like that idea.

So he gave them time to think it over, and said his men would be at home, waiting for an answer, but eager to return to work. Now you can call this a strike, a work stoppage. Call it what you want. Antonio sent a clear message to the bosses: we are united in this effort.

Days later the bosses agreed to give Antonio what he and the men needed. They put all the workers on the job, including Jimmy. Antonio supervised them. And the work got done. The bridge was erected above them. And in record time. And any future grievances—worker to worker or worker to bosses—were brought to Antonio.

My grandfather became a leader, an organizer. What you might today call a union delegate. Although there were no unions in those days—at least that's not what they called them. In the process, he became a foreman, a supervisor, by negotiating with the companies for how much his crew of men should be paid for each job. My grandfather got his hourly wage, plus so much a head for each laborer he brought to the job site. He kept the men employed and happy, the bosses happy, and he was able to support his family.

Antonio made everybody happy. Everybody, that is, but his own son Jimmy, who was becoming increasingly restless and unfulfilled with a bricklayer's life.

Chapter 5

First Prodigal Son

Kids are a pain in the ass. I should know. I was a kid, and I have kids. You love them with all your heart; you do anything and everything you can for them. But they always seem to find a way to piss you off.

Don't get me wrong, I love my three girls. They are my life. You try to guide them. Keep them out of trouble. And the older they get, the more independently they act, the farther they push. What my father displayed to Grandpa Antonio went beyond your ordinary, run-of-the-mill teenage precociousness. It was defiance, plain and simple.

My father was big for his age. By the time he was seventeen, he had a hulking, intimidating frame. That made him a perfect choice, not just for the business of laying out brick, but for another type of business too. The business of laying out people.

Antonio's gentlemanly, trusting way of doing business didn't always work with some guys and with some employers. Sometimes labor and management didn't see eye to eye. Sometimes things got rough. Strikes had to be called for, or at least threatened. With the rising tide of industry in the U.S., came the rising tide, and subsequent power, of labor and labor unions, to be more precise. Laborers for the most part were underpaid and overworked. They went from having to beg for jobs to having to beg for a decent wage, reasonable hours, and fair conditions while on the job.

Antonio was a leader in this labor movement. His desire for diplomacy, and his ability to see both sides, having been in management back in Italy, allowed him to negotiate settlements between labor and management. At least most of the time. He saw labor and management as having common interests and therefore having common goals. If they worked together, he taught to the other workers, kept the lines of communication open and always proceeded from good faith, there wasn't anything they couldn't resolve.

That wasn't always the case.

Antonio's way of doing things, while fair and decent, was becoming just a bit old fashioned. Trust was being replaced with might. Even in the early days when Antonio might go to management and threaten a work stoppage, it was more for leverage, more saber rattling than anything else. He wanted his men to work and so did management. Agreements were ironed out. By hook or by crook, they made it work.

Now things were getting tough because everything was expanding. The country was growing and so was management and labor. Both sides were less and less willing to back down. Both had too much to lose. And their duels in the sun became more and more inevitable, and more and more frequent. Both sides would cut off their noses—in some cases, literally—to spite their faces.

Strikes were bad for business. Everybody's business. They hurt workers and employers alike. Workers hated losing badly needed pay checks and employers hated losing the time and money that strikes brought on them. Strikes were to be avoided at all costs.

Employers saw strikes as strong-arm tactics. As a way for these uneducated laborers and their often crooked leaders to bully them into raising their wages all too often.

Workers saw strikes as an effective tool to use against employers who bullied them into accepting wages that were too often well below what they deserved for the hard work they put in.

So when labor leaders pushed on employers and threatened to pull their men off the jobs, employers found a way to push back. They hired strike busters.

One day on the job, Jimmy's lunch hour rolled around.

Over the sound of laborers clanging away and machinery, Antonio called out to him, "Vincenzo, go to lunch! But come back in an hour. Don't get lost!"

"Okay, Papa," Jimmy shouted back at Antonio.

But Jimmy never did come back. He walked off the work site that day and never returned.

It had been growing inside of Jimmy for some time. This restlessness. This burning desire to do something else, to be something else. To *be* someone else. Not just what his father wanted him to be, but to be what he wanted to be.

He knew he couldn't explain that to Antonio. He just wouldn't understand. Jimmy didn't see himself as a worker bee. As a face in the crowd; as one among many. He saw himself as one. As special. He wanted more for himself. More money, more power, more respect.

Jimmy could never have that on Antonio's job. He could make a living, sure, but he could never make a name for himself. He could never matter. Jimmy would walk away from the worksite, against his father's wishes. He would find another way to make money; to make himself matter. He wasn't sure what he wanted to do, or how he would go about doing it. But at the very least he knew what he didn't want to do. He didn't want to be like everybody else. More to the point, and more painful a realization, for both he and Antonio alike, he didn't want to be like his father.

Employers would enlist tough, young, unemployed guys like my father as enforcers. Their job was to stop union organizers and members from striking. By any means necessary. It would cost the employers more money to get the work done when dealing with a strong union. So breaking the union was in their best interest. When the union men threatened to strike for higher wages, guys like my father would come along, find a delegate, or a leader in the union, or even just an ordinary member, and they would send a message to the union, loud and clear. They would break the guy's head.

A crow bar, a lead pipe, a baseball bat. These were the tools of the trade. Of course, my father, big and strong as he was, needed little more than his hands to inflict significant damage on a man. He could lay a hurting on someone just by looking at them. In this brutal occupation, Jimmy found a place where he could earn respect. Where he could step out of his father's shadow and be his own man.

Jimmy was menacing. He was getting a reputation for being a hell of an enforcer. If a guy saw him coming, he knew what he was in for, and he started running. And if he didn't see him coming, well, then it was even worse.

Jimmy would take a pipe to a guy's kneecaps. Once he had him down on the floor, he'd rap him a few times in the head, for good measure. But he kept the guy conscious so that he could deliver the message he came to deliver. When he pulled the guy's bloody face close to his, he could be sure he had his attention at that point.

"You don't strike!" Jimmy would warn the union guy. "You hear what I say to you? No matter what anybody tells you, if I hear you went on strike, I'm gonna personally come looking for you. And next time, I won't be so kind about it!"

He'd throw the guy to the ground and walk off, pipe in hand. He'd leave the guy with the fear of God in him. Or better yet, the fear of Jimmy in him. He was an effective, efficient enforcer. Word of his ability spread. Everybody on the street knew about Jimmy. The union knew. The mob knew. Only Antonio didn't know. But it didn't take long for him to find out.

One night, after Antonio had gotten word of Jimmy's new job, he came home and confronted him. All hell broke loose in the Napoli house, which was now a six-family building in Williamsburg, Brooklyn that they had moved into from Hell's Kitchen.

When my father was three years old, Antonio took him back to Italy with him to settle up on some real estate he still owned there. Plus, Antonio had stashed away some gold and jewelry when he left Italy in a hurry. Antonio made sure Anna, who stayed in America, had enough money to support herself until he got back. He and young Jimmy were only gone a few months. When Antonio returned from Italy, this time on a nicer, cleaner ship, he brought money back with him. It was enough money to move the family out of Hell's Kitchen. He was able to buy a six-family house in Williamsburg.

Now here they were, father and son, in that house, getting ready for a war.

"*Vergogna!* Disgrace! You are a disgrace!" Antonio screamed at Young Jimmy, who sat, passively taking in the yelling that his father unleashed on him. "Those are hard-working men that you are hurting. Good men. *Our* men. And they've done nothing to you!"

"I'm doing my job," Jimmy said in a soft, self-assured manner, offering little resistance or explanation.

"Your job? It's your job to hurt a man who has done nothing to you?" Antonio blew his top.

Jimmy stood up to confront Antonio. He was now taller than his father. "Maybe you want to work with your hands your whole life, but I don't," Jimmy struck back. "I want more. I'm sick of seeing the signs that read, 'No greasball wops need apply.'"

"How many times have I told you, Vincenzo, there are no shortcuts? Everybody pays their dues. If not now, someday. What you are doing is wrong. Remember what I tell you, Vincenzo. When the chess game is over, the king and the pawn go into the same box."

He wasn't getting through to Jimmy.

Then Antonio laid down the law, once and for all. "If you continue to do this, you are not my son. I disown you. You leave my house right now, and you never come back here again."

Jimmy stared at Antonio for a long moment. Then he turned, without a word, and in an act that revealed the impetuousness of his youth, he stormed out of the apartment.

Antonio rushed to the door and yelled after him, down the long hallway, so that all the neighbors could hear, *"Tu non sei mio figlio!" You are not my son!* He said it over and over again as Jimmy disappeared down the tenement steps and out of sight.

Antonio turned and looked at Anna, who had been listening from the other room.

"Antonio, what did our son do that is so wrong?" she asked in her sweet and innocent tone.

"Son?" Antonio answered her with a question. "What son? We don't have a son."

Anna put her face in her hands and cried as she ran from the room. Antonio went to the window and watched Jimmy walk down the street. As if feeling the weight of his father's stare, Jimmy turned and looked up at the window. They made brief eye contact.

Then, with both of them too proud to give in at this point, Jimmy turned away, just as Antonio brought down the shade.

Chapter 6

Lorimer Street Gang

IN ITALIAN NEIGHBORHOODS, PRIESTS AND gangsters were held in virtually the same esteem. Both were men who helped the community, who lent a helping hand to those in need. Both were loved and feared, and most of all, respected.

When someone was in trouble, depending on the kind of trouble, they either went to their priest or their local wiseguy or street-level hudlum. They were the arbiters of right and wrong. They doled out justice and righteousness. They settled situations that were out of the domain of the law and the courts, which nobody trusted anyway. They were men of honor, who were respected in their neighborhoods, and responsible for solving problems, both big and small. And their word was final.

So when Jimmy Nap left home, he had two choices—go to the church or go to the social club.

He went to the social club.

Jimmy's reputation as an enforcer brought him enough recognition so that the local wiseguys knew him, and would let him and his band of street tough friends crash in their back room. They knew Jimmy was hardheaded. He wasn't going back home. So rather than have him stay out on the street—something the wiseguys would never let happen—they let him stay in the club. They kept him and his friends around to run errands and do other odd jobs and favors for them.

The social club was a dimly lit, smoke-filled gambling den, frequented by the local wiseguys of the day. They talked business over black coffee, while regulars played cards at felt-covered tables, with several games going at once. The espresso machine at the small service bar in the back got a good workout by the old man who pumped out one cup after another.

In the back room, a group of young hoodlums, including Jimmy, laid around on army cots. They smoked cigarettes and counted money—the money they made from the odd jobs they were given. Most of their time they spent waiting to be called upon to run an errand.

When they were needed, the old man would leave the espresso machine and knock on the back room door. He'd pop his head in and call on one of the boys to come out to the front room, where a wiseguy would give their instructions.

The old man stuck his bald head into the room, on this one occasion: "Jimmy Nap..."

"Why's Jimmy get to go again? He just went!" one of them charged.

"It ain't that. And mind your business," the old man snapped back at the hood. "He's got someone here to see him."

"To see *me*?" Jimmy asked, "Who is it?"

"Father Gaetano," replied the old man.

"Father Gaetano? What does he want?"

The old man shrugged. "Says he wants to talk to you."

"All right, well...then send him back."

The old man pulled his head back and closed the door behind him.

"What do you suppose that priest wants?" the nosey hood asked Jimmy.

"What do priests always want?" replied Jimmy. "Money probably."

"Yeah, they got the real racket, huh?"

"All right shush, before he hears. That's all we need is to get God mad at us too."

With a gentle knock on the door, in walked Father Gaetano DiPietro, a tall, silver-haired priest. He was a commanding figure in his black shirt and white collar. Like a movie star in priest's clothing. He spoke in broken English with a thick Italian accent. "*Mi scusi*, Vincenzo. I don't a mean to interrupt."

"You're not interrupting, Father." Jimmy addressed the priest with the proper respect he deserved, at least to his face. "Please, come right in."

"*Buon giorno,* Gentleman," Father Gaetano addressed the other hoods.

"How ya doin', Father?" they said.

"Vincenzo, *per favore*, may I speak to you alone for a few minutes?" the priest asked.

"You heard him. Scram." Jimmy ordered the hoods out. "Ga 'head. Father wants to talk to me."

The hoods gathered their things and headed out of the room.

"*Grazie. Grazie.*" Father Gaetano thanked the boys as they each shook his hand and left the back room.

"Can I get you anything, Father? A cup of espresso?" Jimmy offered.

"No-no, thank you, Vincenzo. What I have a to say, it won't take a long." Then the priest spoke in Italian. *"Posso parlare in Italiano? E' piu' facile per me."* He asked Jimmy if he could speak in Italian. Said it would be easier for him.

Jimmy, who was fluent in Italian, agreed. "*Si, Padre,* of course."

Their conversation was in Italian.

"Your mother and father are very concerned for you, Jimmy," Father Gaetano explained. "You are a young man and they want what is best for you. They want you to come home."

"So they sent you to do their dirty work," Jimmy smirked.

"They didn't send me, Vincenzo. I've come on my own. They love you very much. Your father wants you to come back to work with him. You're his son. He wants you to be safe and happy."

"With all due respect, Father, you don't know what this is really about." Jimmy leaned in and took the priest into his confidence. "I don't want to be the man my father wants me to be. I want to be my own man. I want to be a leader like he is. But I want to do it my way, on my own. I have my own crew now, as you can see. My own men who listen to me and respect me. And I make more money doing this than I made working for him. So please, tell my father if he has something to say to me to come say it himself. He should not put you in the middle."

Father Gaetano nodded. "I can tell him you said that."

Then Jimmy added, "Yes, you tell him. And tell him this too. *Gli dica che il suo ragazzo ora e' un uomo.* His boy is now a man."

Father Gaetano stood up. "If you need anything, Vincenzo, I am always at the church."

Then, Jimmy stood up to meet the priest, eye to eye, and in English responded sharply, "And if you need anything, Father, you know where I am."

The priest stood frozen for a moment, taken aback by Jimmy's brazen but sincere comment. Jimmy was putting himself on the same level as the priest. He was making himself an equal, a peer. It was what Jimmy had wanted all along. It's what made him leave his job; what made him leave his home. To be viewed with respect. By his friends, by his father, by this priest. And here he was now, not asking for it, but in his own way, demanding it.

"Grazie," replied Father Gaetano, as almost if in a whisper. He headed for the door.

Jimmy watched him go. He was emboldened by what he had done and what he had said. He felt strong. He felt big. And at this point in his life, big was all he wanted to be.

Jimmy and his band of hoodlums became known as The Lorimer Street Gang. They prowled the streets of Brooklyn, enforcing mob rules. My father, by natural selection—he was the biggest guy and the boldest of the group—became the leader of the gang. There was no numbers racket in those days, so they made their money protecting storeowners from other gangs in the neighborhood.

Jimmy and his Gang would go into a store, shake the owner down for protection money and leave with either cash in their hands or blood on them. Usually it was the cash.

Then they would head into lower Manhattan and menace the street vendors who sold clothes in the open-air markets. They'd steal secondhand suits off the street racks on Delancey Street. They'd grab a suit, not having time to check for the size and run their tails off, as the Jewish street venders chased after them with broomsticks, cursing in Yiddish. *"De klyner lidegier mamzer! Guy arbeta bissel!"* which meant, "You little nothing bastards! Go work a little!"

Then Jimmy and the boys would return to Brooklyn and walk the streets in their sharp, stolen suits. The suits were usually a little big in the shoulders and sleeves. But they were still the best dressed street punks in their neighborhood.

There were things that my father did back in them days that he would, years later, tell me he wasn't particularly proud of. The stealing, the fighting, the shakedowns— he never seemed to have any regrets about any of that. It was par for the course. It just came with the territory. But there was one thing he did that, even all those years later, stuck in him.

The local wiseguys paid my father to run certain people out of the neighborhood. No, let me be specific. They paid him to run *black* people out of the neighborhood.

As I said, it wasn't something to be proud of, and my father wasn't. But that's just the way it was then. In what had become an insulated and almost exclusive community of Italians, racism and bigotry were rampant. There was no tolerance for those who were different. You stayed with your own, you married your own, and you never mixed with people of other religions or races. Whether you agreed with that or not, you just did it because that's what everybody else did. That's just the way it was. Also, when the wiseguys asked you to do something, you didn't ask why. You did it.

So Jimmy would sit behind the wheel of a big, heavy Ford Model T. It was one of the wiseguys' cars and they would lend it to him for this assignment. His eyes would scan the street, darting back and forth across the windshield, looking for someone who "didn't belong." Or at least someone he was told didn't belong in their neighborhood. A black man.

He waited to see if any black men walked into the neighborhood. If they had, it was probably by accident, or because they had no choice but to cross through the neighborhood on their way to or from some other neighborhood. But it didn't matter. They weren't allowed. And it was Jimmy's job to make sure they stayed out.

If Jimmy saw a black man crossing the street, even if it was a block up ahead of him, he would rev the Ford engine and slam on the accelerator. He rushed headlong toward the black man. Seeing the car coming at him, the black man would run for his life down the street.

Jimmy would chase the man up onto the sidewalk, often just missing pedestrians and other parked cars. The man would scream as the car got closer and closer to him, believing that Jimmy would run him down. My father said that he never would have run a man over just for being black, but the man sure as hell didn't know that at the time.

Coming within inches of taking the man's life, Jimmy would then ease up on the accelerator. The black man would race across a large two-way street, never looking back. He crossed an invisible line, separating one neighborhood from another, blacks from whites. He went back to where he came from, which was what the wiseguys wanted.

My father said he would slump over the steering wheel after he did this, ashamed of what he had done and hoping no one he knew would see him. There were many things, many compromises a man had to make when choosing a life in the rackets. Sometimes you had to follow orders that you didn't agree with. You hurt people who you didn't think deserved to be hurt. My father was learning this the hard way. The hands-on way. He was earning money and gaining respect, like he wanted, like those he looked up to. He was also learning that that respect came with a price.

My father was a wiseguy, in training.

Chapter 7

The Torpedo

My father was a fighter in every sense of the word. Both inside and outside the ring.

Whenever I go to the monthly meetings at The Waterfront Crab House in Long Island City—owned by a protective Tony Mazzarella—and I look out at the members of the Ring 8 Veteran Boxers Organization, which my father founded, I can't help but think about how he loved and respected fighters.

Jimmy Nap founded Ring 8 to help fighters who get old or hurt and can't support themselves. Some of them can't pay their rent or their medical bills. My father hated to see them in that condition. I remember my father saying, "Fighters take a lot of punches and they are going to need financial help when they can't fight anymore. Nobody cares about a fighter who can't fight, and that's a shame."

He made champs like Jack Dempsey, Joe Louis, Jake LaMotta, and Sugar Ray Robinson honorary members. I'll help keep Ring 8 functioning for as long as I live. That's my pledge to my father.

Once, in the nineteen-fifties, in the middle of the night, when the Crab House was closed and completely empty, some young punk tried to throw a Molotov Cocktail through the window. It's a bottle with a gasoline-soaked rag hanging out from the neck. Two of Jimmy's crew members who protected the place saw him. They snatched the cocktail from him and threw the young punk to the ground.

"You want me to shove this up your ass?" the crew member threatened. "Do you? Do you know whose place you're fuckin' with? I should shove this bottle straight up your ass and light it!"

The punk couldn't even respond, and then he was nearly unconscious from the beating. The crew member took the bottle and tossed it into the East River. The next day the punk was brought to see Jimmy Nap for a sit-down at his Hi-Way Lounge.

My father's place was located in the shadow of the Williamsburg Bridge in Downtown Brooklyn, on the corner of Havemeyer Street and Metropolitan Avenue. It was his old haunt. It was his club, his hangout, his *joint*. It's where he did his business all day, every day. Numbers, loansharking, meetings with the likes of Fat Tony, Chin, Rusty, Carlo Gambino. Anybody who was anybody came through the doors of the Hi-Way in those days.

The blue-tinted windows gave the place something of a "members only" appearance and kept any pains-in-the-ass who were unwanted out of the lounge. Put it this way, if you weren't invited in, then you didn't belong. And if you did belong, then you behaved yourself when you were in there. There was no official membership policy, no card to carry, no secret password that got you into the place. If you were a member, if you belonged, then you knew it.

The Hi-Way was my father's roost and he ruled it. His business buzzed around him: number runners came and went. And in a back room, he settled the affairs of local businessmen and others who had problems in the neighborhood. This is where he conducted his sit-downs.

Jimmy Nap presided over the discussion between the punk, whose beaten face and head were bandaged up, arm in a sling, and Tony Mazzarella. My father asked me to sit in, so I sat beside him and observed, saying very little.

Jimmy addressed the punk first. "I'm going to let you live. But there's only one reason for that. Your Uncle Giovanni. He's going to accept responsibility for your actions. If you do anything out of order, against any of my people again, your uncle will make you disappear. He gave me his word on that."

This was the code in the streets. If one of your own does something wrong, the burden becomes yours. This is something my father knew well, because of all my years of getting in and out of trouble.

Jimmy continued talking to the punk. "Now apologize to Mr. Mazzarella over here for what you did. He was your boss. He fired you. So be it. But you don't hurt the place of business."

The punk tried to speak, "I'm sorry, Jimmy…"

Jimmy interrupted him. "Don't apologize to me. He was your boss. Not me. Now go ahead, apologize, so we can put this behind us."

The punk looked over to Mazzarella. "Tony, I'm really fuckin' sorry for—"

My father interrupted him again. "Whoa! We don't use that kind of language in here. This isn't the street."

My father hated bad language to be used in his presence. He never cursed and he never wanted anyone around him to curse. He thought it ill-mannered and vulgar.

"I'm sorry, Jimmy," the punk said nervously, and then he apologized to Mazarella, "And I'm sorry Tony, about what I done…what I tried to do…to your joint."

The Punk and Mazzarella shook hands.

Jimmy wasn't done yet.

"And tell him about how you're gonna come by at least once a week," Jimmy said to the punk, "with your friends and spend a good hundred dollars in Tony's place."

The punk was stunned. "Huh?"

"Tell him. To make up for all the trouble you caused."

"Yeah…yeah, like Jimmy says, I'm gonna come in once a week and spend fifty…" the punk looked to Jimmy, who wasn't satisfied. "I mean, spend a hundred dollars in your place."

"That's very nice of you," Mazzarella said. "I appreciate that."

"Okay, get going. And stay out of trouble," Jimmy instructed the trembling punk.

The punk stood and nodded to Jimmy. He turned to each of us in the room. "Thank you…Thanks…Thank You…"

The punk left, nearly tripping over himself on the way out. Jimmy turned to Mazzarella. "You gotta hurt them in their pockets, where they feel it. To teach them a lesson."

Mazzarella stood and went to Jimmy. He kissed him on both cheeks. "Thank you for saving my place."

When Mazzarella left the room, my father turned to me. "There's nothin' that can't be settled with a sit-down, TN. Remember that. You bring all the world leaders in here, gimme ten minutes with them, there'd be no more wars. I guarantee you that."

I nodded in agreement with him. Not interrupting, just listening as he went on. "We're a government unto ourselves. We should run the real government. Not these button-down Anglos who talk God-this, God-that, and then screw everybody every chance they get. They do it with paperwork and process. Discrete. Behind a curtain, like Oz. Like cowards. Little men. They don't even have the guts to look you in the eye before they hang ya. Where have all the men gone, TN?"

"I wish I knew, Daddy-O. I wish I knew," I said.

"Should be men runnin' things, not these Ivy League sissies." Then he stood. "If only it were that easy, TN. If only it were that easy."

To make a little money when he was younger, my father fought other gang members at the armory. A makeshift boxing ring was set up in the center of what was formerly a large storage area and center for military drills and equipment. As I said, the boxing was as much about pride and street credibility, as it was about the money. To survive on the streets, you had to be able to handle yourself and gain respect. My father could handle himself inside and outside the ring. They called him "The Torpedo."

Young street guys from the surrounding neighborhoods sat in the stands made of long wooden planks placed on top of milk crates. When Jimmy entered the ring, his Lorimer Gang would cheer him on. When his opponent stepped between the ropes, a gang member from another part of Brooklyn, his crew cheered him on. The two gangs would hurl insults at each other in the stands as Jimmy hurled right hands at his opponent in the ring.

"Go back to Williamsburg, you lowlives!" they shouted at the Lorimers.

The Lorimers would go back at them. "Hey, up yours, you Bensonhurst scum!"

One of Jimmy's fights usually went something like this…

The bell sounded and the bigger, burlier Jimmy would stalk the quicker, shiftier opponent. Jimmy was bigger than most but also slower than most. Jimmy would take a few jabs to the head and then return fire, with two straight right hands, that would rock his opponent. Jimmy then cornered him and landed one pulverizing right hand after another. Soon the opponent hit the canvas and was counted out by the referee.

Jimmy would raise his hands in victory and point out to the Lorimer Gang in the stands. The gang celebrated and stuck it in the face of the rival gang. They had bragging rights. They had the toughest gang member and best fighter in Brooklyn on their side. They had "The Torpedo" in their corner. And when you had Jimmy in your corner, you had a friend for life.

Chapter 8

The Other Side of The Family

ON THE OTHER SIDE of Brooklyn, in Bensonhurst, was the other side of the family. My mother's side. Maria and Giuseppe Perrotta. The ones who came over on the same banana boat as Antonio and Anna Napoli.

My grandfather Giuseppe died young of a massive heart attack. Maria, being the heartless witch that she was, didn't waste much time in replacing him.

Maria had a revolving door of men after Giuseppe passed away. One after the other she fed 'em and bed 'em. Until she finally settled on a big fish—the head of the Five Points Gang in Brooklyn, Francesco Ioele or Frankie Yale. Yale had killed a dozen men before his twenty-first birthday. Legend also has it that Yale kept the handles of two knives whose blades were stuck into the torso of a gang informer, and that he proudly displayed them on a plaque on his wall.

You might say Maria knew how to pick 'em. Yale was married with kids, too. Didn't matter to Maria. She was his *goomada*—his mistress. A kept woman. But as long as she was being taken care of, she didn't care.

The only good thing that ever came from Maria was a beautiful little girl named Grace. My mother. Grace was a sweet, obedient girl. Even well into her teens she listened to her mother and treated her with the respect a mother had coming to her. Even when Maria didn't deserve it.

Grace watched the parade of men come and go. A different one at the dinner table every few months. But once Maria started seeing Yale, he became a fixture in the Perrotta house, which was a nice change of pace. Grace appreciated any sense of permanence, even if in the end she knew it was only temporary.

Yale would come over for dinner several nights a week, and they would sit and eat, like something of a family.

Maria could cook, I'll give her that. Yale loved her gravy. "Best gravy I ever tasted," he would tell her, in Italian, as he twirled his spaghetti. "Better even than my own grandmother's."

"You flatter me," Maria would say. She flattered easily.

Grace was a picky eater. But one night she was being even more picky than usual, as she sat at the table and moved her food around the plate without eating.

Maria jumped on her, like she always did, "*Mangia*. What's the matter, Grace? Don't you like the gravy? You haven't touched it."

Grace, always timid and quiet, responded politely, "*Si*, Mama, I like it. I'm just not very hungry. I have to ask you something."

"Ask me something? *Che cosa?* What do you have to ask me?"

"Please don't get mad at me when I ask you, Mama," she said.

"Grace, just ask me or I will get mad."

Grace fought back her nerves, swallowed hard and asked away. "Well, they are having a costume dance for Halloween down at the ballroom and I was wondering if..."

Maria cut her off before she could even finish her sentence, "No. You can't go. No."

"But, Mama, all of my friends will be there. I never get to go anywhere. I promise I'll be home early. Whatever time you want me to be. Please."

"There will be boys at this dance. No?"

"So, what's wrong with boys? You seem to like them," Grace looked at Frankie, who was trying to eat and not get involved.

"Don't you be disrespectful to me!" Maria warned as she slapped Grace's arm.

"*Scusami* Mama, but I really want to go. Please."

Maria looked over to Frankie, "What am I gonna do with her?"

"She's *your* daughter," Frankie commented and returned to his meal.

Grace folded her hands in front of her and begged, "*Per favore Mama*, please!"

Maria stood and paced the kitchen, up and down, tortured by the decision whether or not to let her 14-year-old daughter go to a simple little neighborhood dance. She never wanted to relinquish control over Grace. She wanted her under her thumb and at her beck and call at all times.

She worried that if the girl got a taste of freedom and real life, she'd lose her forever.

Frankie spoke up. "Oh, what's the big deal, let the girl go, Maria. It'll be fun. If she runs into any boys you don't like, I can always take care of them for you."

Maria took in Frankie's words. Then, reluctantly, she gave in. "Okay, fine, you can go. But be home early!"

Grace smiled and leaped from the table in celebration. "*Grazie*, Mama, *grazie!*"

"Thank Mr. Yale too, for sticking up for you."

"*Grazie*, Mr. Yale."

"My pleasure, sweetheart," Yale said with a smile. "Have a good time. And remember, if any boys get out of line with you, you tell me."

"*Si*, I will."

"Now finish your dinner." Maria she sat back down at the table.

Grace lifted a forkful of spaghetti and ate it with a smile, making her mother happy.

The dance was held on the third floor of the Grand Paradise Ballroom. It was full of neighborhood kids dressed up in disguises for Halloween. They danced and drank punch, as a small three-piece band provided the music for the festivities.

Grace paraded around in a Mae West costume, looking oddly like her own mother, Maria.

The lead singer and organ player in the band, Stefano, looked at Grace and winked at her. She flashed a demure smile and kept walking. Stefano fancied himself her date for the evening, but Grace remembered what her mother said: no boys. She took it to heart.

That is, until she caught the eye of the handsome Jimmy Nap, who was the only person in the place not in a costume. Instead he was dressed nattily, in a three-piece suit and tie. He made his way over to Grace.

"Hello there. My name is Jimmy. What's yours?"

Grace hid behind her best Mae West impersonation, "Why it's Mae West, of course."

"Pleased to meet you, Miss West," Jimmy played along. "I never met a movie star before."

"Well, maybe you can...come up and see me some time."

"I'd love to," Jimmy smiled.

"Who, might I ask, are you supposed to be?" Grace asked.

"Me. I'm just me. I'm my own man. I don't need to be anybody else."

Grace dropped the Mae West voice and addressed Jimmy sincerely, "Loosen up. It's a party."

"I'm not one for parties. I prefer one on one."

From the stage, Stefano, the performer, saw Jimmy and Grace talking. When his song was over, he stepped down from the stage and approached them.

"What's the idea?" he confronted Jimmy.

"Excuse me?" Jimmy shot back at him, thinking that this guy apparently never heard of "The Torpedo."

"I say, what's the idea? She's my date."

"No, she *was* your date," Jimmy corrected Stefano.

Stefano looked at Jimmy Nap, and seeing that he was bigger, tougher and now even madder than him, he reached out and grabbed Grace by the hand and attempted to pull her away. She resisted.

"Hey pal, it doesn't look like the lady wants to go with you," Jimmy said out.

"Mind your business," Stefano snipped at Jimmy.

"Ow! You're hurting me," Grace yelled and pulled away.

"What are you going to do?" Stefano grilled her, "Stay here with this two-bit street trash?"

Grace looked away, embarrassed. A crowd circled them.

"Grace? Is that what you're going to do?" Stefano continued to question her.

She moved closer to Jimmy.

"It's just as well," Stefano said, in disgust. "Trash goes with trash."

Stefano turned to walk away. Jimmy looked over to Grace, trying to fight back her tears. Jimmy rushed to Stefano and lifted him from the back of his pants. He carried him to a window and opened it. Holding Stefano by the ankles, Jimmy dangled him out the window.

Stefano screamed, "Let me go!"

Grace and the rest of the partygoers looked on in horror.

"Do you really want me to let you go? Do you want me to drop you on your head, you two-bit organ player?" Jimmy Nap threatened.

"No! No, dear God, no!" Stefano shouted, "Somebody help me!"

Nobody was going to help him.

"Then say you're sorry."

"I'm sorry. I'm sorry!"

"Not to me. To this pretty young lady here, whom you insulted in front of all these people."

"I'm sorry. I'm so sorry, Grace!"

"That's better."

Then Jimmy pulled Stefano back in. Stefano, now a disheveled mess, quivering and shaking all over, looked at Grace and then looked away in shame. He rushed out of the ballroom. The partygoers giggled and cheered.

"Okay, everybody go back to the party," Jimmy said, "The show's over!"

The band played again and everyone returned to the dance floor.

Grace shot Jimmy a piercing stare.

"What? What did *I* do?"

Grace's angry expression gave way to a small smile that she quickly tried to cover up.

Now I don't know if it was the drama of their first meeting but my mother somehow discovered, to her surprise, that she was attracted to this violent, but intriguing stranger. Love is a funny thing.

Jimmy took Grace by the hand and led her onto the dance floor. They danced a slow dance together.

By this time, Jimmy Nap and his crew were expanding their business from small time street crime into a viable money-making operation. They converted Tommy Murphy's Pool Hall on Union Avenue in Williamsburg into an after-hours gambling den. They turned the pool tables into crap tables, by clearing the balls off and covering the pockets.

One night, a tall, heavy-set man entered the pool hall. He was impeccably dressed, with shiny, greased back hair. He was unfamiliar to Jimmy and his crew, but he carried himself like somebody who was important.

Jimmy, seeing the man walk in, turned to a his crew member and said, "I thought you locked the door."

"I thought I did too," the crew member replied.

"Who is this guy?" Jimmy Nap asked.

"Maybe a cop?"

"Let's find out."

Jimmy went up to the stranger, now picking out a pool cue and chalking it up.

"Listen pal, we're closed," Jimmy told him.

The man held out his hand. "Jackie...pleasure to meet you."

Jimmy ignored his hand, "I said we're closed."

"One quick game of Chicago," the stranger named Jackie said, "I challenge you. For fun. No money."

Jimmy Nap didn't like to be challenged. "Listen to me, I'll wrap that pool stick around your head. We need these tables for crap games. So get your fat ass out of here!"

Jackie nodded, placed the pool cue back on the wall and walked out without saying another word.

The crew member asked Jimmy, as he locked the door behind the stranger, "What do you think, was he a cop?"

"No, no cop," Jimmy said. "He was nobody."

My father would find out years later that the man who he thought was *nobody* was actually the Great One, actor Jackie Gleason.

This pool hall was my father's first gambling operation. Local gamblers would come in every night to play. They were mostly compulsive degenerates who would run out of money and get themselves into debt. That's when the place also became a loan sharking den. And when these pathological gamblers racked up huge debts and couldn't pay the money back...well, that's where my father also came in, to help collect.

A gambler who owed money, but wouldn't or couldn't pay, was given a special treatment.

He'd sit on a chair in the back room, his hand trembling as he held a drink that Jimmy Nap poured for him.

Jimmy would address the gambler: "This is a lot of money. You know that, don't you?"

"I know it is, Jimmy. I know it." They always knew what they owed. They knew it was a lot.

"And you know it was given to you in good faith. I mean, when you asked for it, it was there for you, right? No questions asked. Am I right?"

"You're right, Jimmy," the gambler would admit. "But what can I do? I don't have it. Can you take blood from a stone? I don't have it. If I had it, I'd pay it."

They always pulled that 'if I had it I'd pay it' bullshit. Jimmy would then reach into the inner pocket of his suit jacket and pull out a gun. That would shake the gambler up but good.

"Oh God, Jimmy, no, please! I got kids." They always got kids, and they always throw up those kids when they think they're going to be killed.

"What are you talking about?" Jimmy would ask them. "You think I would shoot you? Over what? Over money? C'mon. What are we, animals?"

The gambler would breathe a sigh of relief. "Thank you, Jimmy. Thank you."

"No-no," Jimmy Nap would say, and then he would surprise them by holding the gun out to them. "This is for you."

The gambler wouldn't know what to say. "For me? What am I gonna do with it?"

"Take it."

Apprehensively, the gambler would take the gun from Jimmy.

"Now go out and pull a holdup. That way you can pay back what you owe," Jimmy Nap would instruct them.

"Are you serious?" They always wondered if he was serious.

He was serious.

"Very," Jimmy would reassure them. "And don't come back until you have it. And if you don't come back, I'll come looking for you. Now get outta here."

The stunned and confused gambler would stand and slowly head for the door. "But what should I hold up, a bank or a store or…"

"That's up to you."

The gambler would put the gun in his jacket pocket and leave the back room of the pool hall. A few days later he would return with the money.

I used to ask my father, "Do you think they really went on a hold up?"

He'd say, "I hope not. There were no bullets in the gun. You think I would hand somebody a loaded gun?"

My father knew that these guys could pay what they owed, in most cases. They just didn't want to. They thought a sob story or begging would get them out of paying their debt. They thought they could pull a fast one. They thought wrong. My father used to say that you'd be surprised how much money somebody could come up with when his life depended on it. And he was right too.

So things were moving along for Jimmy Nap in the 1950's. He was making more money, his reputation was growing, and he had a good young woman that he was falling in love with. Grace didn't know what Jimmy did. She didn't ask. He didn't tell. They were young and enjoyed each other's company. That was all that mattered.

It took Grace's mind off what was going on back at home, with Maria and her turbulent relationship with Frankie Yale. If Grace wanted to see what life with a gangster was going to be like, she had to look no further than her own house. Yale was always in trouble. Cops were always looking for him. After a while, even Maria's apartment was uncovered as a Yale hideout. Maria, and sometimes even Grace, got caught in the middle of things.

One day, Maria stood over the stove, as usual, stirring her meat sauce. There was a loud knock at the apartment door. She went to the door with a broomstick in her hand—never sure who or what to expect from Yale and his cohorts.

"Who is it?" she asked.

"Maria, it's me! Open up quickly!" Frankie Yale said.

Maria tossed aside the broomstick and opened the door. Frankie rushed in, out of breath and nervous.

"Frankie, what is it? What's wrong?"

"They're coming! We have to hide it!" Frankie was looking around the apartment and talking fast.

"Who's coming? Hide what?" Maria wanted to know.

"The cops! They're on their way up! We have to hide this," Frankie opened his hand and showed Maria a gun.

"Madre di Dio!" she said to herself and made the sign of the cross.

"We have to hide it! But where?" Frankie searched through the apartment—in the closet, under the sofa, inside the kitchen cabinets.

Maria thought for a moment, and then her eyes settled on the large pot of meat sauce on the stove. "In the pot!" she blurted out.

"In the pot? Are you nuts?" Frankie dismissed the idea.

"They'll never look in there. Put it in!" she lifted the lid.

With no time to argue and no better idea, Frankie placed the gun into the pot. It disappeared into the thick, rich, bubbling red sauce.

Moments later there was a loud pounding on the door. "Who is it?" Maria asked sweetly.

"The police. Open up!"

Maria obliged and opened the door. "Can I help you, officer?"

A police sergeant walked right past Maria and straight to Frankie, who was standing in the kitchen. The sergeant pushed Yale against the counter top and patted him down, while the other officer stood by the door near Maria.

"We know you had that gun on you, Yale," the sergeant who frisked him said. Then he turned to the other officer and ordered him, "Search the place."

The officer went through Maria and Grace's apartment. In her bedroom, Grace heard everything and but stayed out of the way. When the officer came into her room, she sat quietly.

"Please, don't break anything," Maria followed the officer around the room.

"You're wasting your time," Yale insisted to the police. "I don't have any gun. I didn't do nothin'."

"That'll be the day I take your word for anything, Yale. After we find the weapon, you can do all the talking you want, down at the station," the sergeant warned.

The officer returned to the kitchen. "The place is clean, Sarge. I couldn't find anything."

Feeling she had the upper hand now, Maria carried on, "He turned my whole house upside down!"

"What did you do with the gun, Yale?" the sergeant asked him.

"I don't know what you're talking about," Yale played stupid.

"Okay. Okay, fine. Fine, Yale. You got away with one this time," the sergeant conceded. Then he reached into a bag on the kitchen counter and grabbed a loaf of Italian bread. He tore off a piece of the bread.

"You dumped the gun somewhere. I don't know where it is. But I will..." the Sergeant walked to the stove and lifted the lid on the pot of meat sauce...and dipped the bread into it.

Maria and Frankie's eyes looked at the pot.

"...I will find it," continued the sargeant, who talked with his mouth full, chewing on the bread. "And when I do, I'm going to put you behind bars where you belong, Yale."

Maria placed the cover back on the pot.

"Good sauce," the sargeant complimented her.

"Non e' salsa, e' sugo, scemunito!" she said in Italian, so he wouldn't understand. It's not sauce. *It's gravy, stupid!*

The sergeant stared at Maria for a moment, then he shrugged and looked away. "I'll be watching you, Yale," was the last thing he said as he left the apartment, still eating his bread with gravy on it. The officer followed him out.

Maria locked the door behind the police.

"Madone!" sighed Frankie, "That was close."

"Tell me about it," said Maria. "I was sweating like a pig."

"Let me take the gun out," Frankie reached for the pot.

"No, it's boiling hot," Maria stopped him. "You'll burn your hand."

"So, what am I gonna do?"

"Aspetta un secondo," Maria held up a finger. She had an idea. She took two long wooden spoons. She placed them into the pot to fish out the gun.

"Are you sure you know what you're doing?" Frankie asked.

"Si. Watch…"

As Maria attempted to lift the gun out of the pot, she accidentally hit the trigger and the gun went off. Three shots rang out. Right through the pot. Bang!

Frankie hit the deck. Maria leapt back. They listened to see if the cops had returned.

The hot, sauce came shooting out through the holes in the pot and all over the kitchen walls and floor.

"Are you crazy!" Frankie yelled at Maria. "You could've killed us!"

"Maybe we should just wait until it cools off," Maria suggested, with a straight face.

"Oh, you think so, huh?" Frankie joked, as he stood up.

Maria and Frankie laughed, and then kissed. And as she watched from her bedroom, through a crack in the door, young Grace laughed too.

Chapter 9

Al Capone and The Kiss of Death

FRANKIE YALE, WHO RULED THE Five Points Gang in those days, and thereby ruled much of Brooklyn, had taken a shine to my father. He had heard about "The Torpedo" Jimmy Nap from Williamsburg and moved to recruit the young street-tough and bring him into his ranks. A kid like my father, brought into the fold, could be useful to Yale and his operation. A kid like my father, left outside and to his own devices, could be a threat to Yale and his operation. So he brought my father in.

Yale had a direct connection to young Jimmy Nap since he was dating Grace. Yale was only a half step from Jimmy Nap. Reaching out to him was easy. And Yale did.

One day Jimmy was walking Grace home, as he did every day of their courtship. They stood on her front stoop, saying their long, teenage goodbyes until they would see each other again in 12 hours. But when you're young and in love, hours can seem like weeks. So goodbyes tend to take a little longer. They talked and giggled in that special way that only young love-struck kids can. They enjoyed each other's company and they were inseparable. Goodbyes were never easy for them, as they hated being apart. So their farewells would often drag on. But Grace knew she would have to make it upstairs before her mother stuck her head out the window and saw her cavorting with Jimmy. Maria didn't want Grace seeing any boys, especially not Jimmy. Maria could date a hundred men, married or otherwise, and yet she forbade Grace from even talking to boys.

Grace explained as they reached her building, "I'd better get upstairs before my mother…"

"You got a nice building here," Jimmy said. He liked everything about Grace, including the rundown tenement she lived in.

"It's a building," Grace shrugged.

"Ya know, my father used to build buildings. And tunnels. And bridges…"

"Used to?" Grace inquired, "Why, he doesn't do it anymore?"

"I guess he does. I don't know. I don't talk to him."

"You don't talk to your father? How could someone not talk to their father?"

"So I guess you talk to yours, huh?"

"He's dead."

"Oh, I'm sorry."

"But I still talk to him. Every night before I go to bed."

"Yeah, but does he talk back? That's the real question," Jimmy joked.

"Sometimes. I hear his voice. I know he's there."

"I still hear my father's voice too," Jimmy then broke into an impersonation of his strict, heavily Italian-accented father, Antonio: "*Stronzo*, what's a the matter with a you? Be a useful. Pick up a brick!"

Grace laughed. Jimmy could always make her laugh, even when she knew what he was saying was mixed with both humor and melancholy. Jimmy was 17. Grace was 14. She saw him as experienced, worldly, an older man who could love and protect her. And he could also crack her up. What more could a girl want?

Just then, Frankie Yale walked out of the tenement building. No doubt having just come from a mid-day rendezvous with Maria.

Grace quickly stopped laughing. Yale looked Jimmy up and down and then turned to Grace. "Hello, Grace," he said in a low, controlled voice.

"Hello," Grace responded and then looked down bashfully.

"What's so funny out here?" Yale asked without a smile on his face.

"Nothing. Just...laughing," Grace explained.

Yale looked Jimmy directly in the eye. Jimmy did not look away. Very few people looked Frankie Yale in the eye. He was a dark-haired, olive-complexioned man with a round, congenial face, but with eyes that could pierce right through you if you stared into them too long. Yale was Calabrese through and through, which meant he was hard headed, stubborn and didn't like taking "no" for an answer.

"This is my friend Jimmy." Grace offered, to help break an otherwise tense moment. "He's from Williamsbur—"

"I know who he is," Frankie interrupted her, "And I know where he's from."

Then Frankie turned to Jimmy. "I heard some things around the neighborhood about you, kid."

"All good, I hope."

"All good. I maybe could use a young guy like you."

"I'm flattered you feel that way."

Yale turned to Grace, who already had one foot in the building. She was a smart young woman. She grew up in the neighborhood. She knew that when men like Yale spoke they usually wanted their privacy.

"You should probably go up now. Your mother's waiting for you," Yale instructed Grace.

"Okay, I will," Grace replied, already on her way.

Grace looked at Jimmy, who was no longer smiling but was wearing a look on his face that was all business.

"Well, I'll see you tomorrow," Grace told Jimmy, as if she were saying goodnight to a co-worker after a long day, rather than to the young man she was falling in love with.

"See you tomorrow," Jimmy shot back.

Then the teenagers exchanged a short wave goodbye and Grace disappeared into the tenement. Jimmy watched Grace into the building but out of the corner of his eye he felt the weight of Yale's stare. Then he looked back at Yale, who had started talking already.

"I got a job for you, kid. It involves a little travel. You ever been to Chicago?"

"Chicago? I never been outta Brooklyn," Jimmy admitted.

"I want you to bring something to one of my guys out there. His name's Al. Big Al. Do you think you could handle that, kid?"

Jimmy stared at Yale, long and hard. Neither of them blinked. Then, Jimmy gave a slow and certain nod to Yale, which said without any doubt that he could handle it.

The truck barreled down the desolate stretch of interstate ahead. In the driver's seat, Jimmy Nap commanded the wheel of the big rig.

In the back of the diesel truck, stacks and stacks of bootleg beer and whiskey barrels rattled around. With no radio and no passengers, it was a lonely, dangerous run from New York to Chicago for Jimmy. If cops didn't get you, hijackers just might. But for young Jimmy Nap, making the run meant making his bones. Getting the alcohol there on time and undamaged was a job that his bosses in New York, namely Frankie Yale, had entrusted to him. It was also a job the new boss of Chicago, Al Capone, took very seriously.

When Jimmy arrived, Capone's henchmen rushed from the factory to unload the illegal alcohol. They always unloaded under cover of night to avoid attention. But everyone in Chicago knew what they were doing, including many of the police, who were on Capone's payroll. Jimmy didn't help the henchmen unload the truck. It wasn't his job. The henchmen, as the worker bees, would unload one truck and load up another so that the driver, in this case Jimmy, would have a full cab of whiskey to haul back to New York.

A grizzled, older henchman approached Jimmy just as he pulled up in the truck and said, "Big Al wants to see you inside."

Jimmy had never met Al before and knew that Al wanting to meet him might not be a good thing. "See me? What about?"

"Don't ask no questions. When Al asks for you, you just go."

Jimmy hopped out of the truck and headed into the factory.

Inside, Jimmy moved down a dimly lit corridor. His mind raced as he wondered what Capone could want from him. When Capone called for someone, it usually wasn't to give them a raise. Jimmy thought to himself, *What did I do wrong? Did I break bottles? Did somebody set me up for a fall? Am I going to be killed?*

That sense of insecurity and dread was something that was always a part of life in my father's business. Whenever a surprise meeting was called, or a boss sent for you for a meeting, or a *sit-down*, as they are more commonly called, there was always a sense, a fear, that this was it for you. Someone somewhere had said something and somehow you were going to get it. Maybe you didn't do anything wrong. Maybe you didn't deserve to get it. In this life, you never knew for sure if you'd done something wrong. It's a life filled wrought with lies, liars, and damn liars. Guys who sell out other guys to save themselves. The proverbial rat. The stool pigeon. But more often than not a guy can be putting you in more danger by talking trash to someone in your crew, or to a boss, instead of to a fed. And probably he's doing it to throw shade off of himself for something he did.

Life in the mob is all about who talks and who doesn't. A lot of guys in the life are like washerwomen, running back to a captain or a boss with any little tidbit of information they might hear. For some guys it's their only job—to snitch, to gossip, to talk about other guys. And social clubs, they're like tea parties, where neighborhood chit-chat is shared. Who did what, who said what, who disrespected who, is discussed a round robin of verbal one-upmanship. Guys in the mob love to talk. Whether it's to the government, or just to each other. The problem or hard part is finding out who said what to whom and how it might come back to get you.

Sometimes a guy who got whacked didn't even know he was in any trouble at all until the gun went off next to his head. The element of surprise in this business was something that kept its members and associates in a constant state of anxiety. The two biggest fears for anyone in this business—and don't let them ever tell you different—is getting pinched and getting whacked. Nobody, no matter how tough, no matter how hardened, wanted to go to jail or to die.

As my father walked down that dark, dank hall of the factory, all this went through his head. He peered into empty rooms as he passed. His mind was racing through all the possible permutations. Maybe he would get it in the back of the head and it would be over quickly. Maybe they would just break his legs. Or his hands. That he could handle. Or maybe he would get away with just a warning. Then he thought, *for what?* He hadn't done anything wrong. Emboldened by his innocence, and by the petulance of youth, he picked up his pace and continued on, looking for Al's room.

If my father learned anything on the streets, it's that men walk with their heads up, even if they are facing execution. A strong strident walk can sometimes be the difference between life and death on the street. So my father always stood tall, always walked straight, and always kept his head up.

At the end of the corridor, Jimmy saw a room with a door cracked open. Some light streaked out. He stopped for a moment and then gently, respectfully, knocked.

A deep, loud voice on the other side of the door responded," Come in!"

Jimmy pushed the door open slowly. A group of men were gathered around a desk. Their heads all turned to Jimmy as he stood in the doorway. Al Capone sat behind the desk. He was heavy set and balding, but impeccably dressed. He had a deep scar across his left cheek that explained the nickname Scarface.

"You wanted to see me, boss?"

Capone nodded at Jimmy and the men left the room, leaving my father and Capone to themselves. Jimmy stood in silence for a moment as Capone put away some odds and ends on his desk. Then Capone looked up at him. "So you're 'The Torpedo,' huh?" Capone asked.

"Yeah, some people call me that."

"Torpedos take things out. They destroy things. Are you a destroyer?"

"I'm whatever you want me to be, Mr Capone."

"That's a smart answer. You got a good head on your shoulders, huh?"

"I like to think so."

Capone liked everything about my father—his attitude, his presence, his answers. He had heard good things about Jimmy Nap from New York, from Frankie Yale. This was a kid he wanted in his organization. He had smarts and he had balls. Capone moved toward Jimmy.

"I wanna tell you something and you better believe it, kid. Once you're in this racket, you're always in it. You understand?"

Jimmy nodded. He let the teacher teach.

"There's only one way out. A pine box."

Capone stood face to face to Jimmy. "This is a great country, America. This system of ours, call it Americanism, call it capitalism—that's the legitimate racket of the ruling class. Call it whatever the hell you want. It gives each and every one of us a great opportunity. Your mother and father, they came over on a banana boat, just like mine did."

Jimmy attempted to answer, "They di—" But Capone wasn't asking him, he was telling him.

"They did it so we could be anything we wanna be. That's why mothers and fathers break their backs. So their kids won't have to. But you gotta seize the opportunity with both hands and make the most of it. Some kids are born into wealth. Their fathers are lawyers, doctors, congressmen. They got those footsteps to follow into. Other kids are born into poverty. Those kids gotta do whatever they gotta do. They gotta fight their way outta the streets."

Jimmy nodded again and again to let Capone know he was listening closely to his words.

"Don't get the idea I'm one of those goddamn radicals. Don't think I'm knockin' the American system. I'm a businessman myself. All I do is supply a demand."

Capone poured himself a drink. "My rackets run the same like any other business in this country. Only when I sell liquor, it's called bootlegging. When my patrons serve it on Lake Shore Drive, its called hospitality."

Jimmy smiled at the joke.

"Would you like a drink?" Capone digressed.

Jimmy shook his head. He didn't drink.

"We're one in the same, me and you. We're from the same place. You can take the kid outta the street, but you never take the street outta the kid. Capone sipped his drink and put his hand on Jimmy's shoulder. "There's certain people who think this American dream, it don't apply to Dago Wops like us. It's only for some people, not everybody. Some of these people, I hate to say it, they carry badges. But they're not good guys. Believe me. They think they're untouchable. But they're not."

Capone looked straight into Jimmy eyes. "I'm calling on you to do something for me. I want to make sure you're ready."

Without hesitation, without so much as a blink, Jimmy replied, "I'm ready. Whatever it is, I'm ready."

Capone cracked a small smile, wrinkling the famous scar on his face. "That's what I like to hear. That's exactly what I wanted to hear."

Capone put his drink down. He grabbed Jimmy's head between his two thick, strong hands and planted a kiss on Jimmy's lips—The kiss of death.

As night fell on a tree-lined suburban street in Illinois, two men in three-piece suits walked from a modest house. One was federal agent Joe Fuselli, the other was treasury agent Eliot Ness.

They walked to Fuselli's car parked at the curb in front of the house.

I've been told that the Robert Stack television program *"The Untouchables"* depicted this real life event in one of its episodes. The dialogue was probably very accurate.

"Eliot, we've taken down four storage houses in the past two months. Capone's feeling the heat," Fuselli reported.

"We have to shut down those supply routes. That's the only way to stop it. We have to cut it off from the source," Ness insisted. He was always looking for more effective ways to curtail bootlegging in America.

"But how do you stop people from getting something they really want? They'll always find a way," Fuselli responded.

Suddenly, Ness stopped and looked at Fuselli. "Don't you think I have doubts? Heck, doubts race through my mind every day when I consider what my job is—enforcing a law the majority of honest citizens don't even want. So don't tell me about reality."

Ness walked ahead of Fuselli and entered the car on the passenger side. Fuselli, fuming from the reprimand, got behind the wheel and started the car. "Listen, Eliot, all I'm trying to say is, maybe Volstead was wrong. Maybe Wilson was right. All this effort, all this money and bloodshed. For what? To uphold a law that's probably just going to be overturned someday, anyway?"

"It isn't our job to make the laws, Joe. It's our job to enforce them. If you don't like it, then why'd you get into police work anyway? I mean, what the hell, nobody lives forever."

Just then, a car screeched around the corner and stopped right beside theirs. A hooded assassin in the back seat brandishing a machine gun opened fire.

The rat-tat-tat was followed by the sound of bullets crashing against metal, breaking glass, and the screams of Joe Fuselli, who took the brunt of the barrage.

Ness ducked and scampered out the passenger side door. He lay on the sidewalk, unharmed, as he waited for the assassin's vehicle to drive off.

Joe Fuselli's body slumped dead over the steering wheel. Ness stood up and looked at his partner's bullet-ravaged body. He pulled Fuselli from the car and cradled him in his arms at the curb.

Residents came out from their homes. They saw the two government men there, curbside. Ness held onto Fuselli, whose blood was on Ness' white shirt and wool pants. Ness fought back tears as he clung to Fuselli, calling his name repeatedly."

At my home in Forest Hills, I have often watched that episode of *The Untouchables*. I grew up watching it as a kid. But I didn't always realize that I was watching, in some respect, a home movie. That episode is a permanent record of my father's youth, his connection to historic events, and his rise to power.

Announcer Walter Winchell's staccato voice-over capsulizes the episode.

"While Federal Agent Joe Fuselli lay dying on a Chicago street in Eliot Ness's arms, Al Capone was dining and living it up in a Chicago nightclub." Winchell continues, "It would never be known to the world that the man Capone kissed in that back room, in the mafia ritual known as The Kiss of Death, the man who was chosen to commit murder, was none other than "The Torpedo" from Brooklyn, Jimmy Napoli."

Chapter 10

Rise To Power

AFTER THE NESS EPISODE, MY father came back to New York to find that the bosses had a newfound respect for him. He started collecting for them on the streets and was making steady money. He was now their number one enforcer, in addition to the gambling operations he was running. His future in the mob looked bright.

But there was never any real job security in his business. Just look at what happened to Frankie Yale.

On a Sunday morning, July 1, 1928, Yale got a phone call at his Sunrise Club saying something was wrong with his wife Lucy, who was at home taking care of their three-year-old daughter. It was a set up.

Yale rushed out of his speakeasy and into his new coffee-colored Lincoln. He speed up New Utrecht Avenue. A couple of blocks later, Yale stopped at a red light. A Buick sedan pulled beside him. Four men inside the sedan stared at him. Yale sensed trouble just from the look on the driver's face, and he hit the gas, jumping the light. They pursued him. The cars raced through the streets of Brooklyn, Yale desperately trying to get away.

The sedan bumped Yale's Lincoln several times in the back, nearly causing Yale to lose control of the car, but he held on, straightened out his front end and stayed ahead of the Buick. He swerved onto a side street, but his car was overtaken by the sedan. The driver ran him off the street, onto the sidewalk, and into the front stoop of a brownstone.

Yale got out of the car and tried to run away. The four men jumped out of the Buick and opened fire on him. They riddled Yale with machine gun bullets. Neighbors rushed to their windows to see the commotion interrupting the quiet morning. But nobody called a cop, nobody got involved. Nobody ever would in these cases. Then, the four gunmen calmly returned to their sedan and drove off. Yale's bloodied body lay dead on that Brooklyn street. After a minute or two, neighbors came out to gawk and gossip. They gathered round the dead mob boss' body.

Frankie Yale had all of Brooklyn under his control, or at least he thought he did. He was feared and respected and popular among both his peers and his people. But nobody is ever completely safe in the world of the mob. Nobody.

Things go sour in this business, sometimes at the drop of a hat. The relationship between Yale and Capone soured, on both a personal and professional level. Yale didn't support one of Capone's men for a union position in Chicago. Capone, suspicious that Yale might be hijacking some of Capone's booze shipments, assigned one of his men spy on Yale. Yale gunned down the guy.

Capone would have the last word, ordering the hit on Yale. Cops questioned Capone. Nothing came of it. Nothing usually did in these situations. This was mob business. This is how it settled itself.

Yale received a funeral fit for a king, or at least a kingpin. Thousands of Brooklynites lined the streets to watch the funeral procession and pay their last respects to the mob boss. It took twenty-three cars to carry all of the floral arrangements and more than 100 cars were needed to transport all the mourners.

At the funeral, there was quite a stir when two different Mrs. Frankie Yale's came forward and presented themselves as his wife. One was his actual wife, Lucy Yale, and the other was Grace's mother, Maria.

Maria sat in the funeral parlor, in the first row before the casket, weeping, like the widow she thought herself to be. Lucy sat in the same row but on the other side of the room and never once looked in Maria's direction. Maria had no shame. Grace tried to console her, but Maria was hell bent on making a scene and drawing attention to herself, and away from Lucy. She was good for that. Maria howled, but the tears that were half real, half fake. And when someone new came into the room, she became a little louder, a little more dramatic.

"He's dead! *Morte!* Oh my God! Why?! Why him?"

Grace, dying of embarrassment, tried to be a good daughter as she always was. She slid next to Maria, and although mortified, put her arm around her mother. "It's okay, Mama. It's okay."

Maria pulled back on her crocodile tears long enough to butt into Grace's life yet again. She spotted Jimmy out of the corner of her eye, standing in the back of the funeral parlor with some local tough guys.

Maria leaned toward Grace and whispered to her, "Listen to me, Grace...do not get too serious with Jimmy. Never get too involved with a man in the rackets. He is going to spend the rest of his life in jail if he doesn't get out of this business. Or he might end up like Frankie..."

Seeing she had Grace's attention, and never missing the opportunity to exert her voodoo mind control over her daughter, she continued, "Never marry him. He'll never be all yours. A piece of him will always belong to them."

Maria gestured to the back of the room. Grace looked. She and Jimmy made eye contact and she smiled at him. He returned the smile. Then Grace turned to Maria. "Don't concern yourself with me and Jimmy right now, Mama. Don't worry about me. I'm here for you today. Not for me."

Grace hugged Maria, who noticed new mourners entering the room. She turned on the waterworks once again and started wailing.

Luckily, my mother didn't listen to Maria. She loved my father, and nothing her mother or anyone else said was going to change that. Nothing he did for a living was going to change it either.

On November, 29, 1932 Grace and Jimmy Nap were married in St. Mary's Church, on Leonard Street, in Williamsburg. My mother was 18 years old; my father was 21.

The best man was Tommy "Murphy" Napolitano, who owned the pool hall where the reception was held. His wife, Jennie, was the maid of honor.

In the pool hall, Grace and Jimmy had what was known as a "football wedding." That means Italian cold cuts were served and guests made their own sandwiches on loaves of Italian bread. The people who didn't get up to make their sandwich had someone else wrap it for them in paper and throw it to them like a football from the banquet table to the table they were sitting at.

The cold cut trays and pitchers of beer sat on the pool tables. A space in the middle of the hall was set aside for dancing. A three-piece brass band played. Jimmy paid for it all. And in the center of it all was the happy couple: Jimmy in a traditional black suit; Grace in an off-white ballroom dress that hanged down just below her knees, with no train or veil. As they smiled for photos, Maria sat in the corner of the room and scowled.

Grace was becoming her own woman. Maria hated that. She was a bitter, resentful woman and she would stay that way for the rest of her life, until she died of old age at 88. She was laid out with her left eye open because, the funeral director said, "the glue was not able to keep it closed." Even until the end she was a pain in the ass.

No matter how good my mother was to Maria—and she was good to her, believe me, she couldn't stand to see anyone else happy—not even her own daughter. And Grace was happy. She married the man she loved. And the man she loved was in love with her while starting to make a very nice living and nice name for himself.

As one mob boss, Frankie Yale, was gunned down on the streets of Brooklyn, another one, Jimmy Nap, was just beginning his rise to power on those same streets. It was at this time that my father became friends with, and started working with, the man who would one day become the boss of the Genovese family: Anthony "Fat Tony" Salerno.

My father would visit Fat Tony up at his East Harlem hangout—a candy store on east 115th Street where he ran his business. A sign above the front window announced: Palma Boys Social Club. The corner store is still there today—same name, different owners.

Jimmy Nap with a group of guys would enter the store through the cloud of cigar smoke and pass the dusty shelves that had old newspapers and magazines as a front—to a back door that lead to a private, members-only back room. Palma was basically a front for the real business of loan sharking and gambling. This back room always had a lively crap game going after the pool tables were converted. Big money deals were being made—sending and collecting funds from numbers, moving money to and from casinos in Vegas, and handling money from the unions—six days a week. I mean big money deals—even buying and selling casinos in other parts of the world.

Through the smoky haze and toward the back of the room, Jimmy's eyes would land on Fat Tony, who, in keeping with his name, was a chunky fellow, same age as my father, with a cigar that always dangled from his mouth. Fat Tony was always surrounded by tough guys; he barked out his orders and they jumped to follow them.

Jimmy, with the group of guys behind him, made his way over to Fat Tony and cut right through the tough guys.

"Hi Chief," my father would salute him. My father always called Fat Tony "Chief."

"Jimmy Nap!" Fat Tony would call out, and then he would remove his cigar from his mouth just long enough to kiss Jimmy on both cheeks. Then back into his mouth the cigar went.

"I brought you some customers." Jimmy referred to the group of guys that he walked in with. They were basically a group of degenerate gamblers who Jimmy knew would drop a bunch of money in Tony's place.

"Very good. No winners, I hope. We don't like winners in here," Fat Tony joked. Sort of.

"They're gamblers. No gamblers are winners."

"Good point."

Jimmy would point to the crap tables and the guys would help themselves to a night of gambling and boozing. It was really a night of losing, and making a healthy deposit into the coffers of Fat Tony's operation.

Fat Tony would gesture toward a door and Jimmy would follow him into the office. It was a small, makeshift space with milk crates and boxes stacked up everywhere. Tony sat behind a desk in the center of the room and lit his cigar. Jimmy sat in a chair before him.

"I heard about the thing at the track. No more action there, huh?" Fat Tony was referring to an incident where Jimmy got himself in trouble at the racetrack for gambling. News traveled fast in their circles. The track labeled my father a KG—a Known Gambler—and escorted him off the premises. "The Prime Minister ain't gonna be happy about this," Fat Tony informed Jimmy.

The Prime Minister was Frank Costello, who was the head of the Luciano Family which would later become the Genovese Family.

"I'm not so thrilled about it myself," Jimmy said. "They barred me from all the race tracks in the city."

"Sons of bitches. How's a guy supposed to make an honest living if he can't be a bookie?"

"Once the board has you stuck in their throat, that's where you stay," Jimmy said.

"Sons of bitches."

"But I got a few other things lined up though," Jimmy reassured Fat Tony. "A few ventures outside the bookmaking business."

"You do?"

"Man does not live on bookmaking alone."

"So tell me, what else you got up your sleeve, Jimmy Nap?"

Jimmy cracked a small, mischievous smile.

Jimmy Nap was looking beyond the usual mob moneymaking businesses. He was thinking big. He was thinking different. He was eyeing ways that he could venture out into legitimate areas that nobody had really thought of before. He saw industrious mobsters like Costello, Meyer Lansky and Bugsy Siegel spreading out into other areas of the country and into legit businesses: real estate, stocks, casinos and politics. Jimmy knew this was the way to go, to expand, to be more influential.

Jimmy Nap was looking into boxing. It was a sport my father loved and was familiar with. He thought the business offered enormous opportunities. Jimmy Nap was about to enter the fight game.

Chapter 11

A Meeting in The Church

IT WAS IN A CHURCH, just like Our Lady of Mt. Carmel Church, located on Havemeyer and North 8th in Williamsburg, that my father reunited with his family—his mother and father. It was a day he always remembered and spoke of often to me, when he stressed the importance of family and forgiveness.

Mt. Carmel is old but beautiful. It still has saints on display, and you can light a candle. The Catholic churches they put up today—the newer ones—they all look Protestant. Bare. You can't tell if they're churches or auditoriums.

Not Mt. Carmel though. It has character and strength. Like a lot of things from the past, thankfully, it still matters, and it's still here. It can still give you that old feeling. It reminds you that there was a time when people did things right. When beauty mattered. And when a neighborhood still had a heart and soul, and was run by the people of that neighborhood. Not robber-baron land developers.

Nowadays I see people in church with baseball caps on and hot pants. But I'm from the old school, when men wore suits and hats and women looked like women. You take your hat off when you're in church.

I love the sound of the mass. Always did. It's beautiful. Even though I was fired as an altar boy when I was a kid. I was never good at keeping a steady job! I actually did make a few dollars as an altar boy. When I served weddings and funerals the families always threw some money at me. After I got fired, after the priests had had enough of me not showing up, or showing up late, or goofing off, my mother went to my father and said, "You have to get him his job back!"

My father said, "What job? That isn't a job!"

My mother went to the priest herself and told him that my family needed the extra money I brought in to help us survive. She got me my "job" back.

I love the Mass. It hasn't changed since I was a kid. The ritual, the words. It stays the same. There's comfort in that sameness. In having things you can count on in life. Like God. Like family.

It wasn't Mount Carmel in 1930. It was St. Mary's Church that my father entered, the same church he was married in two years later, and stuck a $100 bill in the poor box.

In a pew toward the front of the empty church Jimmy spotted his mother, Anna. She had Rosary Beads in her hands and she was praying.

Jimmy Nap walked up the center aisle to her pew.

Anna turned to him. He already had a tear in her eye. Jimmy sat beside her. He put his arms around her and hugged.

"*Che cosa c'e,* Mama? What's wrong, why are you crying? Are these tears of joy or sadness? Tell me." Jimmy asked of his mother, whom he hadn't seen in years.

"*Tuo padre*...He's dying, Vincenzo," Anna informed him. "He wouldn't want me to tell you. He's very proud. He wouldn't want you to come to him out of guilt. He loves you very much. He always regretted what happened."

"What can I do, Mama?" Jimmy asked. "Can I go to him? Can I see him? Will he welcome me, if I do?"

"You are his son. He will welcome you with open arms, and with an open heart. He's your father."

Jimmy was happy to hear his mother's words. He was happy to see her. It had been too long. He held Anna and the two stayed in their embrace. Jimmy looked up at the crucifix above the altar of the empty church. He knew it was time to make peace.

Jimmy followed his mother into the tenement apartment. The same apartment he had stormed out of so many years earlier.

He saw a sick and frail looking Antonio lying flat on his back in the bed.

Anna spoke to Antonio in a soft voice, as Jimmy stood just behind her, near the doorway. Even though Anna had assured Jimmy Antonio would welcome him, there was a part of him that feared he wouldn't. That their old grievance would rear its head. That Antonio's pride and thickheadedness would kick in, as if by instinct. That this meeting, what Jimmy knew from the look of Antonio would be their last, would end just as their previous one did.

"Antonio, Vincenzo is here," Anna whispered. "Vincenzo, your son. Our son. He's here to see you. May he come in?"

Antonio did not turn to face Anna. He stared straight up at the ceiling. After a long moment, he spoke in a strained mutter. "Si." The word came from Antonio's mouth. Jimmy was relieved. Anna turned to him and he stepped closer. She nodded and Jimmy slowly walked to the bed and stood beside his father.

Anna stepped back, giving father and son their space.

Jimmy turned back to her. She nodded her head again for reassurance.

"*Ciao Papa*," Jimmy spoke, with a slight tremble in his voice. "How are you feeling? I know we haven't spoken in a while. I've been keeping busy. Working. I'm doing okay now. I'm really starting to do okay. I'm becoming a leader of men, just like you."

Jimmy worked hard to fill in the silences between him and Antonio. He wasn't sure if Antonio couldn't speak to him, or wouldn't. "I'm not sure if you can't speak to me, or you just don't want to speak to me. But either way, I want you to know I'm going to be here for you now. I want to take care of all the doctor's bills, and the medicines. Whatever it is, I'm going to take care of it. I told that to Mama. I want to be father and son again. I hope you want that too. I hope you're okay with that."

Without turning to him, Antonio clutched Jimmy's hand, which dangled at his bedside. The father and son tightly held each other's hand in a firm, loving grip.

A tear rolled down Anna's face as she looked on.

They made up.

My father stayed with Anna and Antonio day and night, for almost a year before Grandpa died. My father took him out for short walks around the block and to church with my grandmother.

I never knew Antonio but I was fifteen when my Grandmother Anna died. She used to tell me in broken English that God answered her prayers that day in the church when my father walked in.

Family. That's what it's all about. It isn't all machine-guns and shakedowns. That's what the public likes to hear. They like the juicy stuff. But this is real life. Real people we're dealing with here. And no matter what your line of work, family and the love you feel for them comes before everything.

My father always said family first. And I knew which family he meant.

After losing his father, Jimmy was ready to start a family of his own. He was ready to go from *being* a prodigal son to *having* a prodigal son of his own.

Chapter 12

The Son is Born

IN THE 1930s, MY FATHER started spending more time around the boxing game and visiting Stillman's Gym. He and his boxing manager friend Jimmy Dixon hung around the gym, sometimes standing ringside for hours at a time, watching the various fighters sparring.

Dixon was an impeccably dressed man in his 30s, who had some good-looking, up-and-coming boxers in his stable. One of his most prized fighters was a featherweight named Nicky Jerome. But in boxing, as in a lot of businesses, success often comes down to who you know. Dixon hadn't been able to get a break for Jerome and get him a big fight, or even land him a good payday.

"He looks good," Jimmy Nap said to Dixon, as he watched Jerome take apart a sparring partner. "Strong."

"Kid could be a champ," Jimmy acknowledged. "If he got a shot."

"I hear ya," Jimmy said.

"But you can't get a shot without people trying to take the house out from under you," Dixon offered. "Know what I mean, Jimmy?"

"People? What people?" Jimmy Nap asked.

"People. Certain people." Dixon didn't want to mention any names.

"People like who?" Jimmy Nap pushed him for an answer.

Without saying a word, Dixon gave a head gesture in the direction of the main entrance of the gym, where Frankie "Kid" Bruno stood, talking to Lou Stillman, the gym's owner.

Bruno was a former fighter and a mob enforcer, an all-around tough guy and bully, who strutted around with a chip on his shoulder and who pedaled his influence openly.

Bruno came toward Dixon, who turned to Jimmy. "He's coming over. Don't do anything."

"What am I gonna do?"

Bruno walked past Jimmy and spoke to Dixon. "I like your boy," Bruno said, referring to Jerome.

"Yeah, well, ya know, we're working him hard," Dixon responded.

"That's good," Bruno said. "If you wanna be a champ in this game, you gotta pay your dues. You know that. I'll see ya around."

Bruno gave a cold nod in the direction of Jimmy Nap. He knew him but he didn't know him. Bruno walked off and made his rounds, shaking hands with other boxing managers in the gym.

Dixon whispered to Jimmy, "Like I said, certain people."

"He's giving you trouble?" Jimmy asked.

"He shakes us all down, all the managers. That's what he meant by 'pay your dues.' But I don't want to pay. I can't pay. So my fighter doesn't get his shot."

Jimmy Nap looked across the gym and glared at Bruno, who mingled with the other managers. He didn't like Bruno. He didn't like his style or his way. He didn't like the idea of Bruno playing the big shot role, of shaking down good people, neighborhood people, who were just looking for a break in life. That wasn't Jimmy Nap's style. Jimmy didn't think power and influence should be used as a weapon against the people you know. It should be used to lift people up. Money was money and business was business, but taking money from those who didn't have it, or who needed your help, was something Jimmy Nap frowned upon. He looked down on a guy who took advantage of those who were just looking for a break. Neighborhood people who wanted to raise themselves up. And he swore to himself, right there and then, that he would do something about it. When he had that kind of power—and he knew that someday he would—he would never misuse it in that way.

Jimmy Nap had Kid Bruno caught in his throat from that day on. He waited for the day when their paths would cross again and he would get a chance to show Bruno what he thought of him and his tactics, face-to-face, man-to-man.

That day came a few months later.

Jimmy made extra money working as a bouncer in Tommy Murphy's Mirror Tavern, a local bar that had a regular but sometimes rough crowd. With Jimmy there overseeing the place, people stayed in line and there was no trouble. Jimmy would survey the customers who came in, dissuade any troublemakers with his presence and keep order.

One night, Jimmy walked into the tavern to find the owner, Tommy Murphy, in the back room of the bar, being held by the throat up against the wall by Frankie 'Kid' Bruno.

Jimmy didn't know what was going on or why Bruno was choking Murphy. But instinctively, he grabbed Bruno and tossed him off of Murphy. Bruno hit the ground with a thud.

When he got up, he saw Jimmy Nap standing there. "What the fuck are you doin'?" Bruno asked him, his tough guy swagger still in place. "Do you know who you're touchin'?"

"Yeah, I'm touchin' you," Jimmy Nap shot back, unafraid of the wannabe gangster. "And nobody touches Murphy or anybody else in this joint."

Murphy jumped in and got between the two goliaths, trying to keep the peace in his joint. "It's okay, Jimmy. Me and Frankie, we was just talkin' is all."

Jimmy overrode Murphy and glared at Bruno. "You get the hell outta here!"

"You don't tell me what to do."

"I just did."

"Do you know who you're talkin' to?" Bruno knew Jimmy knew who he was, who he was with, and wanted Jimmy to acknowledge it and back down. Fat chance.

"Yeah, a drunk," Jimmy sneered. "Now take a walk."

Bruno was drunk and he was unreasonable. And now he was pissed off but good. He took a swing at Jimmy's head and missed.

Jimmy punched Bruno in the mouth, drawing blood. Now it was on!

Jimmy and Bruno exchanged punches and began wrestling with one another. Their brawl spilled out into the bar area, where patrons scattered in fear.

Jimmy and Bruno went at it like two heavyweights. They hit each other with fists, bar stools, chairs, fought a good, old-fashioned barroom brawl.

Jimmy fought Bruno with a rage that had been bubbling up in him since Dixon had told him about Bruno in Stillman's months ago. Jimmy would never let himself lose a fight to this guy. He would kill or be killed but he would never lose to Bruno.

Jimmy pulled out a gun and pointed it at Bruno. The bar patrons fell dead quiet.

Bruno was stunned for a moment. He looked at Jimmy and in that instant he knew Jimmy would use the gun. Bruno turned quickly and hightailed it out of the bar, running for his life from Jimmy Nap.

Jimmy, who had anger in his eyes and in his heart, wanted to off this son of a bitch. Here was his chance. No one would miss him, he thought. He aimed the gun at Bruno's back. Then he thought better and aimed the gun a little...lower. Jimmy pulled the trigger and shot Bruno in the right buttock.

Bruno hit the ground like a lump. "Ow! My ass! My ass! He shot me in the ass!" Bruno cried out.

Jimmy Nap didn't want to kill him. He just wanted to humiliate him in front of everybody in the bar.

Murphy, and the remaining patrons, could hardly contain their laughter. Some didn't. The sight of this big bully, now grabbing onto his ass cheeks and screaming for dear life was one many enjoyed seeing. Many. But not everybody.

Bruno recovered from the gunshot wound but he would never rat out Jimmy Nap. That's the way it was in those days. There was an unspoken code, an unshakable creed, a thing called honor, which men of the street—even a louse like Bruno—obeyed. They had laws unto themselves and didn't adhere to any other laws of any other land. They would never sing to the authorities. How times have changed.

Unfortunately, not everyone who witnessed the shooting in the bar was so principled. There was one eyewitness to the shooting who was willing to talk to police. Probably one of the broads in the place. Who the hell knows? My father was charged with attempted murder and went away to Sing Sing from 1941 to 1944.

On May 8th, 1935, Mother's Day, on the top-floor of a tenement apartment at 61 Teneyck Street in Wiliamsburg, I was born. I was a gift to my mother on her day. That's what she always said.

My father now had another hungry mouth to feed and more bills to pay. He was hoping to extend his operation. To branch out. The old work was still there for him when he got out of the joint. He still ran the crap games, broke legs and hijacked the truckloads. The work he depended on before going away for the Bruno shooting was there for him when he got out. He was making money doing it. It wasn't a bad life or a bad living but it wasn't the high life either.

Jimmy Nap was a man who did what he had to do in order to provide for his family. There were obstacles and danger in his business. And competition was fierce. But whatever stood in his way didn't stand in his way for too long. His sphere of influence was increasing. His circles were getting bigger and better. He was establishing himself as a real player in the rackets. And the big score that eluded him for awhile was finally about to come his way.

Chapter 13

The Language of Money

IN 1938 IN HAVANA, THE palm trees were swaying in the breeze, and under a cabana, Jimmy Nap sat with Meyer Lansky and Cuban President, General Fulgencio Batista. And on Jimmy's lap, in the middle of this power meeting, was little ol' me, at four years old.

Lansky was in his late 30s and had already established himself in the New York, Florida and Vegas rackets, as well as in Europe. He was nearly ten years my father's senior and that much more ahead of him in the mob pecking order. Lansky had long been a connection for the mob in Cuba. He had a close business relationship with Batista and other South American dictators to promote gambling casinos in their countries. Lansky was one part gangster, and two parts entrepreneur. My father liked that about him.

My father and Lansky's relationship went back to the prohibition years of the 1920's, when Jimmy Nap drove the trucks back and forth from New York to Chicago for Yale and Capone. During that time, Lansky and Bugsy Siegel managed their own bootlegging operations in and around the New York and New Jersey area with the backing of Lucky Luciano. Together they also formed Murder Inc., which carried out hundreds of murders on behalf of the mob. Their targets usually included informants and mob members who had broken mob rules.

Jimmy Nap and Lansky ran in the same circles, with a lot of the same friends like Yale, Luciano, Frank Costello, and Salvatore Maranzano, the first *capo di tutti capi*—or "boss of bosses" of the American mob. Who Lansky killed under Luciano's orders in 1931. Then after Maranzano's death, Luciano and his colleagues pushed to form The Five Families, which was intended to abolish the position of Boss of Bosses.

Lansky was a short, slight man, always in a suit and brim. He talked in quick, pointed directives and sprinkled his words liberally with curses.

Batista, who was also in his late 30s, always wore his military uniform and turned his unlit cigar between his lips as he listened intently to what Lansky was saying.

"This is the guy I was talking to you about, general," Lansky said, "Jimmy's from New York. He promotes fights in the city. All the big fights. He's the man that can bring a championship bout to your island."

Then Lansky turned to my father. "See, Jimmy, the general here is looking to bring boxing to Cuba. We've been helping him with the casinos and racetracks. Now he thinks it's time to branch out. Championship boxing! A title match, right here on the island. It would be a big draw. Big. Whattaya think, Jimmy?"

"I'm listening," my father said, sincerely, as he bounced me on his knee.

Lansky laughed. "He's listening. He's a funny guy. What I was explaining to the general is that the gambling revenue generated between his fighter, Kid Chocolate, and the kid we bring in from America—whoever you think we should bring in—would be a reflection of the solid relationship between our two countries. A relationship that's good for all involved. It's good for America. It's good for Cuba. And it's good for us because, well, money is always good for everybody. Am I right, Gentlemen?"

The "kid" Lansky was referring to was Eligio Sardiñas-Montalvo, a wildly popular Cuban fighter known as "Kid Chocolate."

Lansky knew how to speak the language everyone understood. Whether Cuban or American, it was the language of money. My father knew Lansky wanted this fight to happen. My father wanted it to happen. They both assumed Batista wanted it too. They got right down to business.

"I got a kid named Nicky Jerome," Jimmy explained. "A featherweight. Tough as nails. You think your kid can take him?"

General Batista smiled and plucked his cigar from his mouth, "Kid Chocolate is one of our great Cuban fighters in history. He has the power in both hands."

Batista put his two hands out to show my father and Lansky. *"Dos Manos!"* Then he looked at me. "Can you say that little boy? *Dos Manos…"*

I repeated the words, *"Dos Manos"* —two hands—then I tucked myself under my father's arm.

"He won his first twenty fights by knockout," Batista said.

"I know who he is," Jimmy acknowledged. "But you have to understand something, general. My guy is from Brooklyn."

The general laughed.

"He's laughing. I'm serious," Jimmy looked from Lansky to Batista. "They call him Machine Gun Nicky, because he throws lightning fast left jabs and left hooks. Fast."

"Kid Chocolate's first twenty one fights as a pro, he won by knockouts," the general said, putting his cigar back in his mouth.

They were now going tit for tat.

"Yeah, but you can't hurt what you can't hit," said Jimmy Nap.

Lansky brought the conversation around to something they could all agree on. "Kid Chocolate is box office gold in Havana, Jimmy," informed Lansky. "We bring in Jerome and it's a match made in heaven. Do we got a deal?"

Batista leaned in. "If Meyer brings you here then I know you are a man of respect and honor. If you say your fighter is the right man and it is the right time, then we have ourselves a deal."

Batista extended his hand and Jimmy Nap shook it. Batista stood and patted me on the head and repeated the two words, *"Dos Manos...*Cute boy."

Then he walked off, followed by two heavily armed guards.

Once Batista was out of earshot, Lansky turned to my father. "Whaddaya think of the general?"

"He's a politician," Jimmy Nap said. "Never trust a politician. You know that."

"He's a good man. He opened up the whole fuckin'... 'scuse my French, the kid's here...He opened up the whole island to me and Charlie." He was referring to Lucky Luciano. "He loves us. We got a stranglehold on a foreign government with this guy in place. Do you know how big that is, Jimmy?"

"Nothing lasts forever, Meyer," my father warned. "These guys cut each other's heads off down here for power. Be careful."

"A lot like the people we know up North, huh?"

"You can't trust them. They don't trust each other."

"This guy's the president here, Jimmy. The main man. That ain't changin'. He ain't goin' nowhere."

"My father used to say something to me." Jimmy shared Grandpa Antonio's wisdom with Lansky. "He used to say, 'When the chess game is over, the king and the pawn go into the same box.' He used to say it in Italian. *Capisce?*"

"So you don't like the fuckin' general? Is that what you're sayin', Jimmy?"

"Meyer, the mouth, please, my son's here..."

"Eh, I'm sorry, Jimmy, but you're aggravatin' me."

"Look, he's a politician, which means he's a crook. Just by nature. He cheated his people out of everything they have. Where we come from, a street guy gets killed for that."

"He ain't cheatin' us, don't you worry about that."

"We'll make the deal, Meyer," Jimmy conceded. "It's good for all of us, like you said. But don't be fooled. He's doing it because it's good for him. It allows him to keep his hold on power here. He's not doing it because it's good for us."

"You're smart, Jimmy. That's why I brought you down."

"And that's why I came."

Meyer and Jimmy smiled at one another. They raised their glasses of champagne and toasted. I raised my glass of milk and they both clanked glasses with me too.

"So, now..." Meyer asked, "Can this Nicky Jerome give us a show or what?"

Jimmy flew back to New York and informed Dixon that his boy Nicky Jerome was going to get his shot, his break, the one he couldn't get before under Bruno.

As Nicky sparred in Stillman's, Jimmy Nap broke the good news to Dixon, who threw his arms around Jimmy. "You got us our shot!" Dixon called out to Nicky in the ring, "Hey, you hear that Nicky, Jimmy Nap got us a championship fight! Only you, Jimmy. Only you could do it!"

Nicky stopped fighting for a moment and lifted his hands into the air.

"God bless you, Jimmy Nap!" Dixon proclaimed, "We won't let you down."

"I know you won't," said Jimmy. "I know you won't."

Other wiseguys and managers looked on from across the gym, as Jimmy, Dixon and Nicky celebrated.

The fight was scheduled for December 18, 1938 at the Sports Palace in Havana.

In the dressing room Dixon taped up Nicky's hands. Jimmy Nap entered the room, unseen by Dixon and Nicky, and he listened from the back.

"This Chocolate is like a legend here," a nervous Nicky said to Dixon.

"Yeah, so?" asked Dixon.

"No, nothin', I'm just sayin'."

"He's a man, just like you, Nicky. He can be beat."

"No, I know that," Nicky said. "I ain't worried about losin.' I'm worried 'bout winnin'."

"Winnin'? What's wrong with winnin'?"

"I don't want there to be no riot in the place. They love this guy. He's like a national hero. The Bon Bon's won 28 straight fights. If I break his ass in front of his people..."

"Just break his ass," instructed Dixon. "Don't worry about nothin' else."

After hearing the conversation, Jimmy stepped forward in the dressing room, as if he had just gotten there. He was dressed sharp as always in a dark suit.

"Ay, look who's here..." Dixon greeted Jimmy.

"Hope I'm not interrupting. Just a fast hello and good luck to you, champ." He walked up to Nicky.

"Thank you, Jimmy," Nicky said. "This is all because of you."

"I'm not the one in the ring. You earned this. With those machine guns you call hands."

"Thank you for saying that."

"Got a lot of supporters out there tonight."

"Really?"

"He was a little worried," Dixon admitted to Jimmy Nap.

"Worried about what?" Jimmy asked.

"Worried he breaks Chocolate's ass and, ya know, the crowd, they turn on him."

Jimmy looked Nicky right in the eye for a few long seconds and spoke three simple words, "Break his ass."

Nicky nodded and cracked a smile.

The Sports Palace had electricity in the air that night. The capacity crowd was antsy and buzzing.

Nicky appeared in the tunnel and made his way to the ring, led by Dixon and his cut man. The crowd cheered. Some even waved American flags. They chanted, "USA! USA! USA!"

Nicky entered the ring. He looked ringside to see the supportive face of Jimmy Nap. Jimmy made a fist and held it up so Nicky could see it. Nicky winked at him. Beside Jimmy sat Meyer Lansky and several of his crew members.

Kid Chocolate came from the other tunnel. The home crowd erupted. Cuban music filled the air. Cuban flags waved in the stands.

Nicky turned and whispered to Dixon, "He's a pretty popular guy, huh?"

"That's all right," Dixon said. "You just do what you gotta do."

Kid Chocolate stepped into the ring. He saw Batista and his military men, all in uniform, sitting ringside. Batista nodded his head in approval. Chocolate acknowledged him with a bow.

The ring announcer introduced the fighters.

Nicky was in the red corner. He fought out of Brooklyn, USA. His professional record was 28 wins, 20 defeats, and four draws.

In the blue corner, was Kid Chocolate. The crows went nuts when he was introduced. His record was 135 wins, nine defeats and five draws; 50 of his wins came by way of knockout...the featherweight champion of the world, Eligio "Kid Chocolate" Sardiñas!

Nicky and Kid Chocolate came to the center of the ring where the referee gave them their final instructions. "Okay, Gentlemen, I've already given you your instructions. Obey my commands at all times. Watch the low blows and the rabbit punches. Let's have a good clean fight. Now touch gloves and come out fighting."

They touched gloves and returned to their corners.

The bell rang.

The fighters met at center ring and exchanged blows.

Nicky then moved swiftly around the ring. He was light on his feet, landing his jab quickly and effectively.

He was faster than the older Kid Chocolate, but Chocolate was the harder puncher. Every shot Chocolate landed was greeted with approval from the crowd. When Nicky connected it was more jeers than cheers.

The two fighters slugged it out. Their styles were different, but they complemented each other. The result was an evenly matched, ten-round brawl that delighted the crowd. Nicky stuck his jab and moved; Chocolate landed hard body shots. In the end, it was clear that Nicky had gotten the best of Chocolate.

By the late rounds Kid Chocolate was cut badly and moved slowly around the ring, as the slightly fresher Nicky Jerome continued to move and land. Chocolate showed heart by not going down or giving up. He didn't want to let his home crowd down.

At fight's end, the crowd stood for the weary fighters.

Nicky looked over to Jimmy, Lansky and their crew.

Jimmy called out to him, "Put your hands up! Dixon, put his hands up! He's the champ, raise his arms!"

Dixon grabbed Nicky's arm and lifted it.

"Raise your arms! You won. Raise 'em up," Dixon told Nicky.

Nicky barely raised them over his head.

Across the ring, Nicky saw Chocolate, sitting in his stool. His trainer attended to the cuts on his face.

The referee leaned over the ring, talking to one of Batista's military men.

Nicky took all this in from the ring and looked to Jimmy.

"Just raise your arms!" Jimmy shouted to the nervous Nicky.

Nicky looked around. He could feel the crowd growing uneasy as they awaited the referee's decision. Something was stirring.

Nicky marched across the ring to a weakened Chocolate, who could barely get off his stool. Nicky grabbed Chocolate's arm and lifted him from the stool. He raised Chocolate's arm in victory and turned to the referee.

Nicky insisted to the referee, "It's a draw! A draw! He's still the champ!

Then Nicky shouted out to the crowd, "He's still the champ!" "He's your champ! Here he is!"

At their seats, Lansky leaned in to Jimmy and asked, "What the hell is he doing?"

"Showing a lot of class," Jimmy informed Lansky. "A hell of a lot of class."

The crowd once again erupted, this time in a chorus of cheers for both fighters. Chocolate was bloodied and puffy but he basked in the glory of the crowd for what would be the last time. Kid Chocolate retired after this bout.

From across the arena, Jimmy Nap and General Batista made eye contact. Batista nodded to Jimmy in recognition of Nicky's act.

After that night, my father, who was a fighter and who loved the fight game, was hooked for sure. My father had stars in his eyes when it came to boxing. And to see two proud warriors conduct themselves as Kid Chocolate and

Nicky Jerome did on that December night in Havana just reinforced everything my father knew boxing should and could be.

When he returned to the states, my father became heavily involved in boxing promotions. He promoted the as Tami Mauriello vs. Joe Louis, Paddy DeMarco vs. Jimmy Carter, and Rocky Marciano vs. Roland LaStarza bouts.

Someone once asked me, if my father had a choice, would he have been a fighter instead of a gangster. I said, *gangster*! My father was no gangster. Don't ever use that word in describing my father. A gangster is a member of a gang. As an adult, my father was his own man. He was a businessman, an entrepreneur.

And anyway, in those days, people didn't have choices like that, about what they wanted to be. They just were. They became. This was before choices were even invented. Back then, people just lived, doing what they did, dealing with what was in front of them.

That was in front of Jimmy Nap after the Nicky Jerome-Kid Chocolate fight: the world and everything in it. That's what he aspired toward. Like Lansky and others before him, Jimmy Nap was beginning to speak the language of money. And it was beginning to speak back to him.

Chapter 14

The 'Fix' Is In

As my father grew in stature in the rackets, he became more than just another neighborhood tough guy who ruled with an iron fist. He never wanted that. My father wanted to be a wise guy, never a wiseguy. He wanted to be a benevolent businessman. He fancied himself a protector of those in need. Jimmy Nap became a guardian of his Williamsburg neighborhood and its inhabitants. My father told me once, "The toughest guy I ever met is a guy who works eight to ten hours a day to support his family."

When I walk past what used to be my father's Hi-Way Lounge and I see what's become of it—now a run down old bar, a dilapidated awning with Spanish writing hanging overhead—I know my father must be turning over in his grave.

The Hi-Way was his headquarters. He was there every day. Same time every day, without fail. One, one-thirty he would pull up to the curb in his white Cadillac. The dapper Jimmy Nap would exit the car and enter the Hi-Way.

The lounge was dimly lit. The familiar faces of regular patrons sitting in red and black trim booths, would welcome Jimmy. They paid their respects and greeted him with smiles and warm hello's as he walked past.

There was always somebody waiting to see Jimmy when he arrived. He spent his first few hours at the Hi-Way meeting with neighborhood people who had a problem and needed his help.

One time, Jimmy arrived at the Hi-Way and his eyes went immediately to a neighborhood woman sitting by herself and weeping in the back of the bar. Jimmy turned to one of his crew members who stood near the back room.

"What's wrong with her?" Jimmy asked.

"I don't know," the crew member shrugged. "She says she needs to talk to you."

"All right, two minutes then send her in."

Jimmy went to the back room, took off his topcoat, hung it neatly on a rack, straightened his tie and sat behind his desk.

The neighborhood woman came in, sat before him and tried to speak through her tears.

"They came...they came...they stole my carriage...they stole my baby's carriage..." the woman pieced together a sentence.

"Who stole your baby's carriage?" Jimmy asked, trying to understand her.

The woman wailed, unable to speak.

"Catch your breath," Jimmy said and then he called out to the crew member, "Get her a glass of water."

The woman took a sip and continued as best she could, "Animals...animals...They saw I was a woman alone, with no husband and they figured..."

She took a deep breath and composed herself. "I don't know what they were. Maybe Puerto Ricans. They all look alike. They took my baby out and handed him to me and they rolled my carriage away. I screamed at them...I begged them... 'Please, please don't take my baby's carriage...I can't afford another one...please!' They just laughed at me and kept going. I can't afford another one..."

She put her head down and cried in her hands.

Jimmy reached into his pocket and took out a wad of cash.

"Take this. Buy a carriage, bring the baby around tomorrow."

The woman looked at the money in Jimmy's hand. Her face lit up. She stopped crying.

"Thank you, Jimmy. I don't know how to thank you." She glowed.

"You just did," Jimmy said and he smiled back at her.

The woman took the money from him and kissed his hand. "God bless you, Jimmy Nap," the woman praised him. "You're going to heaven. Straight to heaven. A lot of people say that men in your...well, ya know...in your *business*. A lot of people say they got no heart and that they're rat bastards. On the street, some people say that. But not about Jimmy Nap. Nobody says that about you."

The woman stood. "I better go. You're a busy man. I'll pay you back. If it takes years, I'll pay you every cent."

"Pay me back by letting me see how happy your baby is in his new carriage," Jimmy told her.

"God bless you."

The woman rushed from the back room, her tears having turned to joy and excitement.

That's who my father was. He was always helping people. That's why everybody loved him and he had no enemies. A good reputation wherever he went.

I took him to a restaurant in Westchester once. Only a few guys were there when we walked in. Before long, they came out of the woodwork just to meet him and greet him. A lot of times, if I was in a different neighborhood they'd say, 'Where you from?' I say, 'Williamsburg.' The first name they mention: 'Jimmy Nap.' Jimmy Nap's neighborhood. My father had a good name. A name of respect. It was important to him. His good name was everything to him.

Jimmy Nap would leave the Hi-Way Lounge every day at 5 o'clock and walk over to Crisci's restaurant. The lounge was mainly for the numbers business. Crisci's was for boxing business. It was his meeting place for boxing managers, boxers and promoters from all over the country. They all came to Crisci's and talk business over a good meal. Jimmy Nap always picked up the check. The FBI thought for a long time that my father as one of the original owners. He spent most of his life there. Six days a week he ended his day's business at Crisci's.

The FBI was always watching him. From the second he left the Hi-Way, he was under surveillance. They followed his every movement, his every step, from the second he left the lounge, until he walked into Crisci's.

Crisci's is still there too. Not the kind of place I would eat in anymore. But in those days it was a hot spot and it was Jimmy Nap's favorite restaurant. Sometimes I look at it and I say, *minchia*, if this place could talk...

Then I realize, this place wouldn't talk. It was my father's place. They'll hit it with a wrecking ball before it ever talks. When my father's dear friend and the owner Cy Crisci died, the stories all went with him. Except for the ones that are still kept alive with me. I know writers hate when stories die, even though everything else dies. That's why for now, through me, they stay alive and well.

Cy Crisci was a thin, balding man who wore thick eyeglasses. He was there day and night and ran the place, giving it that special, personal touch. He was my father's business partner and confidant.

The restaurant decor was simple but elegant. Light brown paneling on the walls, with small chandeliers hanging from the ceiling. The place was always crowded and abuzz with activity, especially at dinnertime. An L-shaped bar with 12 bar stools was always filled with patrons.

You got to the dining room through an arch-way. And to the right, as you entered the dining room, was a table that sat eight. This is where Jimmy Nap held court with his people—having dinner and talking business. At a side entrance to the street where Jimmy's table was allowed his people to come and go without using the main bar area and being seen by too many people.

Most of the dinner meetings at Crisci's revolved around the boxing business in 1958 were between my father and Rocky Marciano. We used to drink at the same places, me and Marciano did, so on my father's orders I brought him to Crisci's to talk to my father about his making a comeback. I remember the first thing my father told him was to stay away from me.

"Stay away from my son," he said. "He's a bad influence. He'll cause you to get a divorce." Marciano laughed it off. My father was serious.

Marciano wanted to talk to Jimmy Nap about a comeback fight that promoters had offered him against Floyd Patterson. Thing was, Marciano didn't want his longtime manager, Al Weil, to manage him anymore. Weil had brought him up from the streets and made him a champ. Marciano said that the promoters were offering him a lot of money to fight Patterson and he wanted my father to make Cy Crisci his manager for the fight. It was to be a title bout, but a one fight only deal.

My father looked at Marciano, the greatest heavyweight of all time, and he berated him for not remaining loyal to Weil. "Go back to your wife Barbara who's sick, and stay in that hillbilly town that Al Weil found you in."

Let me remind you of something. Rocky Marciano was 49-0 in the ring. Undefeated. At this table, he was overmatched.

"You're nothing but a hillbilly who owes his success to a man like Al Weil," my father went on. "Without Al you'd still be a four round fighter who falls on his face every time he misses his opponent with a punch."

Marciano didn't know what to say.

Jimmy Nap reminded him how sloppy he was in the ring at the beginning of his career, before Weil came along. "No promoter is going to offer you anything without Al Weil by your side. Now you stay home on that orange farm with your wife, in Florida." Then my father added, "And don't forget what I told you—stay away from my son TN."

Rocky Marciano never did make a comeback. The Patterson fight went to Ingemar Johansson a few years later. He TKO'd Patterson in the third round in 1960.

Some years before that in the mid-fifties, another meeting at Crisci's was between lightweight contender Paddy "Billy Goat" DeMarco and his trainer Dan Florio and Dan's brother Nick. DeMarco, a broken-nosed bruiser and a real up-and-comer in those days had been managed by Jimmy Dixon. He was eventually confined to a wheelchair with a muscular disease and died nearly a year earlier of heart failure.

"The first lightweight champ from Brooklyn, New York is what you're gonna be," Jimmy Nap told DeMarco. "Are you ready for that? You do the whole borough proud."

"Thank you, Jimmy, thank you," Demarco replied.

"They got you down as a seven-to-one underdog," Jimmy informed him. "But they don't know us Brooklyn guys. We eat that up, being underestimated."

"Let 'em say what they want," DeMarco shrugged confidently. "They'll see what I got when I get in the ring."

"Now listen, you got two of the best guy in the sport here," Jimmy pointed to the Florios. "So you don't need no more advice from me. And I'm not sticking my fingers under my arms or anything, but one thing I learned when I was fighting was this. Always be ready to go the distance. Because—and listen carefully here—if you go the distance and you're on your feet at the end of the fight, then you always have a chance to win. Always. Am I right, Dan?"

Dan Florio nodded in agreement. "Nah, you're right, Jimmy," Florio concurred. "One hundred percent. If you're standin' up, you got a shot on points."

"That's the thing I'm talking about...points," Jimmy Nap said. "If you're on your feet when that final bell rings, anything could happen. You never know how a judge is gonna see it, or score it. Different eyes see different things, you understand? And nobody can tell why or how that score got on the card. But you gotta be on your feet after the fifteenth for the judges' scorecards to mean anything."

"Don't worry about that," DeMarco reassured Jimmy Nap. "I'll be on my feet at the end."

Jimmy smiled and nodded at Paddy. Then he raised his glass and proposed a toast. "To going the distance...May the spirit of Jimmy Dixon be in your corner."

They all raised their glasses.

In the Spring of 1954, a sold-out Madison Square Garden crowd watched Paddy DeMarco stagger back to his corner and flopped onto his stool.

Dan Florio advised him. "One more round, Kid. One more! Keep punchin'. You're doin' great. Watch his left jab, he's tryin' to set you up for the right cross. Don't let him get it off. Stay on top of him!"

Nick Florio squirted water into DeMarco's mouth. DeMarco spit it into a bucket. Then Nick placed the mouthpiece back into his mouth.

"Remember what Jimmy said," Dan reminded DeMarco. "If you're on your feet at the end, you got a shot."

Jimmy Nap and Cy Crisci sat at ringside, as they always did together.

The ring-card girl held up the sign for the 15th and final round.

Paddy stood. The bell rang and he charged out for the final round.

"Keep throwin', kid!" Dan shouted from the corner.

Paddy, like his billy goat nickname, kept coming forward, throwing punches and keeping the pressure on the lightweight champ Jimmy Carter, a lean, quick African-American fighter from the Bronx.

Paddy threw sharp jabs and looping rights at Carter, who stood flat-footed in front of him. Carter swung wildly for a knockout. Paddy made him pay with a stiff right that opened a cut over Carter's eye.

The final bell sounded with the two men still on their feet.

Jimmy Nap and Cy Crisci applauded at ringside. The crowd cheered, with support split between Paddy's Brooklyn contingent and Carter's Bronx supporters.

Moments later, the ring announcer stood at center ring and declared, "We have a Unanimous Decision...For the winner...and...*new*...lightweight champion of the world... Paddy DeMarco!"

Paddy jumped into the air and rushed onto the ropes, with his arms up in victory.

The crowd response was a mixture of cheers and boos.

From the ring, Dan Florio looked down at ringside, where Jimmy and Cy were making their way out of the arena, getting away from the raucous crowd. But that fight brought heat onto my father that he couldn't get away from. He was subpoenaed to appear before the New York State Boxing Commission to answer questions about the fight and its outcome.

A crowd of boxers, ex-boxers, managers and promoters came to lend their support to Jimmy Nap. Of course a gaggle of photographers and news reporters were also on hand.

The Commissioner, sitting beside the other officials on a dais, questioned Jimmy Nap, who sat by himself before them at a lower table, with only a single microphone in front of him.

"Mr. Napoli, you have been called to appear before us today so that we might ask you some questions regarding your involvement, promotional or otherwise, in the boxing game. In particular your involvement with Lightweight Champion Pasquale Giuseppe DeMarco. Also known as The Billy Goat." The Commissioner continued, "Furthermore, we'd like to know what you can tell us about certain perceived discrepancies in the judges' scorecards for the March 5th, 1954 Championship bout between Mr. DeMarco and then Champion Jimmy Carter."

Jimmy Nap cleared his throat and then spoke in a clear, crisp voice, "Mr. Commissioner, first let me say that it is an honor to be seated before you gentleman today, as I am a lifelong and avid fan of boxing. I even fought a little myself as an amateur. With regard to Mr. DeMarco, I was a long-time friend of his late manager, Mr. James Dixon, and at Mr. Dixon's request, I did serve for a short time as Mr. DeMarco's financial advisor."

"Financial Advisor?" questioned the Commissioner.

"That's correct, sir. Boxers often do not handle their money well and Mr. Dixon wanted better for Mr. DeMarco. I was happy to oblige. At no fee, I might add. It was a favor for a friend. A friend whose spirit I believe was in the ring that night guiding his fighter."

"Are you telling this Commission that your only involvement with Mr. DeMarco was as a financial advisor?"

"Well, I'm also a big fan of his, and I was happy to see a kid from Brooklyn win the title," Jimmy Nap added.

The Commissioner stared down at Jimmy for a moment, then muttered something to an assistant sitting just behind the dais. He returned to Jimmy with another question. "What can you tell us about any wrongdoing on the part of the judge's of the DeMarco-Carter Championship bout of March 5, 1954?"

"I believe those judges to all be men of integrity from decent families," Jimmy explained. "They could not be bribed or in any other way persuaded to judge a championship fight in any other way than according to how and what they saw with their own two eyes in that ring. To suggest otherwise would be, in my opinion, slanderous to their character."

"Slanderous?" the Commissioner's voice cracked. "Mr. Napoli, are you accusing this Commission of slander?"

"Mr. Commissioner, all I am saying is, Paddy DeMarco is the lightweight champion of the world. He deserves to be the champion. That's what the judges saw that night. And that's what everybody else saw that night. Did you see the fight, Mr. Commissioner?"

"Yes. Yes, I did."

"And how would you have scored it?"

"We'll ask the questions, Mr. Napoli," the Commissioner snapped.

"Of course. No disrespect, Mr. Commissioner. All I'm saying is, you never know how a judge is gonna see or score a fight. Different eyes see different things. But if a guy goes the distance, if a fighter's on his feet at the end, he puts his trust and his future in those judge's hands. That's boxing. That's how the game is played."

The commissioner turned to another member beside him, "Let's have a recess, please."

Then he turned back to Jimmy. "This hearing is adjourned until further notice." The Commissioner banged his gavel and stormed off the dais.

Jimmy leaned back in his seat with a little smile on his face, his good name still intact.

People have asked me, Did your father fix fights? Fixed is such a harsh word. What my father did was no different then what they do in Wrestling nowadays. He treated it like a movie script. It was truth wrapped in fiction. And everybody won. Even the losers eventually won.

This is how it was done.

It was a show. And my father was the writer, director and producer. Behind the scenes, he would approach at least one of the judges or the referee in charge of the fight.

The offer could be money or it could be to help them pay a certain gambling debt that they owed in the streets. He would school them: not to say anything to the fighters that night.

But the fighter had to go the distance. If his fighter got knocked out, the whole plan went down the drain. The odds were still in my father's favor of winning money. What my father did that made it like a movie script was to let the home town favorite win in close decisions. Then the rematch drew more money.

Take the Paddy DeMarco fight, for instance; DeMarco wins. Eight months later he defends the title against Carter. Who wins? Carter. Everybody's happy. Carter won his title back on November 17, 1954 with a 15-round knockout. Like my father always said, ya gotta be on your feet at the end to have a chance to win.

The fighters never knew what was going on with the judges and the referees. And if they did, they would never talk about it to anyone, or they were barred from getting the big money bouts.

But I wouldn't call it fixing. I wouldn't use that word. I would call it *entertainment*! These were productions. And the boxers were characters in these productions. The audiences loved it. There was always a happy ending.

That's the way it was done in those days. The small boxing clubs around New York were considered the minor league of boxing. So if the managers wanted their fighters to go to the major leagues, which at the time was Madison Square Garden and eventually national television, they had to cooperate. For their cooperation they were paid handsomely and they got exactly what they wanted. If you wanted your fighter to be a champion in the boxing game it meant doing business with Jimmy Nap.

But like I said, nobody loved and respected fighters more than my father. He made them. He made them champions. In many cases, he created them. They weren't pawns to him, interchangeable or disposal, like they were to shakedown artists like Kid Bruno. They were people, in most cases from the neighborhood, whose lives and careers he was advancing. At the same time he advanced his own business and influence in the fight game.

Like a character you create in a book, or a child you rear, you love them. They are a part of you. You want what's best for them. That's how Jimmy Nap felt about his fighters. He cared about them; even when the lights were off and the crowds gone. And even when there was no more money to be made from them, when they were washed up, old, punchy. He still cared about them as people.

He cared about fighters, because he knew a thing or two about love and loyalty. He knew about protecting those he loved. Why else would he have started an organization like Ring 8? Why else would he buy a poor mother a new baby carriage? His allegiance to those he loved knew no bounds. He gave to them with his heart and he gave to them until the end.

Chapter 15

Irreplaceable

THERE ARE SOME PEOPLE IN life that are replaceable—like heavyweight champions and certain wiseguys. And some that are irreplaceable. Like mothers.

Whenever I walk past my grandmother's old tenement building in Williamsburg, where she lived and died, I think of how this angel of a woman left this earth, passing away right in my father's arms.

I can still see the door flying open in 1950. My father holds a sick, frail Anna in his arms. She's eighty pounds and dying of heart failure. He cradles her like a baby. She can barely move. Her arms and legs dangle limply. Her head falls onto Jimmy Nap's shoulder. Her eyelids flutter as she struggles between worlds.

My father paces around the room talking to her and talks to her, as if his words alone will be enough to keep her alive.

"*Non ti preoccupare Mama, sono qui con te,*" Jimmy tells her in Italian. *Don't worry, Ma, I got you.*

Jimmy tries to reassure her, take her mind off her situation. He's not even sure if she can hear him, but he keeps talking, in a soft, certain voice, just the same. "I got you, Ma. I got you." He tells her. "Do you remember when I was small, what you used to tell me? You used to say, 'When a parent helps a child there's laughter, but when a child has to help a parent there's tears.' Do you remember saying that, Ma? You were right. You were always the smart one. Pop thought he was the smart one, but it was you. You were the strong one too. You carried this family. You kept us together. You were our strength."

Anna looked up at Jimmy. Her otherwise blank expression turns to what I can only describe as a tiny smile. A warm, contented grin. A mother's smile. A smile that says, I am going to leave you now, my son, but you are going to be okay on your own.

They laid Grandma Anna out in the same apartment she died in. That's how they did it in those days. Grandma Anna looked like an angel—so peaceful and saintly. There was no replacing Anna in Jimmy's life. There's no replacing a mother.

Some people, however, can be replaced.

Jimmy Nap was tapped by the New York bosses to replace Benjamin "Bugsy" Siegel in Las Vegas, after Siegel was rubbed out.

Bugsy Siegel spent most of his time in Hollywood during the second World War trying to develop and promote the Flamingo Casino and Hotel. He had been sent to the

West coast in the late 1930s to establish gambling rackets in Los Angeles. He was successful and now was looking to expand the operation to the casino and hotel business. Problem was, Bugsy didn't have enough money from the mob back East (Lansky, Luciano, Costello, Joe Adonis) to build the hotel part. He was told to hustle the West coast mob guys for more money. Guys like his partner in crime, Mickey Cohen, who was born in Brooklyn but based in Los Angeles. Bugsy and Mickey had become close friends and business associates from their LA operations.

But Bugsy's vision was a big one. So was the investment he needed to complete it. Bugsy knew he needed a hotel combined with the casino to house people when they came out to the middle of nowhere to gamble. After all, he was in a desert and the only rooms available were downtown flophouses, which were not very enticing to celebrities, wiseguys, and the other high rollers he was hoping to attract to the Flamingo.

Lansky, an old friend of Bugsy's from their lower east side childhood days, had been investing his own money, and mob money, in numerous gambling operations around the world. He was doing that since the early 30s. By the 1940s Bugsy had established himself on the West coast. So he seemed to be the right guy and the natural choice to get things started in Vegas, and Lansky vouched for him and helped him spearhead the endeavor with the New York bosses.

Bugsy had put lucrative gambling operations together with Mickey Cohen. Bugsy and Mickey were close, often traveling by car across the Mojave Desert, 325 miles one way from LA to Vegas, to work on this massive project that Bugsy was overseeing. Bugsy finally got the big money to start developing and building the Flamingo Hotel and Casino. His dream of creating an oasis of gambling and glamour in the middle of the Las Vegas desert was about to come true.

However, in 1947, a series of missteps, affairs, and misappropriations of mob money, eventually got Bugsy a bullet in the eye. His mismanagement of the Flamingo's development caused the New York mob to lose money, patience and in some cases, face. Not even his close and longstanding ties with Lansky, Luciano and the boys back home could prevent them from taking him down.

As Bugsy sat in his mob queen's house in Beverly Hills, an unidentified gunman shot him clear through a window. His eyeball flew out of his head and rolled across the room. It is one of the most famous and brutal mob hits of all time.

Bugsy's murder left a vacuum in Vegas for the New York mob. One that had to be filled so they would have representation there and someone they trusted in place to oversee their portion of the operation. They turned to Jimmy Nap.

My father did time in Sing Sing during the years 1941-1945. While in jail he met and befriended top captains and others who were connected with the powerful East Coast mob bosses. Jimmy served as an enforcer for them in the jailhouse. He protected them. He made sure they were safe and comfortable. These guys are the ones who praised Jimmy Nap to their bosses after they got out of jail. The bosses all knew about Jimmy from the Elliot Ness thing years earlier as well. Now they were hearing it from their own, on the inside: Jimmy was a man who understood the fellowship that men of honor shared.

Jimmy Nap was a man to be trusted, that was clear, and it was Frank Costello who listened to his associates when they said Jimmy should be their man in Vegas to fill the void left by Bugsy Siegel.

The NY mob was searching for two years after Bugsy's death to find someone to carry—literally carry—their money investments back into Vegas. My father actually carried tens of thousands of dollars in cash, in a small suitcase, aboard a plane from NY to Vegas, on his lap, while he sat in his seat.

I was 14 years old at the time and I remember my father getting up early in the morning, like 5 a.m., and taking out of our freezer about a dozen stacks of bills that looked like sandwiches wrapped in heavy wax paper. I knew it was money, because that's where he always kept money if he had to hide it for short time. Otherwise, he'd keep the money in his empty hatboxes on the top shelf in his closet.

I used to make believe I was sleeping on the couch in the adjoining room to the kitchen and peek-a-boo out of the corner of my eye to watch him collect the money and place it carefully into the suitcase. Then he would head out the door to catch his flight to the desert.

Jimmy Nap's foray as a money mule to and from Vegas and his interim replacement for the deceased Bugsy Siegel lasted for some time and solidified his position in the ranks. The East Coast bosses came to know and respect the up and coming Jimmy Nap. They knew he could be trusted and depended upon. They knew the bounds of his loyalty.

My father remained the bag man in Vegas for the New York mob for three decades—from 1949 to 1978. Jimmy Nap's position was created by Fat Tony, Frank Costello, Joe Adonis and Mickey Cohen as the adviser for all five families in the New York area, and he was responsible for all monies contributed to the Flamingo, the Sands and any future casinos.

Jimmy Nap was to be accepted at sitdowns with other family heads from other states allowing him to negotiate big money deals. He worked closely on the West coast with Mickey Cohen. Jimmy schooled Mickey on this venture in Vegas and explained that it was an open door to all families from all over the country to earn. My father understood gamblers and gambling and the casino business better than anyone ever could.

Mickey initially wanted Vegas for only the West coast, until Jimmy Nap showed him that everyone could work together and share the wealth. When I first met Mickey Cohen in L.A. back in 1958 he told me, "Your father came to Vegas in '49 with very powerful credentials from the boys back East. He became their bagman and I became the bagman for the boys on the West coast and the Cleveland boys. We used to call your father The John Wayne of Vegas."

Jimmy Nap made periodic trips to the West coast, and spent some time there, but for Jimmy Nap there was no replacing Brooklyn in his heart. That was home. That was where he belonged. The West coast, with its palm trees and temperate climate, was nice for a respite but not permanently.

His life and work was in New York. That was where he needed to be. Williamsburg. The Hi-Way. His family. That's where his roots were and that's where he wanted to be. That's also where the bosses wanted him to be.

Ultimately, their plans for him would be in gambling, for sure, but not just in Las Vegas. No, for Jimmy Nap, there was something even bigger in the works.

Chapter 16

The Road Not Taken

As a youngster I knew that my father was not your average father. I knew he wasn't a nine-to-five guy. He was something else, something different, something *special*.

I could tell by the way he and his friends dressed to a T; by the pinky rings they wore; the nice cars they drove. For years I thought my father was in the cigar business because he always kept a few boxes of Cuban cigars in the back seat of his car.

After my sixth birthday I didn't know what happened to my father because I didn't see him again until I was nine years old. My mother kept covering up for him by saying, "He's working for the government on special assignment."

She got away with her well-intentioned cover-up because it was during the World War II years, and so it made her excuse plausible. Of course I found out later as I grew up that when he came back to us in 1945 he had been doing time in Sing Sing. He did a lot of time, on and off, a few years at a time usually.

There are chunks of time—from age fourteen to eighteen—where he was conspicuously absent. If you look at family photos of events where my father should have been there and wasn't, you know why. He was doing a stretch somewhere. It's only in hindsight that this absence of his stings. As a youngster, I accepted it as one of the many sacrifices he had to make for his job. But no matter how many times he went away, he always made sure that we were well taken care. He always came back, and. I didn't want for anything. Well, except for a father who couldn't be there.

From age to eighteen, I spent as much time—no, more time—in the gym training to be a boxer than I did preparing for the classroom. My father wanted me to know how to defend myself—but not to become a professional fighter. No, he knew the fight game better than anyone and didn't want me mixed up in it. He always said, "TN, you belong in management, that's the place for you. Don't use your hands to make a living, use your brain."

In addition to boxing in the Golden Gloves, the PAL and in the Catholic youth organizations, I also played on my grammar school and high school baseball teams. When I was seventeen, I tried out for the Boston Braves farm system team as a third baseman. The scout who my father knew was in town looking for future prospects. My father asked the scout to set up a training session for me with their minor league team that was training at a college baseball field in Long Island. They were impressed with my talent and wanted me to go back to Boston and play in the summer time for one of their minor league clubs. But my mother wanted me close to home and close to the family and said, "No way." And that ended that career path.

※

After graduating from high school in 1955, on my father's orders I joined the United States Air Force. He said, "TN, join any branch of the armed forces that you want and defend this great country that my parents risked everything to come to. And one I believe in too. And if you come home alive, then you can think about college or work." My father, like a lot of guys in the rackets, had a fierce sense of patriotism. They loved their country. Even as they were breaking the laws of its land, they still wanted this nation defended and respected.

On October 4th 1955, I arrived at Sanford Air Force Base in Geneva, New York, for basic training. Afterward I was sent to Parks Air Force Base in Oakland, California. for a strenuous, two-month long air police training program in guerilla warfare.

I graduated from Air Police school in March 1956 and was assigned to the Strategic Air Command (SAC) under General Curtis E. LeMay. LeMay was held in high esteem by some but was considered a belligerent warmonger by many others. He had led the bombing campaign in the Pacific in WWII and earned the nickname,"Bombs Away" LeMay. Later, during the Vietnam War, LeMay said that we should "bomb the North Vietnamese back to the stone age." He was a tough-as-nails military man who believed wholeheartedly that might makes right. Not surprisingly,

George Wallace picked him as his vice presidential running mate in 1968. Not surprisingly, they lost.

My first assignment was to escort the general around the Far East on reconnaissance missions. We had to spot the enemy and record their positions. If we were fired upon, we couldn't fire back, because that would give up our own position. In my neighborhood, when someone shot at you, you shot back. But not here. I was learning.

I was also trained to go into enemy territory and try to free our captured servicemen from prison camps. I could cut barbed wire with my shears in the darkness. I was also trained to kill the enemy by choking him around his neck with a thin peace of wire—swiftly and silently so that I could remain unseen and unheard.

The only real weapon I carried was a 12-inch bayonet. The streets of Brooklyn made me tough, but the U.S. Government made me a killer.

When I nearly castrated that punk who touched my daughter at Queensboro Community College, I used the same techniques learned in the U.S. Air Force. All those years later, the training kicked in like riding a bike. That's why I could so easily overtake him.

Eventually I was able to harness my aggression in a more useful way, but that was after years of boxing, street fights, and barrooms brawls. But that killer instinct that I possessed for most of my life was really cultivated and perfected in the good ol' U.S. Armed Forces.

Most of my active duty consisted of a two-year tour in the Far East: Wake Island, Okinawa, Japan, Iwo Jima, and Hawaii. I flew over Korea with the general, spotting the North Koreans, who were our new enemies at the time.

We would drop off equipment and food rations for our troops. Even though the treaty had been signed in 1953 at the 38th Parallel, which divides North and South Korea, we still had sniper problems. And our men were held in prison for years afterward.

After the treaty, I fought on the U.S. Air Force boxing team in the tournament leading up to the 1956 Olympics. My father used to say I had hand trouble. That's what he called it. Even as a kid I was always fighting with somebody.

But the way I look at it, if you're going be a fighter, you better be a good one. And I was a good one, a middleweight. I'd hit a guy with a vicious right cross on the chin and he'd hit the canvas. I had power. A natural, most said.

I did myself, my unit, and my country proud, and suddenly there was a lot of talk about me being good enough to represent the U.S. in The Olympic Games.

I was sitting on the bed in my barracks one time after a preliminary bout, removing the tape from my hands, when General LeMay, who seemed to always have a long cigar in his mouth, approached me.

"Airman Napoli..."

I leapt to my feet "General...sir!" I said, saluting him with a hand still half-taped.

"Please, sit-down, airman."

"Thank you, sir."

"That's quite a fucking right hand you got there," he said.

Where I grew up, general, you either learned how to throw a punch or you learned how to run fast. I ain't much of a runner so..."

"You're a hell of a fighter though, kid. The gooks and the niggers shit their fucking pants when they see you."

"Yeah, well...who would believe it general? Little Tony Napoli from Brooklyn, fighting in the Olympic Games. Madone! But I want you to know, general, as soon as the Olympics are over, I dedicate myself to the Strategic Air Command and I become a full-time soldier again. No more distractions. I promise, sir."

"Tony...listen..." the general's tone changed. "We got a call today...from back home."

"Where? My home? Brooklyn?"

"It was your father. You should call him."

"My father? Is everything okay there?"

"Yes, everything's okay. He just...he wanted to talk to you. Just call him as soon as you can."

General LeMay made his way to the door. Then he turned back. "We're all pulling for you, airman."

"Thank you, general."

I looked down at my hands, which were no longer taped. My knuckles were red and swollen. I clenched my fists and wondered. What it was my father wanted? And would I be able to use these hands of mine for something good—for once—to get myself to the Olympics?

I called home right away. He told me to get home, that my mother had taken sick and she wanted me there.

I arrived in Brooklyn within two days of my father's call. I was dressed in my military uniform with the Air Policeman's band on my left arm, and I carried a small suitcase. I was feeling good about myself, how I looked, and who I was becoming at this point in my life.

Neighborhood people saw me, and greeted me with wide eyes and big hellos. They were looking at me differently now. They were looking at me like I was a somebody. A soldier.

A moment of hesitation came over me as I reached out to ring the doorbell of the Napoli Family house, bought by my father for $15,000 cash ten years ago. I thought of all that I had left behind me—the Air Force, the Olympics, the potential for a different life, one that I had never even dreamed of, but which was within my grasp now. I thought of all that was before me—my mom's illness, my father's business, a life back in the old neighborhood. I seemed to be teetering between all I could be and all I had to be; between one life and another. I sucked in a deep breath and rang the bell.

My father greeted me. There was silence between us at first. He was always a large-than-life, imposing figure. In his big, dark sunglasses that he always wore, he had a way of making everyone and everything shrink in his presence. And that included me, in my military uniform and all. Here I was, standing before him as a soldier in the U.S. Air Force and somehow I still felt like a little boy.

My father broke the silence with an order. "Go see your mother," he said. "She's layin' down in the bedroom. Then come inside. I wanna see you."

With that he walked away. No *how are you, good to see you, how was your trip?* We hadn't seen each other in two years. In my mind, I had gone away a boy and come back a man. In his, I still was, and always would be, just a boy.

I placed my suitcase on the floor and headed down the hallway to the bedroom.

My mother was resting. She looked thinner. She had the cancer in her body, I could tell just by looking at her. It started in her lungs and it was slowly spreading. She opened her eyes as I got closer to her and I placed a kiss on her forehead.

"Hey Brother..." she said in a weak voice. She always called me Brother. That was her nickname for me. "How handsome you look. Look at you in that uniform. You look a little thin though. Have you been eating? Make sure you eat. What happened to your face?"

She was referring to a bruise I had on my face from my last preliminary bout.

"I'm a fighter, Ma, remember?"

"But still...they gotta hit you in the face? Don't they see how handsome you are. Animals. Ga'head. Go eat. There's manicotti in the icebox." She was always more worried about me then she was about herself.

I didn't want to leave her side. "Did you get the picture I sent you?" I asked.

"Yeah, I gave it to your father to put in a frame for me. You look so handsome in your uniform. I can't get over it."

I held and squeezed her hand and she smiled at me.

"Ga' head. Go eat," she insisted. "You had a long trip. Don't worry, I'm not going anywhere."

I knew she would be insulted if I didn't go eat her manicotti. So I left her and walked toward the kitchen. As I passed by the dining room table I saw the picture of me in my military uniform. It was ripped to pieces.

My father approached me. "Sit down," he ordered me again.

"What happened to my pict-" I tried to ask but he cut me off.

"Sit down, I said," he repeated and his voice got louder. So I sat.

He hovered over me and I could feel an anger welling up in him, even though I didn't dare look up at him. I sat there, head down, and just hoped that whatever it was that had put him in this mood would just go away.

Then, without warning, he reached out and ripped the air policeman band off my arm.

"What are you doing?" I shrieked.

"You're home now," he explained. "Your loyalty is here. To this family. *Capisce*? Your fancy armbands don't mean anything on the street."

"Why am I home anyway? Why did you call for me?"

"Because your mother needs you, that's why. Did you see her? She's gettin' worse, not better. And this is another reason I got you out." He held out the air police band. "Did I raise you to be a cop? Is that what I raised my son to be, a lousy stinkin' cop?"

"I ain't a cop. I am an air policeman."

"Same thing. A cop's a cop. I told you to go defend your country, not become a cop."

"You don't understand, in the service you don't pick your job, they pick it for you."

I wanted him to understand. I wanted him to see that I wasn't against him. I wasn't the thing he hated. But it was all falling on deaf ears. My father had spent so much time on the other side of the law, so much time in prison that his aversion to police or anything that even reminded him of the police, ran deep. It was too deep for me to reach. "Yeah, well, around here, *I* pick it for you," he insisted.

"I could have represented my country in the Olympics. I could have won a gold medal. Do you know what that would have meant?"

"No, tell me, what would it have meant?" he asked, patronizing.

"It would have meant I was somebody, and that I did

something," I fought back with sincerity. "I wouldn't just be another anybody in a neighborhood full of nobodies."

"I live in this neighborhood. Am I a nobody?" He looked me right in the face. Now he was being antagonistic.

"I didn't mean it for you."

"Look me in the face and tell me I'm a nobody!"

"I didn't mean it for you," I insisted.

He wasn't having it. He was going to assert his control. He was going to be the boss. I was going to do what he said.

"You don't like this neighborhood? Fine. What neighborhood do you like?"

There was no right answer to this question. In fact it wasn't even really a question.

"I didn't say I didn't like this neigh—"

He cut me off. This was what he was getting at.

"Ya know what, I got just the perfect neighborhood for you."

He had just the perfect neighborhood for me. Had it all planned out. My life. *For me.* I would live it by his rules. All my plans for the service and the Olympics? Finished. Those dreams died that day. That road came to an abrupt end. I was about to go on another path, which was to take me down a road less traveled.

Chapter 17

Crooked Cop

FOUR YEARS LATER, I HAD a crew and my own joint in Union City, New Jersey. It was the lone establishment in a deserted area just outside the Holland Tunnel. The windows were darkened so that no one could see inside. A blue awning hung over the front entrance. In neon yellow, "Club Rag Doll" was printed across it.

Inside was teeming with people and life. Music and merriment filled the big room nightly. An oval bar with 72 stools was full, all the time. A four-piece band played on a small stage in the center of the big bar. In the back of the room was a dance floor. And just next to the front entrance was a booth, labeled "PRIVATE," where me and my crew would sit and hold court.

I was living the life of a knockaround guy, in and around the family business. I was helping my father when he needed me, but looking to venture out on my own too. I didn't want to be in my father's shadow. I also was smart enough to know that being my father's son, in these circles, was a major asset.

I was also starting to drink too much. Which was a direct result of the long hours spent in a bar. I would sit in my booth and down shots one after another to the cheers and encouragement of my entourage. I was an entertaining son of a gun. Everyone loved me. I was a pleasure to be with, most of the time, when I was sober. At least I think I was. But then the booze kicked in and I became belligerent. And the times when I was sober were becoming fewer and fewer.

One night while I was busy impressing my party with my drinking exhibition, one of my guys came over and whispered in my ear. "Captain Mac wants to talk to you, TN."

"Yeah, so tell him to come talk to me then. What the fuck's he want me to do, roll out a red carpet?"

"Says he wants to talk in private."

I looked over to the bar where Captain Mac, a tall, stern Irishman in his late 40s stood. In a cheap suit and a fedora, he slugged back a drink. He was a police captain in Jersey. Not well liked. But a rough guy who was better to have on your side then against you. He nodded in acknowledgment, as I stared blankly back at him.

I took one more shot and I stood, making a head gesture toward the front of the club. Captain Mac put his glass down on the bar and followed after me.

We stood in the vestibule so we could talk in private, away from the noise of the club.

"What seems to be the problem, captain?" I asked him. "Was your free drink a little too strong for you tonight?"

"No-no, the drink was fine. Nice and smooth. As always. And it was a double too," he said, thinking his badge entitled him to his wise cracks and his free liquor.

"You fuckin' Irishmen are all alike, ya know that? Give you one free drink, and you make it a double. You make the moolanyans look classy."

"Let's cut the sweet talk, Tony. I know your father's on the lam. And I know it's because of those murders in Williamsburg."

My father was on the lam for a shooting that happened around the corner from Crisci's Restaurant earlier in 1960. Two brothers were seen leaving Crisci's after having a heated discussion—something about them taking a piece of my father's number business—at my father's table. 'As the story goes, Jimmy Nap told the two brothers to meet him down the block and wait for him in their car. That was about midnight.'

The next morning the two brothers were found shot in the head sitting in the front seats of their car, just down the block from Crisci's.

Nobody talked about the killing of the two brothers anymore. My father was a suspect just like he was always a suspect when there was a major crime committed in the Williamsburg section of Brooklyn. He was always told to turn himself in for questioning when these things happened. The local cops didn't arrest him with handcuffs. They showed respect for him at all times, knowing that after the investigation, Jimmy Nap would be cleared—which was the case most of the time.

My father would go on the lam to take the heat off himself and allow the cops to focus on others who might be involved. It was usually the local detectives who would send a message to my father through his crew when the smoke had cleared. Something to the effect of, "Tell Jimmy Nap it's all clear" and "Tell your father he can come back."

"I don't know what you're talkin' about, Mac. My father's on vacation. He's sittin' in the sun somewhere. Nice and tan. Not like you, you milky white mick."

"That's some vacation. The President of the United States don't even go away for this long."

"Yeah, well, the president doesn't have as many responsibilities as my father does. And he don't have as much power neither."

"Now you listen to me, you fuckin' greasy wop." The captain leaned into me. "This ain't Brooklyn. This is Jersey. And in Jersey, you don't run the show, we do. We got laws here. And it's my job to enforce 'em. From now on, if you wanna stay here and keep this nice little place of yours running with no problems, then you're gonna have to play by my rules. Do you understand me, greaseball?"

I stared at him. If he was anybody else but a cop saying this, I would have cracked his head open right then and there for getting out of line with me. I had this dirty Irish mutt stuck in my throat.

"I'm so sick of your type," he went on, making matters worse with his mouth. "With the fancy suits and the slick olive oil hair. If it was up to me, I'd put you all in a boat and *send* you back to Sicily where you came from."

"My family is from Naples, captain."

He ignored my comment and got right back down to business. "If you wanna stay, then you gotta pay. Do you understand? And the first payment starts right now. Tonight. Otherwise, you go back to Brooklyn. Or, better yet, I'll send you back."

"All right, okay, captain. I don't want no trouble." I had to calm this half-drunk Irishmen down. I had to play nice. At least for a little while. "I hear what you're sayin'. I tell ya what…let's not do this here, out in the open like this. I don't want nobody seeing us. I'm sure you don't want that either. So how about we meet in the parking lot of the Club Capri. Gimme an hour. I'll come there and I'll give you what you got comin' to you."

Captain Mac smiled, a self satisfied 'I got you by the balls' type of grin. He nodded and turned toward the door. Then he turned back and sneered, "You fuckin' guineas make me sick. You ruin every decent business you touch with your dirty hands. I don't even want to take your filthy money. But I will."

I watched him go, with rage in my eyes and hatred in my heart. It was bad enough he was a cop, but a crooked cop, that was worst of all. The day that somebody, anybody, would come into my joint and shake me down would be a cold day in hell.

I didn't call my father. I decided to handle this myself.

I returned to my booth and my party, dropped back drink after drink, and got good and loaded, so I would be ready for my meeting with Captain Mac.

About two hours later—I know I told him one hour, but fuck him, he wanted something from me, he could wait—my Cadillac pulled into the parking lot of the Club Capri, which was just down the road from the Rag Doll. I sat in the passenger seat, plenty tanked up. One of my guys was behind the wheel. It's not that I didn't want to drive drunk. I didn't care about that. Driving drunk was nothing in them days. Everybody did. I just needed a wingman for this assignment.

My eyes darted back and forth as I scanned the quiet parking lot. *Where is that cop? Did he turn chicken on me?*

Come out, come out, wherever you are. In my right hand I clutched a lead pipe.

Suddenly, an enraged Captain Mac came rushing out of the darkness like a man possessed. He slammed on the hood of my car with his bare hands.

"You think I'm stupid?" he screamed, his Irish brogue echoing across the desolate parking lot. "Do you think I'm fucking stupid?"

Simultaneously, my crew member and I hopped out of the Caddy and went on the offensive against the raging Irishman. My guy grabbed the captain from behind and held him while I beat him with the lead pipe.

Then the captain—like any cop would—tried to reach for his gun. My crew member snatched it away from him.

Captain Mac fell to the ground from the repeated blows. I continued to beat him and shouted at him even as he went down. "You try to shake me down?" I hollered, like a goddamn lunatic. I could see my hot breath before my eyes as puffs of smoke burst from my mouth on what was a bitterly cold night. "Who did you think you were fuckin' with? You stinkin' Irish mutt with a fuckin' badge!"

And with each question came another strike to his head, his back, his legs. My temper was now on full display, and all sense of logic, repercussion, or punishment, escaped me. My focus was squarely fixed on delivering pain to this unscrupulous, double-dealing cop, who tried to put the squeeze on me. But like most things in life that I did to excess, this was yet another example of me going way too far.

My crew member, who had more sense in his head than I did and who was sober, grabbed me by the arm and tried to pull me back to the car. "C'mon, Tony, please, let's go!" he pleaded and yanked at me.

I pulled away and looked down at the bloody face of Captain Mac. Then I reached into his pocket and pulled out his badge. And sounding a lot like my father, when he pulled my Air Police band from my arm, I proceeded to berate the semi-conscious captain. "Your badge means nothin' on the street! Ya hear me? Nothin'!" I spit on the badge and threw it in his face.

"Tony, let's go!" my guy called out to me from the car.

I walked back to the car like I was in no particular hurry, the lead pipe, now bent and dented, in my hand.

Back at the Rag Doll, I moved around the club, which was still hopping. Bar people never find time to go home. Blood was still on my face, shirt and hands. Nobody seemed to notice. At least I didn't think they did.

Jimmy Roselli, who was just coming up in the business back then, sang "Mala Femmina" on the stage as unsuspecting patrons swooned. I stormed into the hat check room and opened a trap door in the floor, and went down the steps into a secret room we had built beneath the club.

It was a 15x15 square foot room with a bathroom, a shower, bed, desk, telephone, lighting and a TV set. Everything an underground wiseguy bunker should be. I grabbed a bottle of booze and slugged it down as I flopped back in my chair behind the desk.

After I did the job on that cop, I was prepared to stay in this hideout as long as it took. So long as I had my bottle of Dewars, I was fine. It's all I ever needed. But before too long, I heard the cavalry coming to get me. Sirens. Then footsteps.

After someone tipped off the cops about my secret room, the police broke into the basement to arrest me. They threw me to the ground and slapped the cuffs on me. They were rougher than usual because I had given a beating to one of their own this time. They took it personal. If there wasn't twenty of them I would have given each one of them a beating too.

They led me through the club. The music stopped and everyone got quiet as I was escorted out. Patrons looked on. I knew I had to say something. To make them all feel better. To make myself feel better. To make the cops look stupid. I spoke to the patrons and the band, even as the police pushed me toward the door, hands cuffed behind my back. "Ga 'head, keep playin' the music," I instructed them. "Have a good time everybody. Don't let this put a damper on your night. I'll be back in a half hour. These nice gentlemen just want to take me for a little walk."

Then I called out to Billy, my bartender. "Billy, pour me a six count of Jack and leave it on the bar for me. I'll be back soon."

The police whisked me out the door in a hurry, like they had captured Dillinger rather than a guy who had delivered a much needed beating to a bad cop.

"Ya heard what Tony said. Strike up the band!" Billy yelled out.

I heard the band starting to play again as I was taken from my club. I smiled to myself with a sense of satisfaction, as if in some way I had won.

Some winner I was. For hours I sat in a Union City Police Station by myself. Nobody talked to me, nobody looked at me. They didn't allow me my one phone call no matter how much I harassed them.

Then suddenly I heard a voice, a familiar, female voice, loud and clear, coming from the sergeant's desk. "Take this bail money from me. There's five thousand dollars here. Do what you want with it. I want my son to go home with me."

It was my mother.

"Mrs Napoli, I can't accept your money," the sergeant told her. "You can sit in front of your son's cell, if you want. I'll get you a chair but only for a few minutes. My lieutenant is coming back in a half hour."

He escorted my mother to my cell. I saw her through the bars and my heart sank. "Ma...!"

The sergeant searched my mother's pocketbook. "What's this?" he asked her. "It's warm."

He removed a pint-sized jar of homemade chicken soup from her pocketbook.

"It's for my son. He needs his strength."

The sergeant handed her back the jar. He placed a chair in front of the cell for her to sit in. "Ten minutes only," he ordered and then he walked off, leaving us alone. "Hey Brother..." she said in her soft sweet voice.

"Ma, what're ya doin' here? You're sick and you drove all the way to Jersey."

She handed me the chicken soup through the metal bars. From another cell, a prisoner called out. "Look...He works over a police captain and he's a mama's boy!"

Other prisoners laughed in their cells.

My mother got up and walked over to the prisoner's cell. She stood in front of him defiantly, even in her frail state. "If you don't shut up, I'll get the keys and turn him loose. Then you'll see how much of a mama's boy he is!"

The prisoner shouted back at her, something loud and unclear. The sergeant returned and banged on the prisoner's cell with his club. "Quiet!" Then he escorted Mom back to her seat in front of my cell.

"Ma, you don't have to be here. I don't want you to see me in this place."

"Of course I have to be here. You're my son, and you need me. I'm always gonna be here for you. Even when I'm not here anymore, I'm still gonna be here."

I looked at my mother, her eyes welling up. I wanted to grab her in my arms and hug her, but I couldn't do that through the bars that separated us.

"Eat your soup." She wiped her tears away and looked strong—for my sake more than for her own.

That's who my mother was. The rock of the family. A Rock of Gibraltar.

But months later, back at the Napoli home, out on bail and somehow a free man for the time being, I had to face my father, who was back. If my mother was a rock, my father was a stone.

I sat across from him in a darkened corner of the den, in total silence. Silence was never good when it came to my father and me. I looked down at my shoes, very still, and avoided eye contact—my way when I knew he was mad. He stared straight at me. I could feel the weight of his eyes on the top of my head.

The tension was finally cut. "I spoke to the judge," he said in a low voice. Then he raised it almost immediately. "You hear what I said? I said I spoke to the judge. Look at me when I talk to you!"

I looked up from my shoes.

"He's gonna do me this favor. You're a very lucky guy, ya know that? That cop is in intensive care. Where is your head, TN? I mean, I could see it's on your shoulders, but sometimes I wonder what's inside it."

"He was tryin' to shake me dow—"

"I don't wanna hear it. All I want you to do is get on the next bus out of New York. Go somewhere. Anywhere. Far away. And don't come back until I tell you to. Ya understand? Don't call. Don't send no letters. Just go away. Disappear. When the time is right, you'll hear from me."

I nodded my head in agreement.

"Get your stuff together in your room. Ga 'head. I know it's your birthday but you gotta do what you gotta do. I'll come to your room and get you soon. And before you go, you stop by St. Catherine's Hospital and you say goodbye to your mother. You don't leave without sayin' goodbye to her."

I nodded. "I understand. One question though. Where should I go?"

He stared at me again, as if the question had the most obvious answer. "Go to the last place anybody would ever think to look for you."

Anna Napoli, grandmother

Headstone, Jimmy and Grace Napoli

Jimmy and Grace, Tony's parents, 1947

Tony, age 15

Tony's confirmation, 1947

"Tony Reo" at 160 pounds, 1961

Tony & show girls, Caesars Palace, 1968

Tony 1975

Jimmy Nap (fourth from right) at Crisci's, 1950s

Jimmy Nap, right, with crew at Crisci's, 1950s

Jimmy Nap and Cy Crisci, 1976 FBI photo

Jimmy Nap outside Crisci's

Natty, Rocky Graziano, and Tony, 1980s

Tony and Laura, New Year's Eve 1981

Jimmy and Tony, Lewisburg Federal Prison, 1983

Arturo Gatti, welterweight Gene Ward, and Tony

Tanya, daughter

Helen, youngest daughter

Helen and Johnny Depp

Tony, Tony Danza and Helen, 1996

Tony and Ring 8 president Henry Wallitsch, 2006

Veronica and Carmine, 2001

Laura, Carmine, Veronica, and Tony, 2001

Tony and Juan LaPorte, former welterweight champ, 2004

Tony, 2006

Tony and Gianna, granddaughter

Chapter 18

Welcome To Tucumcari

My bus pulled up on a dirt road, in the middle of nowhere.

Looking out through the dusty window I saw a sign: Tucumcari, New Mexico, Population: 3,500; in the eastern part of the state with a stream of motels parked along Route 66.

I got off the bus, carrying only one bag and wearing sunglasses.

I looked out at the flat open space of earth that seemed to go on forever in front of me. *Where the fuck am I? And what the fuck am I gonna do with myself here?*

My father always said that if a man knows how to take care of himself he can always get by. I needed to get by. Out here in Nowheresville I was going to need to use everything I had at my disposal to get by.

When they're desperate, people fall back on what they do best. So I turned to the one thing, maybe the only thing, I was ever any good at: fighting.

It happened by accident. But soon after getting off the bus, I joined up with a traveling carnival featuring every kind of freak you could imagine. They had midgets, a bearded lady, a fat lady, the lobster man, and Siamese twins joined together at the hip. We had it all.

This is how it happened. While sitting on a park bench, trying to figure out my next move, I saw in the distance a big sign. Bold, black lettering with a white background spelling out "Midway Carnival, The Biggest Little Carnival in the World. Laborers and Fighters Wanted." I decided to walk down a small hill from the park into the carnival area and have a look around.

When I got into the area a security guard confronted me. He asked me if I was there looking for a job. I told him yeah, sure, and he directed me to a large tent near the entrance of the carnival. I saw laborers unloading equipment from boxcars on railroad tracks. I figured here was a job I could do.

Under the tent was a fat bearded slob puffing on a cheap cigar, sitting on a chair behind a long banquet table. There were people standing on line, maybe a dozen or so. The fat bastard in the chair looked at me and yelled out, "You wanna fight for the carnival? If you do, you have to take me on."

I told him, "No, I'm just here to work as a laborer, loading and unloading the boxcars. I can also help to set up and tear down the tents when the carnival leaves for another town."

But the fat slob, who was drunk to boot, came at me. He put his hands under my armpits and picked me up about two feet off the ground. His breath stunk of booze, the cheap kind, like moonshine maybe. My hands were free, so I held his head and bit his nose until he dropped me to the ground.

After that, all hell broke loose. Everybody wanted to see a fight. I danced around the slob, jabbing and kicking him in his neck. He was bleeding and dizzy with all the blows I threw at him. Finally, he went down. Three security guards snatched me and started to escort me off the premises, when a guy with a straw hat, and light-colored suit told them to release me. He offered me a job.

But where the heck did I fit into a carnival?

I became Tony Reo, the Brooklyn Barnstormer. Local yokels paid good money to see if they could go one round in the ring with me.

A master of ceremonies, with a bullhorn and top hat, barked out to the spectators. "Who's next? Step right up! Who wants to try out their fighting skills and dare to go just one round with the great Tony Reo, the Brooklyn Barnstormer? You sir? How about you, sir? Who is brave enough to step into the ring?!"

A lot of these hicks were game. But they were no match for Tony Reo. I'd land one vicious roundhouse to their chin and they knew then they were overmatched. Next thing you know a hick was crashing to the canvas in a heap. I took my aggravation out on them. I sure as hell didn't want to be there doing what I was doing. Somebody was going to have to pay. But since the alternative was jail, I made the most of it.

I would get food and board and a few dollars a night each time I fought. We traveled from town to town on a train, all of the performers together. I would find a quiet spot to myself in the corner of a boxcar and nurse a bottle of whiskey. I turned to the other thing I was good at. Drinking.

After a short while I had had enough and went AWOL from the carnival, deserting the freaks and trash that traveled with the show after we arrived in one particular town, which I don't even remember the name of now because they all looked the same anyway.

I hitchhiked my way from town to town. When I was done in one place, I hit the side of the road with my bag—which had all my earthly possessions in it—slung over my shoulder, and I stuck my thumb out. I barely had enough money to eat one meal a day and keep myself tanked up so I wouldn't dwell on what had become of my life.

You never know what you're getting when you stick your thumb out on the side of a road. Your best bet is probably a trucker, just looking for a little company as he drives across country. Since I knew I could defend myself in almost any circumstance I wasn't too concerned. But this one time a jalopy pulled over for me. It wasn't a surprise really because that's all these hicks drove out here. I didn't see a Cadillac the whole time.

So this shitbox pulled over, with two *dentally challenged* hicks inside. The delinquent in the passenger seat, who had a few more teeth than the delinquent in the driver's seat, leaned out his open window and asked, "Need a lift?"

The jalopy cruised across Route 66 with the hicks in the front seats and me in the back. Loud music—*their* music—filled the car. I guess you'd call it country music. I'm not even sure. All I know is, it wasn't the kind of music I would listen to.

The hick in the passenger seat yelled, "So, you from New York City, ain't you?" without turning to look turning to look at me.

"What makes you say that?" I shouted back.

"You got a New York City face. You look I-*talian*."

"I'm German-Irish."

The passenger seat hick turned in his seat and looked me straight in the face. "You sure look I-*talian* to me," he said, sincerely, as if straining to see if I was telling the truth. He was waiting for me to admit that I was *I-talian*.

We stayed locked in a stare for a moment, neither of us giving in. Then the hick who was driving spoke, looking in his rearview to address me. "You New York boys don't like hillbilliies, do you?"

"I don't know any hillbillies," I said. "I know a few guys from Staten Island, though."

"Yeah, well, we know a hillbilly bastard who's givin' us some real trouble. Ya know what I mean by trouble?"

"Yeah, yeah, I know trouble."

"How'd you like to work him over for us...this hillbilly...we'll give you fifty bucks," the driver offered.

Fifty bucks was more money than I had seen for a while out here. It was an offer I couldn't refuse. The jalopy pulled up to an out-of-the-way-bar—a real dive—that was even more in the middle of nowhere than the rest of this middle of nowhere was.

I followed the hicks out of their car and we headed toward the bar. It was rundown with sawdust on the floor. One of the hicks pointed to a big, sloppy, bearded hillbilly sitting at one of the small round tables in the corner of the bar room with two other hillbillies.

As soon as the hillbillies spoted me and the hicks, they got up from their seats and rushed toward us. The hillbillies started beating on the two hicks with wooden clubs and bats. I took a shot to the head that nearly dropped me to the floor, but I somehow maintained my balance.

Then the two hicks turned chicken shit on me and ran out of the place, leaving me alone to defend myself. My face was already bloodied and the hillbillies continued to rain blows down on me. It was as if the beating that would have been split up three ways was now all being deposited in one place—my head.

Whenever I was in any kind of a fight, in or out of the ring, there was always a time when things slowed down for me; when I could think clearly, sometimes even more clearly than I thought when I wasn't being hit. My mind scrambled to adjust to the situation and I'd always find a way, a motivation, a will, if you will, to keep me going forward.

I started pushing the hillbillies off me, just long enough to spit out a mouthful of blood and speak. I directed my words to the biggest hillbilly, the one I had come for, who had a Louisville slugger in his hand and was ready to keep using it on me. "Hey, Popcorn. Drop the bat and I'll sever your fuckin' eyes outta your head, ya fuckin' ham and egg bastard."

I don't think he understood most of what I said. But the big guy looked to the others. Then he instructed them, "Okay, stand back. I'll take him."

Most guys only know one way to fight—straight forward. It was the same thing with this guy. He came forward, and I began to out maneuver him, out fox him, out box him. Despite my exhaustion and bleeding from head to toe, I reached down deep into whatever strength and pride I had left. I just couldn't let these hillibillies beat me. I was a New Yorker, I was a Napoli. I landed one, last, devastating blow to his chin. He went down like a ton of bricks.

The other hillbillies surrounded me and were prepared to pounce. After all, I took down their leader. Just as they did, the sheriff, and his deputies came busting into the bar. "Okay-okay, party's over!" the sheriff announced, and people began to scatter like roaches when a light is turned on. I thought, thank God this is over with.

The only person they arrested is *me*! They pushed me over a table, handcuffed me and dragged me out of the bar. I was too exhausted to even put up a fight. Take me to jail! See if I care. I'll get a good night's sleep and a meal.

"You got any identification, boy?"

I shook my badly beaten head, indicating "No."

"Where you from, boy?"

I couldn't even respond. I was seeing triple and my head felt like it weighed as much as this fat bastard sheriff's belly.

"I said, Where you from?" the sheriff repeated himself in a louder voice than before.

"New...York...City," I got each word out, somehow.

"Holy shit! New York City? Well, you sure as fuck is a long way from home! Let's go. We gonna give you a place to stay for the night."

They stuck me in a small, cramped cell. I sat on a dirt floor. No toilet. No cot. There wasn't even so much as a broken down mattress for me to lay my aching head on.

"This is what we call a little Western hospitality," the sheriff laughed.

I peered up at him through the bars, through eyes that were nearly swollen shut from the beating.

A good five hours later the hicks who got me into all this trouble showed up. From my cage, I couldn't see them talking to the sheriff. Then, after a few moments, the sheriff walked toward my cell. He opened it. I climbed to my feet.

The sheriff whispered in my ear, "I want you the fuck out of my town, because they're gettin' ready to lynch you, boy."

I stepped out of my cell and I never turned back to look at the sheriff. I just kept walking until I saw daylight. Outside, who did I see parked in front of the police station but the two hicks sitting in their jalopy.

I staggered over to them, my legs wobbly under me, but I was pissed off. So long as I could stand, I was going to give it to these two bastards, but good. I didn't even get a word out and one of the hicks hands me a fifty-dollar bill. I look down at it. All this for fifty lousy bucks. Back home I spend more than that on ice in one day.

I crumbled the bill in my hand and stuck it in my pocket. I got in the car.

The punks, who were suddenly in a celebratory mood, broke out a bottle of whiskey, chugged it and passed it back to me. I threw down a shot. "We did it! We fuckin' did it! Now let's go to California!" one of the hicks howled.

I didn't say a word. I was too beat, too tired. I lay down across the backseat and I fell asleep.

Next thing I know, I heard a slamming sound. I woke up to find myself alone in the car somewhere along Route 66. Some gas station.

My eyes went to the slamming sound and settled on the two hicks, who were beating up on a soda vending machine, robbing it of all its coins and sticking the coins in paper bags.

Then, my eyes went to a gas station attendant, who pumped gas into the jalopy, as he looked on, seeing the hicks committing their penny ante crime. One of the paper bags broke on them, sending coins to the ground and drawing even more attention.

"What the fuck are you doin'?" I called out to them. But the windows in the car were closed and they couldn't hear me. I yelled anyway. "You assholes, what are you doin'? He's watchin' you! Stupid fuckin' hicks!"

The hicks rushed back to the car with a few bags full of stolen coins. They actually paid the attendant with the coins!

The attendant, another imbecile, took the coins and then ran back into the gas station.

The hicks got in the car and I berated them. "What are you guys doin'?"

"Look at all this!" one of them said, so proud of the loose change he robbed.

"The attendant saw the whole thing," I told him. "Let's get the fuck outta here!"

"Oh shit...He's right! Let's go!" says the hick driver, and he threw the car into gear and peels out.

The jalopy moved down the highway at full speed. Suddenly, a siren was heard in the distance, growing closer. It was a police car and it was gaining on them. On us. I couldn't go to jail twice in one day, could I?

"Don't stop! Just keep goin'!" the passenger seat hick told the driver.

"Stop the fuckin' car!" I yelled at them. "You robbed change! That's nothin'. You keep drivin' and you'll go away for sure!"

The police car pulled up to the bumper and hit the jalopy, causing it to nearly swerve off the road.

"Pull the fuck over, you dumb fuckin' hick!" Now I was screaming my head off.

"Don't do it, man. I ain't goin' to jail no more!" I ain't going away for these two again. Plus, I can't take a chance anybody finding out my real identity because of the Captain Mac assault back home. Dealing with the local sheriff was one thing, but this was the state police now.

"You're gonna go away for even longer if you don't pull over!" I tried to talk some sense into driver's seat hick. He had my fate in his hands now.

I peeked into the rearview mirror and saw more police cars chasing us across the desert. One car pulled beside the jalopy and tried hitting us off the road. The driver momentarily lost control of the jalopy, but regained it and continued to out-race the cops.

A helicopter circled overhead.

I was sweating bullets in the backseat because somehow, someway, I knew the guy from New York would get blamed for this!

"Pull it the fuck over!" I was hollering over sirens and helicopters and the idiot in the passenger seat.

"Fuck you! It's too late now," the driver told me with a crazed, distant look in his eyes.

He was right. It was over. Just up ahead was a…

"Road block!" the passenger seat hick pointed out.

I try one last time, "Stop the fuckin' car!"

"No way!" insisted the driver. "They're comin' with us!"

The jalopy drew closer and closer to the road block at top speed and driver hick wasn't slowing down. I could see that the police had drawn their pistols and were aiming them at us.

The hick in the passenger seat brought his head between his knees and covered his face. He let loose a "Ho-lee shiiiitttttt!"

Driver's seat hick screamed and let go of the steering wheel, "Ahhhhhhhhhh!"

The jalopy was now rushing headlong into the police blockade. With no choices left, I reached over the driver's seat and tugged on the steering wheel, causing the jalopy to just narrowly avoid the roadblock. The jalopy screeched and roared, tilted up on two wheels but still going forward as it raced off the road and across the desert, kicking up a blinding sandstorm.

"Where the fuck are we?" the hick driver asked.

"Did we die? Are we in heaven?" asked the other one.

"Just grab the fuckin' wheel and keep drivin', you asshole!" I ordered.

The jalopy made it through the sandstorm, leaving a cloud of smoke behind us.

"We did it! Holy shit, we did it!" the passenger seat hick shouted as he looked around.

What is this "we" shit?

"California, here we come!"

The road ahead looked clear and no one behind us either.

The driver turned to me. "I'll tell ya, that was some nice drivin' there for a city boy, partner."

And just as he turned back to the road before us, the jalopy slammed right into another police roadblock. Sixty days. I got sixty days in the slammer for that.

When I got out, I saw the hicks again—we were released at the same time. One of them asked me, "We wuz...uh... we wuz thinkin'...maybe you still wanna, ya know, come to California with us?"

"Go fuck yourselves," was my response.

The only good part was that the piece of shit car wasn't stolen. It was just four months behind on payments. The hicks agreed to make the payments, pay for the damages to the police cars, and give the coins back to the gas station. After this fiasco, I needed a drink. And I needed a job.

So I put the two together.

I started tending bar at a place called B&M Bar.

On New Year's Eve, 1961, I was mixing drinks when all of a sudden her voice called out to me from across the bar and over the sound of the noisy, drunken revelers. "Brother...Hey, brother..." she said. Goddamnit if it didn't sound just like my mother. She's the only person who ever called me Brother.

I looked up to see a pretty Mexican girl. I got distracted from what I was doing and I envisioned my mother's face in placed of this girl's. I placed the bottle down and went to a pay phone in the corner of the room. I dialed the number but it kept beeping busy. I tried a half dozen times, still busy.

When I got back to the bar, the girl called out to me again. "Brother...Hey, Brother..." She had big dark eyes and a tattoo of a cross between her eyes. She also has a tattoo of an angel on her left forearm.

"Can I help you with something?" I said—impolitely.

"You're damn right you can help me with something, Yankee. You took my job! You think I wanna be a barmaid? Tending bar is where the real money's at. And you took it from me, you gringo!"

I didn't even know this girl and she was accusing me of stealing her job. If she were a guy, she would be decked. But I looked at her curvaceous body.

"I tell ya what...it's New Year's Eve...let's not fight. Why don't you let me make it up to you? After work, let me take you out. We'll go up to the Hill. Whattaya say?"

"No way. I'm not going out with some yankee who took my job."

"C'mon...I'll show you I ain't so bad. Anyway, I think maybe we're meant to be, me and you."

The little Mexican girl laughed. "Oh, yeah, and how is that?"

"Well, for one thing, you called me Brother. My mother is the only person who ever called me that. And when you said it, you sounded just like her."

She smiled and looked down bashfully.

"What's your name?" She pointed to her left forearm. "Angel?" I ask.

She nods.

"That's good," I said. "I could use an angel."

She finally said yes without saying yes and a little after midnight we head up to the Hill, a local nightclub, where New Year's celebrations were still in full swing. We danced, drank and rang in the New Year together.

Then we went back to her place. I held her hand and kissed it. She had a tattoo scrawled across her hand, with one letter just below each knuckle that read "L-O-V-E." I looked at it for a moment.

"It's a Mexican thing," she said.

I liked Angel. She had all those tattoos, and she wasn't even Italian; but I was fond of her anyway. So I stayed the night. Early the next morning, I gently removed her arm from my chest and got out of the bed. I looked down at her sleeping. Then I left the bedroom and headed for the front door.

Well, I left the bar too. I wasn't just running away from Angel. Although I was. But I needed to do more than one job because no one job out there paid enough. So I picked cotton. I pulled broomcorn, used to make household brooms and brushes. I even ran for city councilman.

They loved me out in New Mexico. Especially the workers. Crowds of Mexican workers would gather to listen to me speak. I knew about the awful conditions they were working under. I come from a labor background, like my father and grandfather before me. I knew how they were being treated. They would have to fight to get what they wanted and deserved.

They hung banners around town that read, "Tony Reo, The Barnstormer, A Fighter for City Council."

I didn't win, but I did form a union for the people in the town. I got them a raise from seventy-five cents an hour to one dollar an hour for their backbreaking work in the fields. They came to like me and treat me like one of their own, which I guess, without realizing it, I had become.

Here I was on the lam, living under an assumed name and identity, and I was running for political office. God, you gotta love this country!

I was living what you might call a pretty normal, regular life out there in the middle of nowhere. At times I felt like I was living in the Andy Griffith TV sitcom where he is the wise sheriff of Mayberry. But one thing I have learned is that things don't stay nice and normal for long—at least not in my life. Something or someone always comes along to fuck things up. And sure enough, someone did.

I learned that Angel had been brutally and viciously raped by three guys. Apparently they had followed her home and then chased her through her house. She tried to fight them off, kicking and screaming; but they were too powerful for her. I went to her house.

"Angel...are you here?" I called out to her.

I heard her crying and whimpering in her bedroom. She was curled up in the fetal position on the bed. Her face was beaten up. "Tony..." she barely got my name out. I threw my arms around her. She clung on for dear life.

"Tony...They...They...I couldn't stop them, Brother. I tried...I tried to fight them, but..."

"Shh...Shh. It's okay. I'll take care of it. Don't worry about nothin'. I'll take care of everything."

I held her as tight as I could. She needed it. A fire ran through my veins. I could feel the old rage taking over. I was mad as hell. What they did to this woman, whose voice reminded me of my mother, whose voice I hadn't heard in over a year—no, it couldn't be tolerated.

I comforted Angel, but I was boiling over inside. My rage was not just directed at those sons of bitches, who I knew would pay for what they did, but at myself too. I blamed myself. What if I were here? What if I had stayed? Maybe this would have never happened. And that made me even angrier.

But I couldn't fix the past. What was done was done. But I *could* fix the future. And I could fix their asses for what they did to Angel.

News travels fast in a small town, just like in a small neighborhood in Brooklyn. If you want to know who did something, you go to the source. I put the word out through my Mexican laborer buddies that I was looking for the guys who had raped Angel. Two days later they knew. I asked the Mexicans to bring them to the B&M Bar after hours one night. The lure was a lie about a score they could make if they met with me. I had a good relationship with the owner of the bar and he knew what I wanted to do. He knew what had to be done.

Once the Mexicans brought them to me, the fun began.

I used a metal pipe on the three attackers who had hurt Angel. The bar was closed for business, and a few of my Mexican buddies stayed with me. In the desert there is no justice. There was just us. They screamed and begged, just the way Angel did, I'm sure. But they had no way out.

The Mexicans helped me. They held the attackers as I beat them, one at a time with the pipe, as the others looked on, knowing that they were next. It was what they deserved.

At the end of the beating, I went to the bar and poured myself a drink.

A beating like this was a purging. It got all the bad feelings out of me, all the guilt for not having been there to prevent what had happened to Angel. It was like my own personal blood-letting. I got all the bad blood out.

Sometimes I wondered if I went looking for trouble just to make myself feel better, or if it was just that trouble always found me. But the one constant in my life, for sure, was trouble. There was only one thing that could take the trouble away, if only for a little while. It was in a bottle.

I poured another drink, and then another, and another. I downed them all in a gulp, as the Mexicans dragged the bodies from the bar and out the back door.

I was far from home, but I was the same me.

Chapter 19

Losing My Mother

THERE ARE SOME PEOPLE IN life who are irreplaceable.

I missed home. I was starting to get the horrors in New Mexico. It had been three long years since I had eaten a decent meal, talked to a normal person, or saw my family. I missed it all. I especially missed my mother. She wasn't well when I left and I had no real way of knowing how she was doing. It was killing me. I couldn't call home because my father had told me not to—even though I had tried a few times unsuccessfully anyway. He didn't want any calls being traced. He knew the feds were always watching and listening. He was right. But when you're homesick, you're homesick. And after three years, I was terminal.

My nerves were getting the best of me. I had a bad feeling that I was carrying around for a while with regard to my mother. A sixth sense that was telling me to call. That something was wrong. I knew it in my gut. I sat beside the phone and stared at it. I would pick it up, then quickly put it back down. I didn't want to do anything stupid to get myself caught or bring heat on my father.

This was worse than prison. At least in prison you get visitors, letters. Out here I was in exile. Dead to the world.

I couldn't take it anymore. I had to know how my mother was. I called home.

The phone rang in the Napoli house in Brooklyn. Thank God my Aunt Rae, my father's sister, was there. Chubby and round-faced Rae was always affable and kind. I was happy to hear her voice.

"Napoli residence," she answered with an upbeat tone.

"Aunt Rae?"

"Tony?"

"Aunt Ray...I know I'm not supposed to call, but I really needed to speak to my mother..."

"Tony, how do I know this is you?" she asked, with a suspicious sound in her voice.

"It's me, Aunt Rae," I insisted.

"Well, if this is really Tony, then answer me this..."

"Aunt Rae, it's—"

"Answer me this...if you are Tony. What was your nickname when you were six years old?" It was a good question. Aunt Rae had that sharp Napoli mind, just like my father.

"Ishkabibble," I said immediately.

She used to call me that when I was a kid. I had no idea what it meant then. Years later, I learned that Ishkabibble was actually a stage performer and cornet player of the 1930s and 40s named Merwyn Bogue. Supposedly he took that strange stage name because it meant, "What, me worry?" in Yiddish. He also wore a goofy bowl haircut, which might be why they started calling me Ishkabibble when I was small. But I think they just called me it because it sounded funny.

"Tony...it is you! Ishkabibble!" she shouted, now believing me. "It's so good to hear your voice!"

"Good to hear yours too, Aunt Rae."

"Your father has a reward out for you, if anyone has information of your whereabouts. It's been all over the radio stations. There's been a lot of calls from phonies trying to claim the reward money, so I thought maybe it was a phony who—"

"That's good," I cut her off. She could *talk*. "Listen, Aunt Rae, can I just talk to my mother please?"

Suddenly her tone changed dramatically. "Oh Tony," she said, and then, "My God, I hate to be the one to have to tell you this, but..."

She took a long pause.

"Your mother's gone. She's gone, Tony."

My heart dropped. It fell to my stomach. Then to my knees.

"Your father tried to find you when your mother died but he couldn't," she explained. "He offered a $25,000 reward because he settled all your problems. He did it so no harm would come to you if you showed up at the funeral parlor."

I barely heard what she was saying. Words weren't getting through to a mind and heart that had been pierced by what was my worst fear while I was away: that my mother would die and I wouldn't be able to say goodbye.

"He did it for you, Tony. He was protecting you," she went on, like a good Aunt that she was, trying to make it all better. I wasn't able to take it in. "Tony...you there still?"

"Yeah...Yeah, I'm here, Aunt Rae. I'm here."

I wasn't there. I was somewhere else.

"Your father put a picture of you with her. He put it right in the casket. Right next to her, so she could take you with her. So she'd always be with you. Tony...Give me your phone number there. Wherever you are. I'll have your father call you back. Gimme the number. Your father will get back to you. He'll get right back to you, Tony...okay?"

I gave her the number and hung up the phone without even saying goodbye. Later when I spoke to my father I understood and appreciated what he had done. He told me exactly how he did it.

The funeral parlor had been packed with mourners, who sat quietly and prayed. Some broke off into small groups and chatted softly among themselves. Everybody who knew my mother loved her. Those who didn't know her came out of respect to my father.

My father entered the room dressed in a black suit and his trademark, large dark sunglasses. All eyes went to him and it fell dead quiet. He made his way through to the front of the room and knelt before my mother's coffin. He made the sign of the cross and prayed for a moment.

Then, he stood and reached into his suit jacket and removed a photo. It was an 8x10 of me in my Air Force uniform. It was the same photo he had ripped up years earlier. At the time, I had sent them each one. He had ripped up his but had kept hers. He placed the photo gently beside my mother in her casket.

He said she looked peaceful knowing it was there.

I thanked him. Even though I couldn't be there at her

funeral, I felt like because of what he did, in some small way I was there.

My father told me I could come home. He was coming to get me himself. He wanted me to meet somebody. Two days later a limousine pulled up to the house—the shack—I was renting out in New Mexico.

Through the torn screen door I saw my father step out of the back of the limo, looking as dapper as ever. Following closely behind him was a woman I didn't recognize. She was a striking young blonde. They made their way toward the house.

I opened the screen door and met them halfway on the dirt road in front of the porch.

My father hugged me and kissed me on my cheek. He looked me in the eye. "It's been three years, three months and thirteen days, TN. It's been too long," he said in a loving, fatherly way.

Then he said words that shook me to my core. Words that I could never forget and barely ever forgive. "Meet my new wife," he said, referring to the blonde beside him.

I looked at her and could hardly bring myself to politely nod. I couldn't believe my eyes. She looked like a teenager. More like his daughter than his wife.

Inside the house we stood around the kitchen table, awkwardly. Stuff was in the air. Tension. Things unsaid. Things like, "How the fuck could you replace my mother with this bimbo!" Things that I was better off not saying, for so many reasons. No one could replace my mother. Least of all this…*girl*. Which is what she was.

She was a disappointed singer and songwriter. After my mother died on January 5, 1962 and I was nowhere to be found, my father went looking for me.

His first stop was Miami Beach, where I used to go to romance a lot of the show broads down there. He went around town with a couple of his men going into one night club after another asking the girls and anybody else he could find. Nobody knew anything about my whereabouts. He sent out a message with all those he contacted that if they should see me to tell me that my mother had passed away, and that I should come home, and "everything was forgiven." Which meant the coast was clear. But nobody ever conveyed the message because I was 2,000 miles from Miami Beach.

While he was in Miami, my father stayed at the Eden Rock Hotel and that's where he met Jeanne. This blonde. He told me that they met by chance in the lobby. She was a guest in the hotel too. He said they hit it off right away. They had a lot in common. Jeanne's boyfriend had died about the same time of the month that my mother had died. They were both in mourning. So I guess while they sympathized with each other, they found themselves falling in love.

A year after my mother died, he married Jeanne on January 26, 1963. She was 25 and my father was 52. I knew nothing of their marriage until he came to get me in New Mexico in July, 1964. But it was a huge affair, starting with the ceremony in St. Patrick's Cathedral, the historic church dominating Fifth Avenue and facing Rockefeller Center.

Afterwards the bride and groom and all their 150 guests climbed into silver limos that took them to the Plaza Hotel, for the reception. Just like my father to party in the luxurious landmark across from Central Park that had played host to kings, queens, presidents and celebrities for nearly a century. Jimmy Nap had his own collection of famous guests, including entertainers like Tony Bennett, Della Reese, Frank Sinatra, Julius La Rosa, Jilly Rizzo, Eddie Fisher, Vic Damone, and Glenn Covington. And singer Jimmy Roselli supplied the entertainment. Boxers? How about Rocky Graziano, Jake La Motta, Rocky Marciano, and Paddy De Marco. If you looked for the underworld celebrities of the 1960s, Fat Tony Salerno, then boss of the Genovese crime family was there, and so were Louis "Louie Dome" Pacella, capo in the Genovese crime family, Vincent "The Chin" Gigante, underboss of the Genovese crime family, and Frank "Funzi" Tierri, then considered the boss of bosses.

Politicians, including Congressman Mario Biaggi could be seen at some tables. And the FBI was all over the place. My father arranged a round table in the front foyer of the reception hall for five agents. I heard that he didn't want them "standing around at the front entrance looking like gangsters ready to pull a hold-up." He asked them to remove their fedora hats so that they appeared to be members of the party. The agents refused to eat, and only drank coffee during the four-hour affair.

The wedding cost my father over $200,000 when you factor in the church, the Plaza Hotel, the plane fare and overnight rooms for the traveling guests, the entertainment, and the flowers.

That marriage to Jeanne always made me feel as though he went against his own philosophy. He used to tell his crew members, "Don't ever let a young broad fool you into marriage; keep her on the side as you get older." And now here he was.

They made a striking couple though, I'll give them that. My father in his tailored suit, Jeanne in her fancy dress and all dolled up. I hadn't seen anybody who looked like them in a while out here. The sharpness of their appearance was in stark contrast to the squalid surroundings I was living in. I was a little ashamed, to be quite honest. I offered them something. They refused.

My father took out a wad of cash from his jacket pocket and threw it on the table. "That's your plane fare to New York. There's a furnished house in Jersey that I rented for you. It's time you got out of this place and came back home."

I looked at him, then down at the bills. Yep, it was time to go home.

My father got me a huge beachfront home in Point Pleasant on the Jersey shore. It was more than I needed for myself. But my father was like that. Generous. Also I think he put me out in Jersey to keep a small distance between us and to keep me away from trouble in the city. But I could find trouble anywhere.

It was winter and I sat and watched the waves crash against the desolate shoreline. Seagulls, in pairs of two, descended on the vacant beach looking for food. I threw some bread out to them. In the distance the pizzerias, ice cream parlors, and penny arcades all had their gates drawn and signs up that read "Closed For Season."

The amusement park rides stood spookily still. The Ferris Wheel cars swayed ever so slightly in the ocean breeze. This was the New Jersey shore in winter. Dead.

The boardwalk was empty except for me. As I stood alone looking out into the ocean I could swear I heard my mother's voice in the ocean waves.

"Brother...I'm so happy your home now...I love you..."

I looked deeper into the ocean, as if I expected to see her there. But I didn't. I would never see her again. Except in my mind and in my dreams.

My gaze went to the horizon. My focus shifted. It was time to put things back together again. Or at least try to.

I went to work for my father here. He put me in charge of his building company that turned empty sand lots into affluent coastal communities filled with luxury, waterfront homes. This is the company he turned over to me. And I soon destroyed it because of my drinking, gambling, and womanizing.

Sure, I was making a lot of money with the building company. But then I started in with the old life again: showgirls, whiskey, late nights, trouble. Before I know it, the money ran out. Nothing good ever lasted too long for me.

I was drunk and upset with my father again. I had a disagreement with him about my life style. He wanted me to walk the straight and narrow—to stay in the building business—but by my doing so, I felt that I would be another puppet, just like the rest of his crew. I wanted to control my own crew, be my own boss. He objected and he told me if I couldn't change my ways I should end it all by jumping out a window.

After our heated exchange, how could I possibly tell my father that the money from the building business had run out?

I left him that late afternoon at Crisci's Restaurant and started drinking heavy in different bars. All I wanted to do was get drunk. Later on in the evening I wound up in Queens and couldn't remember how I got there. I paid a visit to this bar I knew out there. The Roosevelt Bar.

I was drinking there for a while and the place started clearing out. I was running low on cash and I had a piece in my jacket pocket. Calm and cool, I took the .38 caliber out of my pocket and pointed it at the bartender. "Everybody get the fuck in the bathroom. Let's go."

I forced the four frightened customers and the bartender into the bathroom. "Get in there. And stay in there until I tell you to come out," I instructed them.

I raided the cash register behind the bar. I stuffed fistfuls of fives, tens and twenties into my jacket pockets and headed for the door. Just as I tried to leave the bar, the bartender, who tried to play hero, comes running out of the bathroom and straight at me.

I pistol whip the dummy and split his nose in two, sending him to the ground.

"See, that's what you get for tryin' to be a fuckin' hero," I said to him as his blood covers the floor beneath him. I grab a dishtowel and throw it onto the floor beside him.

I looked at the bathroom door. Nobody else was coming out.

Then just as coolly as I entered the place, I walked out of it. About a grand richer. If that.

I walked along the street and entered another tavern just up the block from the Roosevelt. The bar area was crowded. And wouldn't you know it, the band was playing Sammy Davis Jr.'s "I Gotta Be Me." Well, I'll be a son-of-a-bitch! If that wasn't a coincidence.

I walked over to the bar and called out to the bartender, "Double martini! And another round for all these nice people."

I reached into my pocket and pulled out the stolen money, throwing bills on the bar. I downed the martini that the bartender placed in front of me. "Another!" I called out to him.

The song, my song, came to an end. I got up and walked over to the bandleader. "Play it again!" I ordered him. "Play that same song again!"

I dipped into my pocket, pulled out more bills and handed them to the bandleader.

"And keep playing it until I tell ya to stop!"

Then I began singing along with the band. Soon after, like always, the frickin' cops busted in and spoiled all the fun. The band stopped playing. The old routine: the cops grab me, handcuff me, and lead me out of the bar.

"Keep playing that song!" I shout out to the band. "Don't stop playing it until I tell you to. I didn't say stop. Keep playing it!"

The band continued playing "I Gotta Be Me" as I was marched off by the fine men in blue.

At the police station in Queens I sat handcuffed. Too drunk to really know what was going on. On the other side of the room, I can see a police captain talking to two rough looking, but well-dressed men—my father's men. They shake hands with the captain, who gestures to another cop. The cop removes my handcuffs. The men escort me out of the station.

They lead me right to a Cadillac that is parked outside the station house. They open the back door and I get in. Jimmy Nap was sitting in the backseat. Not happy. He stared at me—a piercing, icy stare. I looked down, avoiding direct eye contact with him, like I always did when I was in trouble.

I peeked up. My father's top lip barely moved, as he spoke in a soft, but firm, tone. "Up to your old ways again, huh, TN?"

I still didn't look all the way up.

"You're going back to New Mexico so you can't embarrass me anymore."

Now I lift my head up. Not another exile!

"All you do is burn up money and hurt people. I can't even look at you. You make me sick. How are you my son?" My father looked away, out the car window. I looked at him with my mouth open, but no words would come out. "I want you to remember something, TN. Alcohol gives a man false courage. You enjoy drinking, then go ahead and drink. But don't drink to give yourself courage. Because you gotta *have* courage, with or without the alcohol."

He was right. He was almost always right.

"Here," he said. He handed me a set of car keys. I took them. "It's a Lincoln. Take it. And take this too." He handed me another thick wad of cash.

"I'll have two hundred a week sent to you. That's all you'll need to live out there."

I was speechless. A tear welled up in my eye. I didn't want to leave. I knew I couldn't stay.

"Go back," my father told me. *"Go back to New Mexico. For everyone's sake."*

Chapter 20

Stick-Up

No way. There is no way I'm living like this again. No fucking way. That's what I kept saying to myself over and over again for the whole long, lonely ride out West. I talked myself into pulling another robbery.

I pulled the Lincoln Continental my father gave me up to the old house I was expected to live in. This was a different old house than the other old house I was living in. This one was just outside Albuquerque. Same thing. It all looked alike.

I made my way to the house and stopped on the porch. I looked out on the scenery. The same scenery I had looked out on for three and a half years—a leveled landscape shadowed by mountains, with the Rio Grande flowing along nearby.

No tenements. No people. No action.

No way.

My best escape out here was to get loaded. I would sit in the Grand Canyon Bar, on what these yokels considered to be a main street (that meant there was a bar, a bank, and a grocery store), and drink my days and nights away.

Most of the time I was in there by myself. Just me and the bartender. One day when I was in there, inebriated as always and bored out of my mind. I called out to the bartender. "Hey Guy, let me ask you somethin'...Could I ask you somethin'...?"

"Ask away," he said, as he wiped down the bar top.

"You got a piece?"

"A piece of what?"

"A piece of what? Fuckin' yokel...A piece. *A piece.* A gun!"

"Shh...yeah. Yeah, I got a piece."

Not sure why he was shushing me, there was nobody in the joint.

"Good. Gimme it," I demanded.

"Give you it?"

"Yeah, gimme it. Don't worry. I'll bring it back."

He looked at me, long and hard for a moment. Then, realizing I wasn't kidding around, he said, "You're serious, ain't you? Okay. Okay, fine. But it'll cost ya."

"I'll be right back," I said, as I stood suddenly from my bar stool. "Don't go nowhere. I'll be back."

I rushed out and stood outside the bar, taking in a few deep breaths and opening my eyes wide, trying to sober myself up a little. Then I looked across the street, to a building with a sign on it that read Beneficial Finance Company.

Still sufficiently buzzed I crossed the street and entered the building. I approached a guy sitting at his desk who looked important, or at least who thought he looked important. Like a manager or something. He wore a suit.

"Can I get a loan form?"

The manager man paused and looked up at me, carefully taking in my condition. Then he professionally and dutifully responded, "A loan form. Yes, sure. Here you go." He reached into his desk and handed me one. "Just fill that out and return it at your earliest convenience." His tone was somewhere between serious and condescending. He was doing his job, but he was also just trying to get rid of me.

I took the form from him. Then I leaned onto his desk, grabbed a pen, and started quickly filling it out.

"Sir, you can have a seat to do that, if you want to be more comfortable."

This was his way of saying, "Get off my desk!" Ever notice how business people never say what they mean, and rarely mean what they say? I ignored him and kept on filling out the form.

"Sir..."

I handed the form back to the manager. "Done."

"Okay, Mr..." he held the form up to his eyes and read it. "Reo. Anthony Reo. We'll process this and see if it's approved. You want five hundred dollars?"

"Is that a problem?" I snapped at him.

"Shouldn't be, sir, no."

"How long's it gonna take?"

"We can usually have an answer to you by the end of the day. But it's almost the end of the day now, so it should be tomorrow, at the latest."

"I'll be back before you close today," I informed the manager. He sat there speechless. I turned and made for the exit. Then I turned back. "Hey, Popcorn...Here's your pen!" I threw the pen to the manager. It bounced off his chest and fell to the floor.

After that, I stood outside the finance company formulating a plan. I put my sunglasses on for this. I decided that when I got the loan, I would leave New Mexico for good. The money my father was sending me wasn't enough. And I had already sold the Lincoln to support my drinking and gambling habits. So with the loan money, at least I could buy a car and head somewhere else, somewhere decent. Another city, another town even. Anywhere was better than where I was. I had had enough of living out here in the middle of nowhere, like a nobody. I needed this money to make my break. And by hook or by crook, I was going to get it.

I headed back to the bar, where the bartender gestured for me to follow him to the back room. There were a few patrons in the joint now and he wanted us to have some privacy. Once back there he handed me a gun.

"Twenty five dollars and it's yours," he bargained.

I looked down at the weapon in my hand—a snub-nosed .38 caliber. Nice piece. I reached into my pocket, pulled out some crumbled up bills and handed them to the bartender. He didn't even count them. I gripped the gun tightly, then placed it into my jacket pocket. I charged out of the back room and through the bar. Just before heading out the front door, I stopped and downed one of the bar patron's drinks.

"Hey, man..." the patron protested.

I slammed the glass back down on the bar top in front of the patron, shattering it. He looked way, in silence. I wiped my mouth and headed for the door. I felt powerful.

I was on a mission, as I crossed the street back to the Beneficial Finance Company and barged in through their doors. I walked right up to the manager's desk and announced, "All right Guy, I'm here for my money!"

The manager looked up from his desk, "Yes, Mr...Reo, was it?"

"That's right," I nodded.

"There were a few problems with your application." I saw that he was nervous.

"Problems? What problems?"

"Well, for one...your name." The manager shuffled some papers around his desk. "The social security number that you gave us belongs to a Mr. Anthony Napoli, not Anthony Reo."

I got stumped for a second but then I pushed on, "Yeah, that's me."

"Which one is you?"

"Both of them. I got alotta different names I go by."

"I'm sorry, sir, but you cannot give false information on a loan application."

"It ain't false, I just told you, that's me."

"Sorry sir, you were turned down for the loan."

I looked down blankly at the manager, at his white bread face that seemed almost gleeful hiding behind the façade of professionalism to reject me. He would never have had the guts to reject me man to man, on our own terms. He could barely get the words out, he was trembling so much. But he did get them out and he enjoyed getting them out. I could tell. He didn't want to give me that loan from the second I walked in there. He was only too happy to find an excuse to not give it to me. His power came from his ability to reject people—to cower behind rules, regulations, and technicalities in order to decline people, to deny them money, and thereby deny them a way out. I was filled with rage. Now I was going to show him where my power came from.

I reached into my jacket pocket, pulled out the .38 and stuck it right in his face. "Come with me!" I ordered him.

The manager stood, shaking in his loafers. I snatched the loan form from his desk and got behind him. I led him behind a long counter where three female clerks were working. I pushed the manager toward the clerks, who were scared to death of me and my .38.

"Now gimme that fuckin' five hundred out of the register," I commanded the manager. Now *I* was making the rules.

"You won't shoot me. You don't have the guts," the manager challenged me. I guess he was trying to be brave in front of his staff. Brave, but stupid.

"You wanna bet your life on it?" I asked him.

Then I cocked back the pistol and pointed it at his head. He swallowed hard and then turned to the register and began taking money out of it. Too much money.

"Just the five hundred, Guy," I said to him.

He left $500 in tens and twenties on the counter and put the rest of the money back into the register. I snatched the bills and shoved them into my jacket pocket. Then I placed the loan form on the counter with a pen. "And okay my loan while you're at it," I instructed him. The manager looked down at the form.

"Take a pen and okay the form, like you should have done before!" I shouted. "I don't wanna take nothin' that ain't mine."

As the manager signed the form, I turned to the clerks, who cowered in a corner. "Ladies, we could have all been saved this trouble, if this ham and egg bastard would have just approved it to begin with."

The manager held the form out to me.

"And stamp it too, Guy. What do I look like?" I said to him. He thought I didn't know it had to be stamped to be official.

The manager took a rubber stamp and stamped the paper. I pulled the form out from under him and announced, "Okay, now everybody into the back room."

"No, please don't lock us in. There's no air in…" one of the Clerks tried to speak up.

"Just get in the fuckin' room!" I hollered.

I led them all to a small back room and then slammed the door behind them, and locked it.

And I left.

But I didn't leave town. I didn't even leave the same street. I went right back to the bar, which was now a little more crowded than before. I threw money on the bar and called out to the bartender, "A round of drinks on me!"

Why the heck didn't I just get the heck out of Dodge, right? Wasn't that the point of taking the money in the first place—to escape? The answer is, I don't know. Sometimes I just didn't think right. I felt indestructible. Like no one could touch me.

The bartender brought me over a drink. I slid the gun to him across the bar top. He stuck it under the bar. I got drunk.

I knew people had seen me come into the bar from the finance company. I didn't care. I knew the second the manager and his staff got out of that back room, they would be calling the police and they'd be coming to get me. I just didn't care. So much for a plan! Maybe I wanted to get picked up. Who knows? I just couldn't take this life anymore. Maybe it was the alcohol doing my thinking. But I just didn't give a shit. If they wanted me, they could come get me. And sure enough, they did.

Less than an hour later, the local cops busted into the bar and grabbed me. They slapped the handcuffs on me and led me out of yet another bar, but this time this one was far from home. This time I was fucked. The bar patrons booed as I was taken away. Their free drinks were being taken away.

When the police car pulled up to the county jailhouse, a crowd of news reporters were gathered in front. I looked out the back window and thought, what the heck is going on here?

As the police removed me from the car, reporters and photographers converged. Flash bulbs exploded. Reporters hurled questions at me, as the officers escorted me into the jailhouse.

"Are you really a Mafia kingpin's son?" shouted one reporter.

"Are you the son of Jimmy Nap, mobster from New York City?" called out another.

I didn't respond.

This was the most action they had had in this shit kicker town their whole lives. I didn't want to spoil their fun.

The jailhouse cell was cramped and crowded, with 10 bunk beds, one toilet, a small shower, 19 Mexicans, and me. I sat on a bottom bunk, keeping to myself.

It was supposed to be an overnight holding pen for local prisoners who were waiting for bail to be set. I ended up spending three weeks in that cell. Other prisoners came and went, and there I stood. Guys came up to me and said they knew who I was.

One of the Mexicans approached me one day. "Hey Man, I saw you and your father in the paper and on TV."

I just nodded. He nodded back.

I figured my father was going to send one of his crew members out here for me. But, it had been three weeks, what was taking him so long? If I was guessing, I figured it would be Big Red. Red was a barrel of a man, nearly 300 pounds, short and round with red curly hair. Red handled a lot of things for my father. But after three weeks, no Red. No body.

Then the angel Gabriel himself appeared, as if a prayer was being answered.

Early one morning my father appeared before the metal bars early. I thought I was dreaming. But I wasn't. It was him. I got up to greet him. He spoke to me through the bars, never raising his voice above a whisper. "If you want my help. Then you gotta ask for it now, from me, or I leave you in here. Ya understand?"

"I want your help, Daddy-O," I said. "Just get me outta this shit-hole."

Outside the jailhouse a Cadillac was parked. We got in. The Caddy took us to the airport where a private jet was waiting. We got on the plane together and my father started talking in concrete terms. No yelling, no screaming, just a plan of action.

"I got you a lawyer from F. Lee Bailey's office," he explained, "Because you're my son, bail was set at $50,000 for the half-ass crime you committed. For that amount, you should have robbed the whole place."

I let out a small laugh that my father didn't return. My father told me that he had lunched with the New Mexico senator, Jerry Apodaca, who would later go on to become governor. "He told me to bring you to the airport and to put you on a plane. He told me to send you somewhere else until you come to your senses. If you ever do. Those are his words, not mine."

Then my father handed me an envelope. The envelope had money and instructions about what I was to do when I got to wherever I was going. Everything I needed to start over. I never saw New Mexico again after that.

My father let me out of the plane. He stayed on. This was my stop, not his. He was going back home to Brooklyn. I was going somewhere else—to the place where all addicts and degenerates go to get better. Or to die.

Las Vegas, Nevada.

Chapter 21

Prince of Vegas

THE STRIP GLOWED. IT WAS electric. I took it all in from the backseat of a limo. I watched the lights and sights go by, my eyes wide open to a new life.

Earlier that day I had been sitting in a filthy cell with no money and no hope. Later that day, I'm in Las Vegas. The charges against me from the stick-up were dropped. My father made a deal with Senator Apodaca. In return, his gambling debts at Caesars Palace would be straightened out, and I walked. God, sometimes I loved being Jimmy Nap's son.

The limo pulled up to the casino at Caesars Palace. The limo driver got out and opened the back door for me, and suddenly I was greeted by a casino representative.

"Mr. Napoli. So good to see you tonight. I was told to give you these immediately and escort you up to your room."

The Casino rep handed me a small box, which I took from him. "Right this way, Mr. Napoli..."

I followed the rep into and through the palatial casino. He led me past slot machines, poker tables, roulette wheels, to the hotel side and up to my suite. The suite was large, extravagant, luxurious. I could hardly believe my eyes. I was living in a shack hours earlier.

"I'll have your bags sent right up," the rep said.

"I don't have no bags."

"Okay, well, then is there anything else I can do for you, sir?"

I thought for a second. "No. No, I'm...I'm good."

"Very good, sir." The casino rep headed for the door.

I called out to him, "Uh...excuse me...I'm sorry..." I reached into my pocket to tip him. I had been in the sticks for so long I had nearly forgotten my manners.

"No-no, please, that won't be necessary, sir. Everything has been taken care of for you." Then he smiled and left.

I looked about the room, stunned by its opulence. I went to the window and pulled back the curtain. All of Vegas glittered before me. I was the king of the world. Then I remembered the box the casino rep gave me. I opened it up. Inside the box were business cards. I took out a card. It read: Anthony Napoli, Casino Host.

Yep, sometimes I just loved being Jimmy Nap's son.

I got myself some decent clothes and met with three casino bosses who showed me around the palace. The bosses taught me about the every day operations of the place. They were cordial, white bread guys, in bad suits, and untinted eyeglasses: Jerry Zarowitz, president of the casino, Bill Wineburger, boss of the food and beverage department, and Ash Resnick, boss of casino operations. They were legitimate looking guys who didn't draw any heat from the control board or the feds. They were smart guys too, who really knew their business. They were good at what they did. But there were certain jobs they weren't cut out for, that they just couldn't handle.

Like collecting money owed to the casino from guys connected to the New York families. These guys would throw their weight around. Figuring the guys in suits weren't going to do anything, they'd rack up losses and think they could just walk out without paying their tabs. Until they saw me, that is. Then these loud-mouthed tough guys who were losing their shirts knew it was time to pay up.

That's where I came in.

All I had to do was make my presence felt. I'd walk by the high stakes poker tables and they'd see me and stop talking. They would nod in acknowledgment. They knew there were no more free rides.

I was also in charge of markers. That's an agreement between the player and the casino. We gave them the advance so they can play. A guy would come to me and ask for a marker, say $10,000. If I approved it we'd go to a cage. I would initial a small piece of paper with the figure $10,000 written on it. The guy would give the slip to the cashier, who would push $10,000 worth of chips through the window for him.

But, when they leave the casino they have to satisfy the marker first. They have to pay us back. If there's anything left over they can keep it. But that's when some of them get greedy. They want it all.

Sometimes I'd see a guy starting to win and he starts slipping chips into his pocket. Either that or he hands some back to his friend, who heads over to a cage to cash them in. Hustlers always think they can hustle a hustler. So when I caught somebody doing something like this, stealing from the casino, trying to get around paying his marker back, I had to use my muscle. Teach them a lesson, so nobody else got any ideas. That's why I was there.

In a case like this we'd have two security guards escort the guy away from the table and bring him up to one of the executive suites. They'd sit the guy down on the bed and I'd talk to him.

"Was I good to you?" I would ask the guy. "When you asked me for the marker, did I give it to you?"

"Tony, I..." he would try to explain himself. I wouldn't let him. "If I call the boys back in New York, what do think they're going to tell me?"

"There must be a misunderstanding..."

They always got nervous when I mentioned New York. Before I came around these guys would throw New Yorker's names around, trying to intimidate everybody, trying to play the tough guy role, make themselves out to be big shots to get what they wanted.

"You know the rules. The rules are the same. They never change. Especially for scumbags like you who live off of somebody else's name. So since you didn't want to pay for your marker the right way, now you're going to pay with your real estate."

Then I'd cock back and punch him in the mouth. "I'm the broker who made the deal. I vouched for your marker. You want to make me look like an asshole to New York?

Is that what you want? You want to steal from this casino? When you steal from this casino, you steal from me. Do you want to steal from me?"

The guy would wipe the blood from his mouth. Some of it always ended up on the bed and floor. "Do you know what we do to people who steal from this casino? We bury them! And you wanna see the cemetery we bury them in? Come here, I'll show you."

I grabbed the guy by his arm and dragged him to the window. "It's called the Mojave! And that's where you'll end up! Head first in the fuckin' sand, you ever try something like this again. You understand?"

Then I always got an apology. "I'm sorry, Tony. I'm truly, truly sorry."

"You're sorry, huh! Truly sorry! Well, ya know what? I'm gonna accept your apology. Go clean yourself up. Ga'head. I have a little deal to talk over with you. But first I gotta go see your friend."

We'd drive the guy out into the desert, kicking up a trail of dust behind the Cadillac as we did. The minute he saw where we were taking him he'd start to squirm. "Tony, I never meant to do any…"

I would tell the driver to pull over in some random, isolated spot. I'd reach into my pocket and pull out a blackjack, which is a small lead weight covered with black leather, with a loop that you put your hand through to keep it in the middle of your palm.

Once he saw the blackjack, the apologies really started to flow. "Tony, please…what are you gonna do?" Then we'd get out of the car. "Whatever the beef, I can make a call to my cousin in Queens and we can straighten this whole thing—" There they'd go again, using somebody's name to get what they wanted. In this case, he wanted to live.

In mid-sentence, I'd slap the guy on the top of his head several times with the blackjack. His screams would echo across the desert. Those blackjacks hurt like hell on top of the head. Blood trickled down his face and he'd go down to his knees. Never met a guy who didn't go down after getting the blackjack on the head.

"Get up. Get up, you fuckin' mutt!" I'd pull him to his feet. "Now run! Run like the filthy, deceitful dog that you are!"

"Run? Run where?" the guy would ask.

"For your life!"

I'd pull back to slap him with the blackjack again. He'd jump and start running. It was a huge, open plain of earth before him, with no one and nothing in sight. He would stumble a little, not sure what direction to even run in.

"Run! Before I change my fuckin' mind!"

He'd just take off running, with the blazing sun beating down on him and blood still dripping from his head. Then I'd get back into the Cadillac and be driven away. Out the window I could see the guy running aimlessly into the heart of the vast, empty desert. I often wonder if he'd made it somewhere before the heat got the best of him. But I didn't really wonder for too long.

Back in Vegas, I'd open a bottle of Jack Daniels and down a mouthful. That took away any wonderment and concern I might have had about anything. I had to be careful with the bottle out here though. I could never look loaded on the casino floor. I could never show them that side. It would get back to New York, to my father. It would also make me look weak. And out there in the desert, you couldn't look weak.

I was making plenty of money in Vegas and was treated like a prince because of where I came from and because of how I was enforcing rules. But I also found a way to make a few more dollars for myself on the side. Occasionally I'd find a guy losing at a poker table. I would use a guy like this. He couldn't get any more credit from the casino. So instead of cracking his head open, or tossing him out on his ass, I would okay him for a dime, one thousand in chips, and let him go back and gamble at one of the tables. If he lost, I would put it on record that he satisfied his marker, even though he lost it all. I would put a slip in the money box of the table he played at, saying, so and so "satisfied his marker." But if he won, well, then I got half the winnings. I was in control of the markers. In casino language, it's called skimming. It means I myself was beating the boys in New York out of money. But hey, that's the name of the game. Like I said, hustlers hustling hustlers.

But there's one group of hustlers that nobody seems to have figured out how to beat yet, and that's the United States government. You could spot these ham and egg sandwiches a mile away, walking around a casino in basic Brooks Brothers blue suits.

They would walk across the floor toward me. They wanted to talk to me, harass me, make their presence felt. I wasn't going to give them the chance, if I could help it. I'd walk away, heading down a long row of slot machines. We'd play a little cat and mouse game, as they followed me through a maze of slot machines, roulette tables, money wheels, and crap tables. I'd give them the slip, disappearing behind a cashier's cage and into a back room office with no name on it. Then I slammed the door shut.

But it wasn't all beat-downs and FBI bullshit. Believe me, Vegas was a lotta fun too.

I was also an assistant entertainment director. In the showroom I oversaw the rehearsals of the chorus line girls. It was my responsibility to hire the entertainers for the big showroom; and for the small lounge shows in the Palace too. And I took my responsibility very seriously.

As I watched the choreographer in rehearsal with the girls, I'd sometimes throw my two cents in. "Excuse me, I have an idea. If I may..." I'd approach the choreographer.

"Please, be my guest," he'd say, always open to a fresh idea, as good creative people are.

"I think the problem is, when you girls cross in front of each other, you're blocking the ones in the back. We want to see you all. What you have to do is slide, like this...slide. Then you girls in the back slide up like this and then everybody slide, slide, slide."

I even went so far as to demonstrate the dance moves to the dumbfounded stares of the dancers and the choreographer. "Go ahead...try it. Trust me...if it's okay with you." I always deferred to the choreographer. I didn't want nobody stepping on my toes, I didn't want to step on anybody else's.

Reluctantly, but politely, the choreographer would try my suggestion. "One, two three," he counted, leading them into the movement.

The showgirls would execute the dance moves I had demonstrated. I'd wear a big smile across my face and cheer them on. When I left they probably forgot everything I showed them. But who cares, I was having a ball.

I became friendly with many of the entertainers who performed at the casino—like Frank Sinatra. Again. Actually I had met Frank about ten years earlier—in February 1958—at the Sands Hotel in Vegas. That's when Fat Tony and Frank Costello had okay'd my father sending me there to be a captain of the waiters in the Copa Room at the Sands. The Copa Room was a showroom in the Sands Hotel and Casino. It was named after the Copacabana nightclub in New York City. That was also the year that Costello started moving most of the employees from the Copa in New York to the Sands in Vegas. Costello was always the man behind the Copa.

It didn't seem that long ago—ten years. When I got to the Sands back then, Sinatra was booked to perform there. Jack Entrotta, formerly the entertainment director at the Copa in New York, was now the entertainment director at the Sands. He booked Sinatra as the starring act and comedian Pat Henry as the supporting act. Not many people knew that Pat Henry was actually Italian and that his uncle was Frank "Funzie" Tieri, the underboss of the Genovese Family in New York at that time.

Sinatra convinced the hotel to send out gold-lettered invitations to his close celebrity friends and mob guys for his opening. When they arrived at the Sands, it was going to be my job to accommodate them, with complimentary suites and all the trappings. But come opening night, Frank never went on stage and neither did Pat Henry. We all got drunk because Frank had a fist fight with the casino manager, Carl Cohen. Carl knocked out a few of Frank's teeth. Then Pat Henry, in support of Frank, refused to go on stage.

It all started when Sinatra lost $50,000 on a marker at the crap tables. He refused to pay. So Carl Cohen thought he would teach him a lesson. He brought Sinatra back to his suite and knocked out his front teeth.

Frank argued that he shouldn't pay because he felt he was acting as a shill for the house to draw customers to the crap table. At the table were celebrities like Eddie Fisher, Sammy Davis Jr., Dean Martin and Vic Damone. Frank wanted credit for drawing these celebrities. Plus he was also drawing regular customers to the crap tables.

A couple of days later, my father called from New York to ball me out. He told me that I was management and didn't belong partying it up with those degenerate entertainers. He heard that I was drinking and dancing up a storm with actresses like Lauren Bacall, Shelly Winters, Lana Turner, Natalie Woods, and some of the showgirls who worked as dancers in the Copa room. We had no show in the showroom so we put on our own show. My father was hopping mad. He said, "I recommended you to Costello and the Fat Man. How could you do this to me?"

I knew I was on my way back to New York, so I decided to keep drinking and partying it up for a couple more days. After Sinatra got back from the dentist the next day, he thanked me for supporting him and joining him in the party he threw in his suite. Pat Henry made a lifetime friend in Sinatra by not going on the stage that night. They had no replacement act during the three-day commotion. The only show you could see was in the lounge: some mediocre band and a few half-ass comedians.

Anyway, after three days and nights of partying, I finally passed out in my room. When I woke up I called the front desk for any messages. I found out that I had to catch the first flight back to New York City, on my father's orders. I was all shook up and I started coming to my senses. I had been asleep for about 17 hours from a bad blackout. I jumped out of bed and started toward my bathroom, stumbling over naked female bodies, all passed out on my floor. They were the three show broads from the Copa room. Then I remembered that I had told them they could use my suite. I took my shower and after getting dressed and packing my clothes, I found it very hard to leave all those beautiful pieces of art lying on the floor without running my hands all over them.

Inside the car waiting for me outside the casino were Eddie Fisher and Vic Damone. They were flying back to New York with me to see my father. They couldn't pay their markers of $25,000 each at the crap tables. They wanted me to talk to my father to make a deal to pay it back at so much a month. Little did they know, I was in worse trouble than them. That was when my father assigned me to the Rag Doll in Union City, New Jersey.

But this time around in Vegas, I'd gotten to socialize even more with Frank and his crew and under slightly less insane circumstances than those days at the Sands. We drank together after performances. I spent time with him in his suite and in his dressing room shooting the bull about broads like Lana Turner and about who really stabbed and killed Johnny Stompanato. He was a hustler who worked for Mickey Cohen and was romancing Lana Turner back in the 50s.

Turner's 15-year-old daughter Cheryl was accused of killing Stompanato. She told the cops that she stabbed and killed him because he had been physically abusive to her mother and threatened to kill them both. But most of us who knew Stompanato felt that Lana had called her ex-husband, her daughter's father, before calling the cops. When her ex-husband, Stephen Crane, arrived at the apartment and saw all the blood and a dead body, he called his lawyer.

Frank told tell me, "The kid took the rap for the mother 'cause the lawyer probably told them that the kid's under age and won't do any time if she was protecting her mother from an abusive boyfriend." And that's just what happened in court to Lana Turner's daughter—the jury ruled that it was a justifiable homicide.

Often I traveled with Frank on his private jet from Vegas to his home in Palm Springs, California, which was only a half hour plane ride from Vegas. We had wild parties with Dean Martin, Tony Bennett, Sammy Davis, Jr. and a lot of other celebrities. Frank had cabanas at his poolside with names over each doorway. And each cabana was named after one of his hit songs, like *Strangers in the Night*, for example. He let certain entertainers have keys to those cabanas, so when they came to visit, the security guard would escort that person to their own bathhouse.

Frank balled out Tony Bennett for using marijuana; he could never use it in Frank's house. Frank used to say to Tony, "You're always telling club owners that you want the stage to be high and above the audience. That's why you smoke that weed, 'cause you think it makes you high, too."

Well, my father used to chase Tony out of his townhouse in New York for smoking pot in his living room. Tony was friendly with Jeanne, my stepmother, because of her music business affiliations.

It was always exciting to be around the show business types. Of course, it wasn't helping my drinking situation, which I seemed to be doing even more than ever before. But I could never be totally zonked while I was on the casino floor. I had to keep my eyes on the tables. So I could be tipsy but not smashed while I was working. These guys from New York would never pay back the legitimate bosses what they owed if they thought I was out of it.

It wasn't long before the boys in New York found out that I was made a boss at Caesars. I was being paged every half hour over the casino PA system. "Paging Mr. Nap... Mr. Tony Nap."

They all wanted favors. "Get me into the Sinatra show. Get me a hooker. Get me a line of credit." Comp passes for the room, food and drinks. You name it, they asked for it. And I don't think I ever turned anybody down.

Because of the continuous paging of my name, the FBI, and their nosy agents in the blue suits who wandered aimlessly around the casino, finally got wise to what was going on. They caught on to who I was and found a way to get me. They arrested me for not having a work permit, which was required to be an executive on the floor of the Palace.

The feds brought me in and questioned me about my father's business affairs and about the robbery in Albuquerque. So I put a call into New York. My father had the governor straighten everything out. *Again.* But he told me I had to get out of there ASAP and get back East. Somebody was talking and it wasn't safe for me out there in the West anymore.

My father sent a limo, and within two days I was on my way back home.

Chapter 22

Laura

BACK HOME IN BROOKLYN, 1968 at the Hi-Way Lounge, I sat at the bar, late one night, drinking, as usual. The place was clearing out. A pretty little cocktail waitress, one I'd never seen before, walked past me. She resembled Elizabeth Taylor, with long dark hair and big black eyes.

"Gimme another Dewars on the rocks, please, doll, and make it strong this time," I called out to her as she zipped by me. She was maybe ten years my junior and real cute.

"Sorry, we're closed," she said, point blank. She had a mouth this one.

"Maybe you didn't hear me. I said, Get me a drink."

"And maybe you didn't hear *me*. I said, We're closed."

She was sassy. I like sassy. "If you don't get me a drink, I'll pour it myself."

She moved toward a pay phone at the end of the bar, looking to call somebody, as she had been instructed, I'm sure, to deal with troublemakers like me. I grabbed her arm.

"I'm Jimmy Nap's son from Vegas and I need a drink, all right?" I spoke in a whisper, through gritted teeth.

Regulars who were heading toward the door turned back as they were leaving. I shot them a look and they kept going.

"Oh," said the waitress, as she put the phone back down on the hook. "So you're TN, the prodigal son, huh?"

"What did you call me?"

"The black sheep of the family. Yeah, I heard about you. Why don't you do your father a favor and get the hell out of town again?"

"Listen honey, I do whatever I want."

"Oh, do you now?"

"That's right."

And just to prove it to her, I headed for the safe behind the bar.

"What are you doing?" She hurried after me.

"I'm going in the safe to take out money. I know the combination."

This pretty waitress, who had some pair of balls on her, tried to physically stop me. But I overpowered her and snatched the money from the safe. Then in another act of power I pulled her close to me and began feeling her up.

"Get off of me!" She was a fighter. "You're a dead man! When I tell your father about the money..." She pushed away from me. "And that you're hand-happy, you bastard!"

She ran back to the phone and picked it up. This time she dialed, "Yes, I need a car...The Hi-Way Lounge...Havemeyer and Metro—"

I grabbed the phone and hung it up on her in mid-sentence.

"I can't wait until tomorrow to tell your father that you took that money from the safe. Then what are you gonna do, huh? What are you going to do then, tough guy?"

Yep, she had a mouth on her, let me tell you. And she had some guts the way she spoke up to me. I knew men who didn't have the courage to speak to me that way. I didn't even know her name yet and I was in love. "Nothing," I responded to her question, even though I think it was probably rhetorical. "Because *you're* going to replace the $500 I just took. Tomorrow morning, before he gets here."

"What! Why you fuckin' bum bastard! I'll have you killed first! And your father would thank me."

She hit below the belt too. What a woman! "Enough of your sweet talk. What's your name?"

"What do you care?"

"Because when I dance with a broad, I like to know her name first."

"You think I'm going to dance with *you*? Yeah, you wait."

"Yes, I do."

Everyone was long gone by now and I locked the front door. Then I went over to the jukebox and put on a song. My song. Sammy Davis Jr.'s "I've Gotta Be Me."

I moved over to Laura and took her in my arms. She resisted but didn't exactly fight me off. She knew, as I did, that there was something between us that was instant. It was in the air. Even through the arguing and the threats, there was chemistry.

"Laura," she whispered in my ear. "My name is Laura."

I held her close and sang along with the music. I kissed her neck and worked my way up to her lips. Laura kissed me back. Before I knew it, the wall clock over the bar read 5:00 a.m. and we had fallen asleep in each other's arms in one of the booths. I looked over to Laura, who was also awake, her head nestled in the crook of my arm.

"Listen, Popcorn, I don't usually apologize to a broad like you but...I'm sorry for what I did to you...puttin' my hands all over you and all."

Laura peered up at me. "Ya know something? I think I liked you before I ever even met you."

"How so?"

"Just by hearing the stories about you. Ya know, living like you wanted to live. Doin' what you wanted to do. Not like the goons I see in here everyday. They got no balls. No minds of their own. All they ever say is, 'Yes Jimmy. Whatever you say, Jimmy. I'll do whatever you want, Jimmy, because I need your help.' Those aren't men."

"You remind me of my mother, ya know that? Strong. You don't take no shit off nobody. She was the strength. She kept the family together. She was the real backbone behind Jimmy Nap. Not these half-assed tough guys, you're talking about, who pretend to look out for him. You could have an army behind you and it don't make you as strong as having one good woman does."

"Oh, you're a charmer all right," Laura joked.

"I'm serious. You got her kind of strength. I see it."

"Yeah, well, we better keep it between us. You know your father's policy. None of his help dates any of his people or they're fired on the spot."

"I'm not one of his people. I'm his son. Whoever objects to us being together or tries to separate us with threats... we'll fight 'em off."

"So you're a fighter too, huh?"

"My whole life. I fight anybody that stands in my way. Including Jimmy Nap. So...are you with me?"

Laura gave me a quick kiss on the lips to seal the deal. And the deal stayed sealed. We kept a low profile for a while. But some people in the neighborhood knew. Some people in the neighborhood know everything. And once one person in the neighborhood knows, everybody in the neighborhood knows. They'd see me in the bar, talking to her. They'd see how we looked at one another, laughed with one another and how most nights we left with one another.

I assumed my father knew about me and Laura, but we never talked about it. He probably also assumed that she was just another broad, one of many, in his mind, and that we would never last. She wasn't. She was the one.

On August 13, 1970, I proposed to Laura. We decided to get married as soon as possible. We didn't want to make a big thing out of it. So we started calling close friends and relatives personally to invite them to a simple ceremony in church. I had promised Laura's mother, Angelina, that I would marry her daughter at the altar. We didn't even want a reception. Laura's mother took care of her friends and relatives the same way. From the pay phone at the Hi-Way Lounge, I called my father at his town house uptown in Manhattan. It was about 9 p.m.

I'll never forget; I asked him to come to my wedding, and told him that we weren't doing it up big, weren't sending out invitations, just calling immediate family and friends.

He called me a bum who had "no right to disturb Laura's life." He said, "You caused nothing but heartaches since I found you and brought you back from New Mexico. All you've done was to cause me embarrassment and you owe money to loan sharks and bookies all over the neighborhood—who I've been paying off for you. You beat up on some of my controllers with your drunken rages, for no good reason. You even owe money to Laura, who helped pay some of your debts off and now you want to marry her? Do you want to ruin her life, too? Well, before that happens, I want you out of town. There'll be no wedding. So pack up and don't call my house ever again."

My answer to him was simple and defiant, "Nobody's going to stop this wedding." I not only hung up the pay phone hanging from the wall, I ripped it off the wall, yelling, screaming and cursing at the stupid Polak of a bartender, who used to be one of my crew. I downed a double Scotch on the rocks. The bartender ran out the front door as I went behind the bar and chased the other customers out of the place as well. I jumped over the bar and picked up one stool at a time, throwing them and breaking all the blue-tinted mirrors. I went crazy. I said to myself that he's my father, and I'll never put my hands on him, but I will wreck his untouchable bar. I cursed him up and down, comparing him to Mussolini and every other tyrant I could think of.

Then, when I was done wrecking the Hi-Way, I walked up to Crisci's Restaurant. I stepped into the bar area where my father's crew was sitting around. I told them what I had just done to the Hi-Way and challenged them. They couldn't get up fast enough, rushing out the side door, some running in full sprint toward their cars. They all wanted to be the first one to tell my father what I had done. They wanted to deliver the news first hand to him at his townhouse. I called out to them and made everybody look. "Go ahead, you cowards! You can't wait to tell Jimmy Nap first. Look at you. The race is on to see which one of you gets there first!"

Then I called Laura at her mother's house and told her what I had done. She came to pick me up with a friend and took me to the friend's house for protection—as if anything could protect me from my father's wrath once he found out what I did. I told Laura and her mother that night that we were getting married at the altar as planned. Laura's mother cried all night thinking I was going to be killed. I told her that my love for Laura was too strong for anyone to break us up. Anyone.

The next day my father called Laura. It was about 2 o'clock in the afternoon, a day before our wedding. He told Laura to put me on the phone. I was sleeping in my clothes on the sofa in her living room. I had had a blackout and when Laura woke me and told me that my father was on the phone, I started remembering everything I had done the night before. I got up and with the phone in my hand, I heard him say to me, "I want to see you outside Laura's mother's house in 30 minutes." He told me he wanted to talk to me about the wedding. So, I was excited, thinking he was going to come to our wedding and that all was forgiven.

I stood up, straightened my look in the mirror to be presentable and I told Laura and her mother that my father wanted me to wait for him outside the house. "He probably wants to talk to me alone so he can give me his blessing," I explained.

As I stood in front of the stoop outside the house waiting for him, his driver pulled the Cadillac over to the curb, hopping the curb and going up on the sidewalk a little. My heart actually sank a little as I imagined my father coming out of the car, arms open wide, and offering me a congratulatory hug. "TN, my son," he would say, "You are on the road to straightening out your life. I'm so happy for you and so proud of you."

No such luck. My father jumped out of the front seat of the car with a crowbar in his right hand. I was shocked. He unleashed a barrage of blows, hitting me on my head, and across my shoulders and back. I put my arms up to protect my skull and all I could hear him saying was, "You son-of-a-bitch, you wrecked my Hi-Way!" Over and over again, he said it. Over and over, he hit me. It's not like I didn't deserve it. But no matter how hard or how much he hit me, I refused to go down, or hit him back.

I was bleeding pretty good from my head and I remember three Puerto Rican passersby who tried to help me. "No!" I yelled out to them. "He's my father! Go away!" That's when my father threw the crowbar onto the ground. He looked at me. "You're a disgrace. Change your name and get out of New York—you and her!" He pointed to Laura, standing in the doorway of the building, crying. She rushed toward me.

"This is what he is. You see him?" my father said to Laura. "This is the man you love. Take a good look. You'll be on the receiving end of him one day." Then he stared at me. "Change your name and get out of New York, you and her. You're not my son anymore!"

My father picked up the crowbar and swung it one more time. One last blow that brushed my shoulder and connected with my temple, bringing me down to one knee. Which is what he wanted.

He went back to his Cadillac and his driver took him away.

Laura saw and heard it all. My father didn't care. He wanted her to hear. He wanted that to hurt me even more than the beating.

Laura held me. Blood oozed from my head and onto her, as she cradled me in her arms. If my father's intention was to break us up, it didn't work. He only brought us closer together.

I looked at her through squinted eyes, and spoke through my pain, "Like I told you, together we'll fight 'em all off."

She shushed me and wiped the blood off my brow with a wet towel her mother threw down from the window.

"But Laura..." I went on, "I think we might have just lost round one. That's okay. That's okay."

I passed out in her arms, barely hearing the sound of the ambulance.

Like I said, the beating my father gave me was a day before my wedding. I had to wear a toupee to the ceremony, because I needed 21 stitches to close up my head. As we exchanged vows and posed for our wedding photos, I kept thinking that the toupee received all the attention. But nothing could take my concentration off of Laura. She looked so beautiful I couldn't take my eyes off her. Guys will understand this. I had one of those moments where I looked at her, the one and only woman in my life, and wondered what the heck this amazing lady wanted with me. But I'm glad she did want me. Even if no one else did.

Laura and I went down to Cape Coral, Florida for our honeymoon. God knows we needed to get away from it all and have some time to ourselves. One night, we were enjoying a nice, romantic dinner at the Tiki Lounge restaurant down there. There was a vase on the table with 12 long stem red roses in it that I bought for her.

Laura excused herself from the table and I escorted her to the ladies' room. I disappeared into the men's room myself.

Moments later, I returned to the table to find Laura sitting there. Inside the vase was just the long stems but the roses themselves were missing, as if they had been clipped off.

"What happened to the roses?" I asked her.

"I don't know. It was like that when I got back," Laura said, looking upset and confused.

I looked inside the vase, under the table and around the floor of the restaurant. Then my eyes went to the next table where a strikingly handsome man wearing a cowboy hat and a thick mustache sat. The man gestured with his head toward a group of drunken men sitting at another table. They were wearing roses on the lapels of their jackets.

"Sons of a bitches..." I said, under my breath.

"Tony...please..." Laura tried to cool me off.

I walked over to the table and confronted the biggest one of the bunch. "Did you guys take my wife's roses?"

"Roses? What roses? We don't see any roses," One of drunks said, as he sniffed the one attached to his lapel.

The other drunks laughed, as they sniffed the roses on their lapels. They didn't know who they were fucking with. I stared at them for a moment. I looked over to Laura, who was praying, hands folded in front of her, that I would just let it go. Then I caught a look at the rose-less stems in the vase and I lost it. I cocked back and punched the big fat one in the jaw. The others stood and came at me. Big shittin' deal. Like I never had four guys come at me before! I held my own, knocking down a few of them. But the rest of them grabbed me from behind and threw me through a sheet rock wall.

Laura got into the fray, swinging her heavy black purse, hitting some of the guys on top of their heads until I come back through the wall to continue the fight. What a team!

Cops rushed into the place and grabbed me and slapped cuffs on me. Four on one and they grab *me*? Do I have *jerkoff* written across my forehead?

Luckily the guy in the cowboy hat at the next table intervened. "Officers, the guy was just protecting his wife," the Marlboro Man look-a-like explained, "These guys took her roses. Those were her roses. I saw the whole thing. And this little woman here sure can fight."

The cops looked at me and Laura, then at the drunken men. They take the cuffs off me. I thank the guy in the cowboy hat and I take Laura back to the hotel. Dinner ruined.

The next morning the owner of the Tiki Lounge sent Laura a dozen long stem roses with an apology note. She risked getting hurt to help me. What a woman. And that good-looking mustached guy in the cowboy hat who vouched for me would go on to become Magnum, PI himself, Tom Selleck.

Laura and I settled down in Cape Coral for a while. It was a nice area just a couple miles from Fort Myers, with only a small bridge that separated the two.

One night, while we were alone in the living room of the apartment we were renting, I told Laura that I wanted to go straight—stop gambling and drinking and living a life of crime. I told her that I would like to go to that college on the other side of the bridge in Fort Myers—Edison Community College. I could use my GI Bill to pay for my education.

Laura supported my decision. I not only majored in accounting, but before long I was asked by the dean of business to start working as an accountant for the college. He felt that my grades made me eligible to join the team of two other accountants in his office.

I took the accounts payable position and began attending evening classes. I had to lie on the employment application. On the form was the question, "Were you ever arrested for a crime?" I wrote No. I figured if I told the truth, I'd never get the job. I figured nobody would really check and I'd be okay.

After working in the accounting office for a few months I introduced a way for the college to earn interest on money we kept in a checking account. The money came from the state and from small businesses to be used for students who qualified for low income scholarships. I noticed that between sessions the money was not being used for three-month intervals. A regulation in the state's manual that said when using state funds for low income scholarships we could invest the money and put it up for a 90-day interest income at a local bank. It had to be a federal reserve bank. We earned a half point on our money after 90 days and we added that to the scholarship fund.

Eventually the FBI got wind of my employment. They came in and told me to resign my position immediately because I had lied on my application and it could lead to a jail sentence. Also, with my background and record they told me I wasn't permitted to handle state or federal funds.

I went home and told Laura what had happened and her answer was, "They just won't let you go straight, will they?"

I was once asked what I would have wanted to be in life, other than the direction I had first chosen. My response: an accountant. But it wasn't to be. So I decided to stay in the family business. I didn't have any other choice.

Once back in New York, Laura and I started on our own family. Our newborn daughter Veronica was the light of our lives. But she had a problem. The doctors told us that Veronica needed an operation to correct her right hip. Without the surgery, she might grow up with one leg shorter than the other. I didn't have the money for the operation and we were stressing out that our little princess might not get the care she needed.

One day, at Laura's mother's house, Angelina sat there with the rosary beads in her hand and she said to me—in Italian, of course— "Go see your father. I know he still loves you very much. Make amends. Tell him you're not there for yourself. Tell him you're there for Veronica. Right now he is the only one who can help with the doctor's bills."

I took in her words. I put my head down for a moment to think. I knew it was the right thing to do, for my baby daughter, for my relationship with my father. But I didn't want to give in. There was a stubborn streak in me that just didn't want to be the one to break down and go to him.

But then I looked into Laura's sad eyes and over to the Veronica in Angelina's arms and I knew what I had to do. I walked into the Hi-Way and all eyes went to me. I avoided eye contact with everybody and made a beeline for the back room.

Jimmy Nap was sitting at his desk, surrounded by his crew. They all went silent for a moment, as me and my father looked at each other across the room. My father slowly got up from his chair and walked to me.

There was a tension in the room as the crew members looked on, unsure what he would do. He stood in front of me for what seemed like forever and he stared in my eyes. I didn't look away. He threw his arms around me. He greeted me with open arms and everything that had happened before disappeared in that embrace. Thank the lord, my daughter ended up not needing the operation. But Veronica's health scare brought my father and me back together. Sometimes out of something bad comes something good.

Soon after our reunion, my father had another assignment for me. "I'm sending you back to Reno to do what you do best, casino operations. You take Laura and the baby with you. There will be plane tickets waiting for you at the airport."

I did as he said. And off we went to Reno.

Laura, with healthy little Veronica in her arms, and I entered Harold's Club and Casino. It was an old sawdust joint that had been out in Reno for decades. It was more atmosphere than anything else. Like a relic from a time gone by. It needed a facelift. But it still brought in crowds.

The founder of the place, Pappi Smith, was an eccentric. Well into his 70s, he would ride through the casino on his white horse, in a Stetson hat and chaps. People in the casino stopped and stared at the geezer. Some applauded. A mop bucket hung from his horse's neck. Pappi would ride the horse over to the bar and yell, "Fill 'er up!"

The bartender then would fill the bucket with beer and the horse would drink it, as Pappi rode off, through the first floor of the casino and out the front door.

We were greeted by Harold Smith, Pappi's tall son who had taken over the day-to-day operation of the place. He also wore a cowboy hat. They all wore cowboy hats!

"TN?" he asked me and then introduced himself, "Harold Smith. Good to have you and your family here at our place. Come with me."

After showing us to our room, Harold wanted to talk to me in private. In his office he poured me a drink. "As we both know, our fathers go way back with each other. Of course, as you saw, my father is a little...let's just say...senile now, and has nothing to do with the day-to-day of the place. We just let him ride through a few times a day. Keeps him happy. I run the show. And if I can be perfectly honest with you, I really don't want someone like you working for me. Guy like you can jeopardize the place with your name."

I stared at Harold without saying a word. Then I downed my drink in one shot. My hand trembled with rage. Harold jumped in, sensing my sudden change in mood, "Now before you break my head open and leave me for dead—yeah, I know all about your reputation—let me finish my thought. I said I don't want you working *for* me. But I would be more than happy to have you working *with* me. Why don't you invest in the place? This way, if any heat comes down, I can always say you're an investor. One of the owners. The place is as much yours as it is mine."

I pulled myself back from the brink of violence and asked a sensible question, "What's the buy-in?"

"Ten million. But, hell, that should be no problem for a big shot like your father, right?"

I stared at Harold again. I wasn't sure how to take this guy. He had that bullshit good ol' boy persona but I could see a snake underneath it all. He slithered around the desk and poured me another drink. "Think it over. We'd love to have an I-talian like yourself as a partner."

Even the way he said I-talian. I hate that shit. I could never tell if he was being sincere or condescending. Once you get out of New York, it's hard to tell who's for real and who's full of shit. They all sound like bullshit artists. I like to deal with New Yorkers because they're straightforward. What you see is what you get. These guys out West were double dealers. Undercover scumbags is what I call them. Beneath the syrupy, goofy charm beat the heart of a killer. Something wasn't right. But I ran the deal past my father to see what he thought. I called him right away from my hotel room. "What do you say, Daddy-O? The buy-in is ten million."

I could just see him, sitting in his big chair in that fancy upper east side Manhattan townhouse with the phone in his hand. "I tell you what, TN, listen to me very carefully. Here's what you do. Go to the local bank out there. Tell them you're my son and get your ten million."

And with that he hung the phone up on me.

I went back to Harold the next day. I told him my father wasn't interested in being his partner. He said just as well. He had gotten an offer from Bobby Maheu, who was Howard Hughes' man. Ten million was a drop in the bucket to a guy like him. It was a brush-off all around.

So I left Reno without a deal. My father told me to get to Vegas for another assignment. I packed up Laura and Veronica and off we went.

Chapter 23

Trouble with The Cleveland Crew

I HEADED BACK TO CAESARS Palace, family in tow. We carried the money that came from Fat Tony and the New York mob, and my father was held responsible for both his end and Fat Tony's who represented the New York mob.

We were greeted warmly by Jasper Speciale. He was tall and thin. His hair was jet-black and he had a spinal problem that affected his walk. Jasper owned the Tower of Pizza, a restaurant on the strip. He was my contact out there. He had to give me money and clue me in as to what my father wanted me to do and whom I should report to.

At Caesars this time around, besides overseeing the floor, I was involved in the boxing shows and the big show room. The Jewish mob had taken control of the hotel end of the Palace and the guys back home had to pay them rent to operate the casino. Jasper said that my father told him, "When they see TN on the floor they might want to leave town."

So it was my job to make them feel uncomfortable. I prowled the baccarat pit and high roller rooms where they stayed and played, making my presence felt. Of course, I spent most of my time drinking and partying it up. I hooked up with Sinatra and his entourage. We drank into the wee small hours of the morning, telling stories and laughing. We were boisterous and rowdy and always drew a crowd and plenty of attention. Especially from the men in suits—both the casino bosses and FBI agents—who watched from a distance but didn't dare approach us.

One time Sinatra put his arm around me and gestured toward the agents. "Look at them, TN," Ol' Blue Eyes said, "Standing around watching us, with their cheap suits and polyester ties. They got a problem with me being with guys I know my whole life. They don't know nothing about loyalty. Come on, let's take a picture. Come here. All of you. Let's burn their asses. Give the bartender the camera."

The guys gathered around me and Sinatra. The bartender took the camera.

"All right," Sinatra said, "On three, everybody look at our buddies over there and say, "Bah-fonghoul. Ready? One, two…three!"

We all yelled out, "Bah-Fonghoul!"

The bartender snapped the photo. The agents walked off. We laughed.

I would meet Jasper at his place, The Tower of Pizza, so he could brief me on goings-on over a few drinks and a plate of macaroni. "It's getting tight out here, TN," Jasper informed me at one meeting. "Between the corporate Jews, who own everything, and now the Cleveland guys moving in on the action. Before too long New York won't have a fountain to piss in."

"There's no respect because there's no fear. You can't have one without the other," I said. "That's why I'm here.

But your father said, 'Please, tell him not to use his hands.' Let that be the last resort."

"My father thinks you can solve everything with talk. That's where he and I disagree. I think people listen a lot better when you got them by the throat."

Two feds walked into the restaurant and headed right toward the back table where we were sitting.

"We got customers," Jasper, who was facing the door, said. I knew what he meant without even having to turn and look.

The agents approached the table and addressed me directly. "Mr. Napoli, we'd like to ask you a few questions."

"Yeah" I said, "Well, I'd like a lot of things too." I looked at Jasper with a smug smile. Then the agent dropped a bombshell on me. "Mr. Napoli, your father and 44 of his men were picked up in New York City today. You need to come back there with us for questioning."

I stopped smiling.

"I'm not going anywhere without my wife and kids."

"We'll pay their plane fare. But you're going back with us."

I deliberated, needing a moment to gather my thoughts, as the agents hovered over me. "Let me just finish my drink first."

The agents nodded in agreement and stood next to the table, as I slowly finished the drink, making them wait. Jasper pulled the napkin from under his chin and tossed it onto the table and into his dish.

It was at moments like this that I would turn to my father for advice and guidance. Now I couldn't. I was on my own.

Back in New York, I was questioned in the district attorney's office by FBI agents and an assistant DA. "So, Mr. Napoli," the DA said, "Can you tell us about that phone call you made to your father?"

"What phone call is that?" I asked him.

"The one where you asked him for ten million dollars."

"Ten million dollars?" I looked around the room. "You guys are dreaming."

"Don't bother denying it," an eager agent jumped in. "We have it all on tape."

"Yeah, well, if you got it on tape, then what do you need me to tell you about it for?" I snapped back at him.

"Mr. Napoli. We'll have you read from this paper and match your voice to the wiretap from your father's apartment to identify you as the person who called him on January 7th, 19—"

"All right, calm down, Popcorn. Yeah, I called my father. I call him all the time. Big deal. And yeah, I asked him for ten million."

"Oh, you did, huh. So then what happened?"

"He told me to take a walk."

"Take a walk where?"

"That's an expression."

"In that phone call, your father mentions a bank. He tells you to go to 'the bank.' What bank is he referring to?"

"Bank? What bank? He gave me a brush off. He told me to go to the nearest bank. To take a walk, in other words. To get lost. What bank was I gonna go to?"

"He meant a numbers bank, didn't he?"

"A numbers bank? Where's a numbers bank in Reno, Nevada? If you know of one, tell me, because I'd like to go there myself. We'll go together."

The agent's and district attorney's faces dropped. They thought they were going to get me to cooperate about some big secret numbers operation in Reno. They had nothing. All they had was a phone call with a father telling his son to take a walk for himself. Stupid bastards. Hustlers hustling hustlers.

They dropped the charges against me and I went to the Hi-Way to tell my father.

We were surrounded by his crew as I told them all about the DA's questioning me.

"So I told them, yeah, I asked you for the ten million. They already knew about it anyway. They got your phones all tapped. And I told them you didn't give it to me. You brushed me off. That's all I told them. Yeah, they had nothing, Daddy-O. What were they going to do, arrest a son for asking his father for money? No law against that."

The crew members laughed and sang my praises: "You done good, TN," "You got a stand-up kid here, Jimmy."

My father was quick to temper their respects. "Don't give him too many compliments," Jimmy Nap said. "He's got a better deal with me than with them."

The crew laughed again.

"Here, take this," my father said, sliding an envelope filled with money across the table. "Get back to Vegas. They'll lay off you for a while now. But you go back to The Trop this time. Food and beverage. Take your family with you. Handle everything for the house. Discourage Cleveland. Ya know what I mean?"

I knew what he meant.

"But for Chrissakes, TN. Be good."

"Ain't I always?"

My father smiled.

So I moved the action from Caesars to The Trop because Fat Tony back in New York told my father that we should "follow the money." So I followed the money, to protect the New York mob's investment. We took our money from the cage in Caesars and deposited it in the cage at The Trop. A few of my crew members and I transported one million dollars in cash inside attaché cases, escorted by deputies from the sheriffs department.

It wasn't unusual in those days to move from one casino to another. It made sense to invest money for a short stay in order to bank the games. The hotel owners wanted nothing to do with banking the games themselves. They'd rather collect 10% of the take before taxes with none of the headaches of hiring dealers and floor bosses to watch their money. The money we moved was from the New York mob with the Fat Man holding my father responsible for all profits and losses.

New York deposited a mil in cash into The Trop cage to bank all the bets made at the tables. We had a one-year lease with the hotel owners for us to bank the gambling and handle the food, drinks, and entertainment for the house. We were giving the hotel owners 10% of the take from everything we did. That was considered our rent. The only problem was, the Cleveland Mob was our landlord and this big prick, casino boss Jim Snow, thought he now had some power over us because Cleveland was backing him. He thought he was untouchable. He thought wrong.

I couldn't stand Snow. He was stocky and gray-haired, with a sarcastic mouth. A typical exchange between us was usually edgy. Snow would see me on the casino floor and call out to me, "Nice suit, Tony."

"Thanks, Snow."

"You almost look like a boss in that suit. Almost."

He would throw his digs and I would let them roll off my back. "Yeah, well, you gotta dress the part," I'd say and keep walking past him, because if I stopped I might break the scumbag's neck.

Then he would move closer and take a pot shot at me. "Well, keep dressing the part, and keep playing make-believe. Because you and your boys from New York, you're never taking control of this casino away from Cleveland. They just wanted me to tell you that. In case you had any big ideas."

"Are you a messenger boy now, Snow?"

"Yes. And it's my job to deliver you back to the dirty streets of New York, where you came from."

One night I was hanging around the Tropicana Hotel lounge getting loaded with some of my crew. I was talking about Snow and how he was getting fresh with me. "This fuckin' Snow has some balls talking to me like that. He thinks because he's with Cleveland I won't rough him up. Popcorn bastard that he is."

"I just saw him at the crap tables. He's mouthing off again. Guy's got a big fuckin' mouth. He's got no manners."

"He said somethin' to you?" I asked, looking for any excuse.

"Me? No. But it's the way he treats people. The help. Busboys, dishwashers...he treats everybody like garbage. He thinks we're all beneath him. He tells everybody New York does what I tell them to do."

"You just saw him? Where is he?"

"He's at the crap tables."

"Gonna go have a little talk with him." I stood and headed out of the lounge.

"Tony, where you goin'?" one of my crew members asked. "Tony, don't do nothin' stupid."

I ignored his words and headed toward the casino floor, right to the craps table where Jim Snow sat, puffing a long cigar, and talking loud and tough. As I approached, Snow looked up at me. "Look who's here. I thought I smelled something."

An awkward silence fell over the table. He laughed. I didn't.

I moved closer to Snow. He blew his cigar smoke in my direction.

"Ya know, I was just tellin' everybody here about you and your boys," Snow said.

"No kidding."

"Yeah, I was telling them how you New York guys belong in the basement where we keep our nigger help."

That was it. He went too far. I knew it. Everyone at the table knew it. And he knew it.

I landed a right hand onto Snow's jaw, knocking him onto the table. Then I jumped onto the table after him. I grabbed his head and tried to bite his ear off. (This was years before Mike Tyson sank his teeth into Evander Holyfield in their 1997 bout in Vegas). Players snatched their chips up from the table.

Snow screamed, "Get him the fuck off of me!"

Security guards rushed to the table to try and remove me from Snow. But a group of big, burly blackjack dealers ran over from the pit and formed a circle around me, so no one could get to me as I continued to gnaw Snow's ear off his head.

Attacking that piece of shit Snow got me put on the black list by the gaming board, barring me from all gambling casinos in Nevada. That was March, 1974. I never again went back to Las Vegas. Needless to say, my father wasn't happy with me.

I sat across from him in the Hi-Way.

"You think you're a hero for what you did? Is that what you think?" he asked me. "Well, I don't care who praises you for standing up for us. To me, you're no hero. All I know is, you became a fool by using your hands on that man. You lost your job. They blacklisted you. You're lucky you're not in jail. Or dead. Tell me something, how the hell do you do the things you do and get away with it?"

There was a long awkward silence. Then I looked up at my Jimmy Nap and I smiled.

"What the hell are you smiling about?"

"If you had a daddy like I got, you'd do anything you wanted too."

My father fought back a smile of his own. "Use your head, TN. Not your hands. I'm not going to be around forever."

Daddy-O was right. He wasn't going to be around forever. Shortly after, he was sentenced to 7 years in jail for racketeering and promoting gambling without a license. While he was gone, the meat and potatoes of his business—the numbers rackets—fell into my hands.

My father controlled one of the largest gambling operations in the United States. He was the banker, agreed upon by all Five Families in New York. Even while he was away, the bosses protected my father's numbers business against any wannabes who would try to steal the business out from under him while he did his time.

Unfortunately, they couldn't protect it from me.

Chapter 24

A Gambling Empire

My father's $150 million a year gambling empire was run from the back room of his Hi-Way Lounge. It was the main office. The people in the numbers office were average working joes, who usually had a legitimate job but wanted to make extra money on the side. These workers counted money and stacked bills in neat piles on felt covered card tables that were set up side by side in precise rows along the back wall. They were systematic, efficient, fast. They had to be, as the action was heavy and it came in waves throughout the day. My father paid one person in the office $2,000 a week and that person could hire as many people as he needed to complete the tally, or the breakdown for the day's "action."

There was an army of number runners who were dispersed throughout the city. My father always said, "The number runner is the backbone of the numbers business." The runner goes out into the streets at eight o'clock in the morning and makes his rounds. He visits various locations to see his usual players. He goes from job site to job site: trucking companies, factories, bars, restaurants, pizzerias, social clubs, the stock market.

The runners and bookies adored my father, and were fiercely loyal to him. One bookie who knew my father for almost 50 years was David Trecanolli, or "Davy Treck" as everybody knew him. Davy was a bald, roly-poly guy, who was known as the Don Rickles of the neighborhood because of the jokes he was always telling. When it came to my father though, he could have had Rickles' other name, Mr. Warmth, because of all the warm feelings he had for Jimmy Nap. Davy said of my father, "When Jimmy Nap was in jail it's Christmastime." So the people in the neighborhood got a card and we all signed it. I put down a little note saying: 'Jimmy, It may not look like Christmas where you are, but we got you in our Christmas hearts.' But like I say, if you were in trouble, and you knew him, you didn't have no trouble. One time Jimmy Nap says to me, "If you have a whole loaf of bread and somebody comes and asks you for a little piece of that bread, rather than have an enemy, because you ain't gonna eat that whole loaf of bread, you're gonna throw some of it away, or maybe eat it the next day. Rather than have an enemy, give that person a piece of bread. That way you made a friend, instead of an enemy.' That was Jimmy Nap. That's who he was."

Jimmy always shared his bread with others, especially those who worked for him in the numbers business. He especially respected what the Runners did every day. He considered them the foot soldiers of the operation.

The runner would take the "action" from the player. That means he took their bets and money. He wrote down the player's three-digit number. The player could play the number straight or in combination. For example, take the number 816. A player could play it straight, 816, or in a six-way combination. That means the number could come out 816, 861, 618, 681, 168, 186. Either way, the player "hits the number" and wins. The odds are 500-1. The player can tell the Runner to keep the number in for a day, or for a whole week.

The winning number for the day came from reading the horse racing results in the *Daily News*. After the final race at the track, the last 3 digits of the "total mutual handle of the race track" is considered the winning number for that day. This is referred to on the street as the "Brooklyn Number." It's totally random. Has nothing specifically to do with any one horse or any one race. It is just those last three digits of the total amount of money taken in by the track on that given day.

And on most days, most players lose. And that was good for my father's business. This was back in the days before New York state got in on the action in 1967 and started running their own numbers racket three times a day with the lottery. For years the government told everyone that gambling was wrong. Except for when they run it, of course, then it's suddenly not so wrong.

Jimmy Nap, who was the banker of the numbers business, gave 35% to his controllers who brought in more than $10,000 a week. The runners got 25% of the controllers' 35%, leaving the controller with 10%. Jimmy Nap got 65% of the collections. But being the banker meant that he had to make all the payouts from his 65%. There were times after all his payouts he had only 10% left over for himself. Of course, that would be 10% of the two million they would bring in every week. There were also times when Jimmy Nap had to put his own money into the business. That was very rare. Luckily, he had a big volume that covered his payouts. My father had thirty-three controllers, who handled 900 runners in and around the five boroughs.

Because my father couldn't get to see all his runners every day, the controllers would handle collections, payments to the runners, and payouts to the winning players. Each controller had to handle a minimum of $10,000 a week from his runners to be eligible as a controller. A controller could have as many runners as he was able to handle as long as the controller's business from all his runners totaled more than the $10,000 a week. The controller would then report the win-loss to his supervisor. Then the winnings were brought to the Hi-Way Lounge to my father.

But with my father getting pinched, I began to oversee things. About six months after my father went away, controllers came to see me, saying they were having a problem—or a "beef"—with their supervisors.

One controller told me, "TN, some of the supervisors... they're not doing right. They're not letting us hold onto the money every day like your father did. So we can't make the payouts on time and that's causing us to lose business. Your father paid out the next day to his players. Now the supervisors are making them wait. Meanwhile, they're going to the track, going to private crap games. They're blowing the bank's money. And I don't mean any disrespect on this, TN. I know some of them are family."

That was the thing. The supervisors were relatives and close friends of my family, hand-picked by my father. He allowed them to make a living because they had no talent or knowledge of how to run a business on their own. My father allowed them to live high as long as they used some of the money for their families. Now with my father away, their bad habits were destroying the business. What was I going to do? What would my father do?

I reached out and put my hand on top of the controller's hand. "Don't worry about it," I assured him, "I'll take care of everything."

"Thank you, TN. Thank you for being understanding," the controller said.

I did what I thought my father would want me to do.

I stuck up for the supervisors, who were family, and I passed the blame onto the controllers. I made it look like they were the ones who were taking the money. I bombed their stores...I captured their runners...I set their cars on fire.

And why'd I do that? Because these were my father's wishes. He always told me not to harm anyone in the Napoli family, no matter what. You take care of your own. That's what he always said. I said that the controllers were the problem. They weren't handing in their paperwork on time to the supervisors. I had to make an example out of them. And that's what I did. And how did the bosses react?

Fat Tony Salerno called me in for a sit-down in his place up in Harlem.

At a small table in the back of an under-furnished room, I sat across from Tony as he chomped on his cigar. At this point, he was the underboss of the Genovese Family. I wasn't sure how his opinion would go. Whenever a boss calls you in, you hope for the best, but the worst is always somewhere in your mind.

"You saved face for the family, TN," the Fat Man said, to my relief. "What you did with these renegade controllers...and standing up to those Cleveland guys. If you have any beefs, you come here, we handle it for you. It's time to put you on the honor roll."

The honor roll? *Me.* This was one of the proudest moments in my life to that point. That meant if all the other bosses agreed, I would become a made man. A fuck-up like me could finally become a man of respect. I was on cloud nine. I was taking care of the family business, just the way my father wanted me to.

Taking care of the actual family was a little more difficult. While my father was away, wild parties were underway. I got wind that his music business wannabe wife Jeanne was hosting nightly festivities at his townhouse. The parties included lots of the "beautiful" people: celebrities, models, singers. And a lot of drugs.

Jeanne was a former Copa girl, and a disappointed actress. So while Jimmy Nap was away, she started dabbling in producing musicals on Broadway. That meant throwing my father's money around like it was water. And she hosted these big parties almost every night of the week at the townhouse.

I knew my father wouldn't have approved of these activities in his house. It was disrespectful. It was wrong. It made the family look bad. So I took it upon myself to handle it—in a way that I thought my father would approve of.

In a drunken rage and accompanied by several of my crew members with baseball bats, I crashed one of her bashes and chased the partygoers from the townhouse. As they raced out the door, I screamed at them as I swung my bat, "In my father's house? How dare you do this in my father's house? *Disgraziata!* I'll kill you all!" We missed some targets on purpose, but a few bats landed on heads, kneecaps, and rib cages—both men and women.

Jeanne rushed over to me, hollering, "Tony, these are my friends! This is my house! Get out of here! This is my house!"

"No, this isn't your house," I shouted back at her. "Nothing is yours. This is my father's house. And it will always be his house!"

She rushed off into another room, crying, as me and my boys continued clearing the house of all its guests. When they were all gone, I headed over to the bar, grabbed a bottle of whiskey and downed it. I would've sooner killed every one of them bastards before I would've let them disgrace my father or his home. I would do anything for my father.

One Thanksgiving, when my father was still in the federal prison in Danbury, Connecticut, I did something I knew he would like. I got together some singers and dancers and a group of wiseguy's girlfriends. I filed them into three limos and took them up to the prison, which was the lowest-security prison in the Northeast and sometimes referred to as Club Fed.

In the cafeteria, Jimmy Nap and his crew members ate Thanksgiving dinner, surrounded by pretty, familiar faces and being entertained by the singers and dancers.

The warden and the guards stood in the back of the cafeteria, watching everyone enjoying the festivities. My father leaned over to me, "How the hell did you pull this off, TN?"

"I just did."

"I don't believe it. You brought the girls too. You're something else."

When dinner was over, my father's crew members lined up in the back of the cafeteria and kissed me. Even the warden thanked me. "You brought the best entertainment we ever had up here," he said, with a smile. He was willing to let me do something nice for my father and the other men. He knew some of them for some time and there was a mutual respect there.

"Thank you, warden."

Then my father approached me. "When those limos pulled up we thought it was the governor coming to see us. I'm very proud of what you did, TN. You did a very nice thing for me and the boys. You gave us a nice holiday. We won't forget this."

Then the warden led Jimmy Nap away. I watched him go and was reminded that with all his respect and power, at the time, my father was on the *Forbes* magazine power and influence list, he was still living behind bars.

I would've done anything for my father. That's what family is all about. You do things you might not normally do. You go out of your way. You also put up with things you might not normally put up with.

For example, when my daughter Veronica got married years later in 2001, she had a beautiful reception at Leonard's of Great Neck on Long Island's exclusive north shore. It was a fancy, crowded affair. She looked beautiful. Everything was perfect. Well, almost everything. Veronica married a cop. I didn't like the idea at first. But she fell in love. Like I said, when it comes to family you have to learn to put up with things. Things you don't necessarily like. So on one side of the wedding hall was all cops. On the other side? All gangsters.

What can I say? That's family.

When my father came out of prison, he resumed his rightful place at the top of his empire. I faded into the background, by design. I wanted to approach my father about what the Fat Man had told me but didn't know how to bring it up. But he brought it up to me first.

"This thing about you on the honor roll," my father said to me, as we sat in the Hi-Way one day.

"Yeah, what about it?"

"I went to the west side and had a sit-down over it," he informed me.

"What did you say?"

"I told them you're my son. You belong to one family and one family only, the Napoli family. And as long as I'm alive and kicking, and even after I'm gone, my wishes are for the New York families never to propose you again. Do you understand?"

Maybe deep down I understood. Maybe I didn't. But at that moment it was like my knees went out from under me. "So they took me off the honor roll?" I asked.

I didn't expect an answer, and I didn't get one either. I knew the answer.

My father didn't want that life for me. He wanted me to stay out of it. He knew that for me to be made meant that I would have another ruling body over me, another boss. He knew that my loose cannon ways would probably get me into even hotter water than I'd already been in, and if I was made, not even he could get me out of it.

As far as my father was concerned, there was room for only one Napoli on the honor roll, and that was him.

Chapter 25

Jimmy Nap Is Made

It was a brutally cold November Night in 1976 when a convoy of town cars pulled up to the front entrance of the Hi-Way Lounge. From the backseat of each car came a different boss and capo in the Genovese family. They were all dressed sharply in cashmere overcoats and tinted sunglasses. Smoke bursting from their mouths into the frigid night air, they moved quickly from their cars to the lounge.

Gathering in the back room were the bosses and capos, the underworld luminaries: Vincent "The Chin" Gigante; Anthony "Fat Tony" Salerno; Frank "Funzi" Tieri; Louis "Louie Dome" Pacella, and other members of the Genovese family. They came for the secret ceremony of Omerta performed for my father.

Fat Tony stood beside Jimmy Nap. Tony took a photo of Mary, the Blessed Mother, and placed it on a table before Jimmy. Then he took Jimmy's hand and sliced a small cut onto the top of his finger. The blood from Jimmy's finger dripped onto the photo of Mary. Fat Tony struck a match and set the photo on fire.

My father said, *"Che io bruci nell' Inferno, se tradisco la famiglia o spezzo il nostro codice,"* which means, "May I burn in hell, if I betray the family and break our code."

The bosses and capos looked on, as the photo of the Blessed Mother mixed with Jimmy's blood burned to a crisp.

Like my father always said, we were a government unto ourselves, with our own rules, codes and ways of behaving, including our own ceremonies and rituals. It was on this night that my father became a made man. He was 65 years old. He never wanted to be made before that. He never needed to. For years, he stood above the commission, above the Five Families, as the banker, the controller. Because of his position he could move between families and be treated as a man of respect by all.

With my father facing more time in jail, this time a seven-year sentence, for promoting gambling without a license, income tax fraud and bribery, the Five Families recommended that he be recognized by one family, to protect his street business and crew while he was away in jail.

My father was allowed to pick the family he wanted, which is an unusual occurrence and a sign of the level of respect with which my don was viewed. He chose the Genovese Family. They were considered the Rolls Royce of the Five Families. My father went straight to the position of capo, or captain, with the Fat Man sponsoring him. He was the first man to ever do that. Once you become a made man, you are supposed to prove yourself by bringing in your monthly earnings. My father had already proved himself for forty-five years.

Bosses and capos congratulated Jimmy Nap that night with hugs and kisses on the cheek. They celebrated with him, by drinking espressos with anisette and a lemon twist. Although my father had enjoyed all the privileges and reverence of a made man for many years, it wasn't until that night in 1976 that he officially became a made man.

Shortly after, he was convicted on gambling charges and got seven years in Danbury federal prison. Then my father was transferred to maximum security in Lewisburg, PA because he was the leader in a food strike in Danbury after the prisoners found roaches in their food trays.

My father never discussed with me how he felt about being made. It was not a big deal for him personally, because he had held the rank unofficially for so long. He only took the button to protect his crew from anyone who might try to capture them while he was in jail. He was made about a year before he went to jail. He used that time out on the street to reorganize his crew and tell them what he expected from them while he was away. He wanted them to be careful with their gambling habits and not get too involved with the loan sharks until he was done serving his time. He didn't want them to get hurt. He took the button to protect them too, not just himself. But, in the end, they all deceived him and went crazy gambling the money while he served his seven-year bid.

My father did his time in two different prisons. First he was in Danbury Federal Penitentiary. Then, in 1981, he was transferred to Lewisburg Maximum Security Prison in Lewisburg, PA, where he did the rest of his sentence with guys like Phillip "Rusty" Rustelli, boss of the Bonanno family, and Jimmy "The Gent" Burke, who was immortalized by Robert DeNiro in the picture Goodfellas. It was seven years of disaster for my father's beloved numbers business.

Chapter 26

Out of Control

RICO. THIS WORD BECAME a permanent part of most of my life. This four-letter word struck fear in the hearts of many friends and associates of mine. It also directly affected the Napoli and Genovese families.

The Racketeer Influenced and Corrupt Organizations Act is a United States Federal Law enacted in 1970 as part of the Organized Crime Control Act. The intention of RICO was to provide the government with greater powers and stronger penalities for going after individuals who they perceived as performing unlawful acts as members of a larger criminal organization.

To me, and to many others, it was just another example of the government bending the rules, or better yet, *rewriting* the rules, to stop businesses that threatened their own stranglehold on power and control. Ever wonder why RICO charges have never been brought against the U.S.

government itself? Can you think of a more conspiratorial criminal entity than them?

So the good 'ol U.S. government made up the RICO law—like they do every law—because they couldn't figure out how to get guys like us any other way. So when you're losing, what do you do? You change the rules. And that's exactly what they did.

The real consequence of RICO was that it put Italians in jail. Lots of them. G. Robert Blakey, the scumbag who drafted the original RICO bill, once said, "We don't want one set of rules for people whose collars are blue or whose names end in vowels, and another set for those whose collars are white and have Ivy League diplomas."

Bullshit.

The intention of RICO was to go after organized crime. *Italian* organized crime. The Mafia. This was its original intention and this is how it has mainly been used since it came into law. Heck, the damn law itself ends in a vowel.

What's more, it was named after Edward G. Robinson's Italian gangster character "Rico" in the 1931 film *Little Caesar*. While no one, including Blakey, has ever admitted this, no one in government has ever denied it either.

One thing that there is no question about is how RICO hurt our people. Once the government was armed with the broad sweeping powers of that law, they used them liberally and frequently against us. RICO didn't stop anyone from conducting business, mind you. It just made us more careful, more aware, and in some cases even more defiant.

During the seven years that father was jailed on RICO charges—between 1978 and 1985—I had a hand in taking control of some of his numbers business. His controllers and supervisors, some of whom were blood relatives, had started their shit again. They were not paying the hits to the bettors on time. With my father gone, they went back to their old ways. So the bettors came to me to bank their action until my father came home. I had to go get permission from the west-side faction of the Genovese family. And the bosses gave me the okay to bankroll the parts of the numbers business that those bastards were losing on us.

Some controllers were trying to break away with what they considered their share of the numbers business because they claimed that they weren't getting paid on time with Jimmy Nap gone. Those are the ones I was ordered to go after. I was to get that business back and hand it over to the Genovese bosses. As for my father's business, I would have to bank the business myself and not ask for any financial help. If I couldn't do that then they would get someone else to replace me. It would still be considered my father's business until he returned home from jail, but I knew that once control of his business was handed over to those outside of the immediate family, he would probably lose his hold on it forever. I couldn't let that happen.

I went with my crew into the Brooklyn and Queens areas where most of the insurgent controllers were located. They had left us to take part of the business with them. I had to use force on them. I wrecked their clubs. I broke some heads. I had to do what I had to do to keep my father's business from crumbling. I knew these were guys who wouldn't respond to talking. They had to be treated like the rebels they were.

So my crew and me used strong-arm tactics: smashing the windows of their clubs or grabbing guys out of their cars and working them over by pistol-whipping them; or using solid pieces of metal pipes to break their heads. I would be yelling to the bastards during the beatings I gave them. "Hey Popcorn, and the rest of you fucking ham and eggs, that guy is still alive." I meant that my father was doing time but he wasn't dead. He'd be back. The word on the street from some of these rebels that I worked over was that Jimmy Nap was history and no longer in power. After I was done with them they knew different.

After beating them, I emptied out their pockets and took their money to help pay expenses for my crew. I also took over their bars for weekends and emptied out their registers. I needed the cash for more of my expenses.

They had nobody in the streets to complain to or get help from who was above me. And those who were above me wanted nothing to do with these rebels. They were happy I was putting the shitheads in their place.

So I was able to recover a quarter million a week in action, which was considered about 25% of the business at the time. I was praised by the bosses for saving both face and business for my father and for the family.

Also during these years, while my father was in jail, I was operating after-hours places in the city. That meant a lot more drinking and gambling for me. I was collecting money from loan sharks at a rate of 10% to 20% of the collections. I took over some neighborhood bars by using strong-arm tactics on the junkies who were causing problems for the owners. People came to me with domestic problems and thanked me for teaching their drug addict kids a lesson by giving them a beating. Some of these kids were stealing and actually beating up their mothers and fathers to get money for drugs. I kicked the shit out of them.

I had my crew drop them off in some deserted areas in Long Island and made them find their way home. These tactics put the fear of God in them.

I was drinking more, gambling more, and becoming more violent than ever. I was out of control—desperate to maintain my father's honor and not let him lose control of his numbers business while he was away. Plus I was hell-bent on maintaining my own reputation on the street.

But I wasn't the only one out of control.

Before Jeanne's marriage to my father, she had been a marijuana smoker, but my father never knew. Then a few years after their marriage, and each time he went to jail, she started using heavier drugs. She gave those drug parties in the townhouse when he was away, or even when he just went out of town on business. But after she gave birth to their second child in 1967 she started using cocaine. And then in 1978 when my father got sentenced, she started taking heroin.

When he found out, all he said was, "My wife has a disease." He would never call her a junkie, or disparage her in any way. He had the courage to say, "She has a disease." I always admired him for that.

So, with Jimmy Nap away, things were really coming unglued, on both a personal and business level. RICO had taken one Napoli man from his family and livelihood. Then it aimed to take another one.

Chapter 27

Giuliani Time

IN AUGUST 1984 A GUY named Bill Breen came to me with a "serious problem." He said that he owed $500,000 to a finance company called Capital & Resources located in Lake Success, out on Long Island.

Breen found me through his limousine driver, Joe, who was a union man with a local that I had some influence with. He told me, "We both could make some big money with this guy." I looked into the matter and sure enough there were some wiseguys behind the scenes associated with Capitol & Resources. Breen told me that he got a half-million dollar loan from the company on the basis of some property he owned in Texas. When he couldn't keep up the payments, the wiseguys grabbed him and told that him he had to pay one point a week until they sold the property—or else they'd kill him.

Breen was supposed to use the money to build a discotheque in the Hotel Diplomat in midtown Manhattan.

The place was going to be big; holding 1,500 people after remodeling was done. It would have two floors, six bars, and a stage for live music. This was back when discos were still hot, with places like Studio 54 being the preferred spot for New York celebrities and trendsetters. Breen, who was a hick, wanted to call his joint the Cowboy Palace.

I took Breen around with me, trying to impress him by inviting him to my private crap games and after-hours places. I made a deal with him: I would get the wiseguys off his back for $50,000 after we opened the disco together. I would see to it that Capital & Resources would get all their money back within a year after our grand opening. So I put a special meeting together in the building where Capital & Resources had their offices. Little did I know that the office I used for the meeting with six other wiseguys (from three other New York families) was bugged and had a hidden camera behind the wall facing the long executive table where we sat.

During the meeting, which was being taped by the FBI, I presented my plan for them to get their money back. I told them to go back to their bosses with my idea. They all said there was no need for them to see their bosses, because when I said something they knew where it was coming from. They figured I was speaking for my father, which I wasn't. On tape it made me look like a boss.

The next morning at 5 a.m. I heard pounding on the front door of my house: "FBI; you have one minute to open this door or we'll break it down."

I told Laura to stay with Veronica and Tanya while I talked to these guys. Still in my pajamas, I opened the front door to see four agents flashing their badges. One was a female agent. I guess they sent her in case my wife got out of hand. One of the agents said, "You're under arrest; we'll tell you why after we book you." They had no search warrant, but I went with them peacefully anyway. I didn't want a scene in my home. They took me to 40 Foley Square, to the office of the U.S. Attorney for the Southern District of New York. I looked at the name on the door: Rudolph W. Giuliani.

Giuliani. A paesan. One of us. A guy raised not that much different from how I was raised. Like me, he was born to a working-class family in Brooklyn, the grandson of Italian immigrants. Here was a guy who could understand me. We had a lot in common.

We had nothing in common. Giuliani is what I call a self-hating Italian. A guy so driven by political ambition that he singled out his own ethnic group for prosecution so he could break any and every possible tie to them. He could make a name for himself as a tough and unbiased prosecutor. He could look the world in the eye and say, "See how fair I am. I even go after my own."

Giuliani was aggressively prosecuting organized crime. No, more to the point, *Italian* organized crime. He racked up a record of 4,152 convictions as U.S. Attorney. Many of them were people whose names ended in vowels. He was brimming with ambition. He had the mayor's office in his sights. And he'd get there too, running as a tough-as-nails law-and-order man. This is the same "fair" man who would stage public arrests of people to humiliate them on camera. The same "fair" man who, as mayor, would see his own police force turn into brutal bullies. In one highly publicized case, an NYPD officer beat and tortured a suspect he had in custody—a Haitian immigrant named Abner Louima—by sticking a plunger up his ass in a precinct bathroom, all the while shouting "This is Giuliani time!"

My arrest was part of his round-up for what would become Giuliani's famous Mafia commission trial, in which he indicted eleven so-called organized crime figures, including the heads of New York's five families: my father's old buddy, Anthony "Fat Tony" Salerno (Genovese Family); Paul "Big Paul" Castellano (Gambino Family); Carmine "Junior" Persico (Colombo Family); Anthony "Tony Ducks" Corallo (Lucchese Family); Phillip "Rusty" Rustelli (Bonanno Family), and their subordinates.

Giuliani used his favorite toy, the Racketeer Influenced and Corrupt Organizations Act or RICO, designed to make it easier to prosecute organized crime figures. The charges included extortion, labor racketeering, and murder for hire. Time magazine called it the "Case of Cases" and possibly "the most significant assault on the infrastructure of organized crime since the high command of the Chicago Mafia was swept away in 1943."

They quoted Giuliani: "Our approach...is to wipe out the Five Families."

And now here he was, my *goumbah*, the honorable Rudy Giuliani, coming after me. Giuliani tried to make a deal. "Bill Breen was part of a sting operation, he bleated." I put my head down and asked his two assistants to put me in a cell. If Breen was a rat, fine. But I wasn't talking.

My trial started in January, 1985 with 14 other defendants. That's when my lawyer told me that Bill Breen belonged to a gang that had robbed banks in the Texas area and that he and his gang were responsible for shooting and killing a federal judge in a Texas courtroom.

After eight years of doing time for bank robbery and murder in Lewisburg federal prison, Breen had made a deal with Giuliani's office to infiltrate the Genovese crime family in the New York area. They made a deal with a judge killer! You have to love the U.S. government's morality.

Giuliani brought five counts against me under the RICO Act. I was facing five years on each count for a total of 25 years if I was convicted. The trial against me and my 13 co-defendants lasted four months. Some of the other guys on trial had names and titles like Michael Franzese, a capo in the Colombo family; Benny Aloi, a capo in the Colombo Family; Jim Rotundo, a capo in the Genovese Family; Lenny DeMaria, a capo in the Gambino Family, and Frankie "The Hat" DeStephano, a capo in the Gambino Family.

Stool pigeon Bill Breen took the witness stand against six other Italians and me. In cross examination he said that he told Giuliani's Assistant DA's that he should have stayed with me because he had a better deal with Napoli than with Giuliani and the government. He told the jury that Giuliani offered him $35,000 to testify against me and that he never saw a penny of it. He also informed the jury about how I invited him to the best Italian restaurants in the five boroughs. How I gave him money to gamble in private crap games and always made sure that he had a woman to escort him around town with my limousine service.

Breen described how I saved his life. That was the turning point. He explained that there was a contract out on him because he owed some of the defendants in the case $500,000 and how I called the contract off. He quoted me telling them, "Why kill a guy who owes that much money? Let's give him time to recover his assets and pay back so much every month." I stuck up for him because I thought he was worth more alive than dead. Of course, if I had known he was a rat I would have gladly had them put a bullet in his brain. Breen laid out, in detail, the specifics of the sting operation he was a part of, working closely with the FBI as an informant to infiltrate the New York mob.

During the trial I was out on a $125,000 bail that my father put up for me. It lasted from December 1984 to April 1985. My father had been released from prison in February 1985, right in the middle of the trial. So every day after court I was able to go over to the Hi-Way Lounge to see him. He demanded that I report to him with an update of what had happened in the courtroom each day. My lawyer had orders to accompany me to see my father, and the case cost Jimmy Nap about a quarter of a million dollars in legal fees.

When I saw my father after those long days in court, he would say to me, "Giuliani doesn't want you, he wants me. Stay strong and sober, TN, until this thing blows over."

He was right. Giuliani really wanted my father and tried to use me to get at him. He knew Jimmy Nap was just out of jail and back on the street. The government knew what his influence was and how large a gambling racket he ran. They wanted to put him back in jail. They wanted Breen to get close enough to me and, by extension, Jimmy Nap and his business so he could bring the whole operation down. Or better even, they wanted to flip me, get me to testify against my father. Against my own father! Imagine these bastards. No way they were going to run that game on me.

The words my father shared with me every day made me feel as though everything was going to be okay and that I would be acquitted of all five counts. He kept telling me not to worry and that it was a very intelligent move on my part to advise the other defendants in the case not to hit Breen. "Otherwise you would all be in a murder trial," he reminded me.

Jimmy Nap was glad he was home to be with me during the trial. He couldn't be in the courtroom but he was waiting for me every afternoon at the Hi-Way. His presence gave me the strength to face that trial and to believe I could go free. He told me that over and over again, and in the end he was right.

In April 1985 after almost four months in court, six other Italians me and were acquitted of all charges brought against us by our countryman Giuliani. Even with the stoolie Breen spilling his guts on the stand day in and day out, the government didn't have anything on me. I hadn't done anything to this guy. None of us had. He came to us, we didn't go to him. If anything, we tried to help him. His, or rather the FBI's, screwball scheme went up in smoke.

It all came out in the trial. It had taken Breen nearly two years to convince the boys that it was a good deal. He had given the boys the deed to his property in Texas as security for the half-million-dollar loan. It was a project that he initiated, with the help of the FBI to infiltrate the mob and to get the mob to lend him their money to complete the disco. It was a definite and clear sting operation, but one that never really led to anything significant. Bill Breen's property in Texas, we learned, was part of the operation as well—all created by the FBI.

Before Bill Breen died of a brain tumor in 1991 he told his story to writer Donald Goddard whose book, The Insider: The FBI's Undercover Wiseguy Goes Public was published in 1992. He was a judge killer and bank robber who the FBI knowingly worked with so they could come after guys who were committing lesser crimes. He was a rat who flipped to shorten his sentence; a rat who they turned into a hero. And one who came up a little short in his efforts to put me away.

As I walked out of the courtroom that day in April, Giuliani stood by the back doors of the court room and growled, "Napoli, I'll get you the next time."

The next day Channel 7 news portrayed me as the mouthpiece for the mob when I told their reporter John Johnson outside the courthouse, "Giuliani is a Gestapo and the FBI are a bunch of peeping Toms." Where I'm from you were taught to fight fire with fire. I'm sure Giuliani understood that. After all, we were just two guys from Brooklyn looking out for ourselves.

On the night that I was acquitted, my father threw a big party for me at the Hi-Way but I didn't attend. I was exhausted and I just wanted to stay home with Laura and the girls, drinking my martinis. I missed those martinis. I missed feeling like a free man. When you're on trial and facing the loss of your freedom, you think about the things you might never see again, like your family. You know what you are and what you're doing when you get into this mob life. I knew what I was. But no matter who you are, you are never ready for the loss of freedom that comes with imprisonment. It hangs over you like a drape. For the time being, that drape had been lifted.

My father called and asked Laura if she was coming to the party with me. She told him that we wanted to be alone. Jimmy Nap reminded her, "Tell my son now he realizes that the DA can indict you for eating a ham sandwich." He was right. When they want you, they'll move heaven and earth to get you. My father agreed with Laura that it was best for me to rest and meditate about my future—one he was planning for me. Soon I would see that the future he had in mind was for me to be close to him every day—for the rest of his life.

Chapter 28

Father Knows Best

WHEN MY FATHER WAS RELEASED from prison in 1985, he could not put up with his wife Jeanne and her bad habits anymore. Her drug use had become more than he could bear. He would never divorce her, because he believed it was his responsibility to care for her. He had taken care of my mother, who suffered from cancer, for seven years before she died. He felt a person on drugs needed the same help as a person with cancer. So he supported Jeanne until the end. But he couldn't spend too much time with her anymore. He went home to his townhouse only late at night to sleep, when she was passed out from all the drugs in her system. He spent his days with me and my family.

I had opened up the Society of San Paolo Club. It was a two story red brick building, located in Williamsburg. It sat directly across the street from Crisci's Restaurant, which was one block off of Metropolitan Avenue. Inside was part social club, part catering hall. The front of the place had several tables and chairs set up for our regular customers. An archway in the back led to a small kitchen and prep area where Laura did all the cooking.

We ran private parties out of the San Paolo, but it was never open to the general public as an every day business. We never ran any illegal activity out of there either because I lived upstairs in a five-room apartment with Laura and the girls. All the dinners we served were to were friends or those recommended to us by friends.

I would sit with my father at one of the tables in the front, while Laura cooked all his favorite dishes in the kitchen—like *Pasta e Lenticchie* (Pasta with Lentils), *Pasta Piselli* (Pasta with Peas), boneless chicken baked in olive oil, and garlic with linguini on the side, and *Prosciutto Pomodoro*. My father was now in his mid 70s, and while he'd always displayed a strong physical presence, for the first time in my life I could see that he was starting to look older and more fragile.

When he first came to the San Paolo, I asked him, "What do you think of the new place, Daddy-O?"

"Nice," he said, looking around. "It's not the Hi-Way, but it's nice."

It was during these days spent in the San Paolo, just sitting there eating our meals, playing cards, and talking, that I came to really know my father. Far from the maddening crowd—and the business that had taken us all over the world and back—we were able to connect as people, man-to-man, father-to-son. Our business had taken us away from our families for long periods. It was a business filled with deceit and danger, where looking over your shoulder was always part of the deal. The stress of living that kind of a life cannot be understated. If it wasn't some hoods who were out to get you, it was the feds. Over time, living like that takes its toll on your mind and body. It was refreshing to just sit here with him. No rush. No wire taps. Eating pasta fagioli, with no fear.

"I've been meaning to tell you, TN," my father said to me one day. "You did good while I was away."

"I did my best."

"You did good."

"Thank you, Pop."

"Look at me, TN. I'm an old man now. I don't have my club anymore. I've seen men I loved and trusted and put in positions of power, disappoint and betray me. I've missed years of my life in the joint. But the one thing I'm proud of, the one thing makes me know I lived my life the right way, is that when I leave the face of this earth, it'll be of old age, and not because of a hole in my head."

"Want me to put that on your tombstone?" I joked.

"It's up to you. Put what you want. Then again, with you, who knows what the hell you'll put on my tombstone!"

We shared a laugh. It was great to listen to him, offering fatherly advice, and a perspective second to none. My father had lived a hard life but at the same time, a charmed life. He had seen it all, done it all, and he had wisdom to share. It was wisdom that I was finally old enough and smart enough to understand, even if it took me a little longer to actually follow it.

Then Jimmy Nap put his spoon down and turned serious again. "This thing I had, TN, it's all over with now. All the debts are settled. The last bets have been put in. The windows are closed. I turned everything over to the west side. I told all the supervisors that too. I told them, go out and find another way to spend your old age. Do something legitimate. Stay outta jail. Kiss your kids, for Christ's sake. Don't let them see you rot away in a cell somewhere. I tell you that too, TN. That's why you can't be in this business anymore. There was only room for one tough guy in this family and that was me."

My father was telling me to straighten myself out. He was giving me advice wrapped in a warning. I could hear what he was saying and he was right. But I was still too close to it all. His words were clear and correct. They were the words of a smart man, who knew the path I was headed down if I didn't change my ways. But I wasn't there yet.

"Could I tell you something?" I said to my father. "I think you were too easy on everybody. All the scum who used your name, your money, your clout to get what they wanted. Including me."

"Don't include you with them," he shot back. "I knew all the while what was going on with them, misusing my money, running around like the degenerates that they are. But you, I still can't figure you out. How the hell do you get by?"

"How do you think? I get by because I'm your son, Daddy-O. That's how I always got by."

That wasn't the last thing I ever said to my father, but I'd like to believe it was. I'd like to believe that my father knew how much I loved him, and all that he meant to me. I lived under his name, under his protection, under the cover of the respect that being his son afforded me. For much of my life I never felt like anything more than a prodigal son to him—exactly what Laura called me on the night I met her at the Hi-Way. But during those days in the San Paolo, I think he came to see me as something more.

As not just a parasite who took from him, but as a loving son who cared for him, deeply, until the very end.

My father never complained of any sickness other than feeling weak due to old age. I spoke to him on the telephone a day before he died. He told me he wasn't coming to the San Paolo and that he was staying home. I knew something was wrong because he never wanted to stay home in the daytime. He stayed with me and Laura and the kids from 11a.m. every day and a crew member of his would drive him home to his townhouse so he could sleep in his own bedroom, alone, without Jeanne. On the telephone that day he sounded like he wanted to be alone in his thoughts. So I let him be.

The following day, December 29, 1992, my father died in my arms in his townhouse in Manhattan. Actually he was in both mine and Laura's arms. He suffered heart failure at the age of 81. We were both holding him as he lay on the floor of his den. The EMS workers, who had been talking to Jeanne when we arrived, told us that he was already dead. Laura and I just couldn't believe it, so we both got down on our hands and knees on the floor where he was and put our arms under his head, tilting it up toward the ceiling. His body still felt warm as I spoke to him. "Dad," I whispered in his ear. "I'm so sorry. Can you hear me? I love you so much."

Tears fell from my eyes, down my cheeks and onto my father. Laura tried to get a reaction from him. She told him how much she loved him too. But he never spoke a word as his eyelids stayed closed. He didn't move. He was gone. Laura and I felt that he heard us when we said how much we loved him. I hope he did. I hope he knew. I just clung to him. I didn't want to let go, didn't want him to go. No matter how old you are you never want to lose a parent. Especially one who has been everything to you as my father had been to me. I had never had to face this cold world without him. Now I would. I clung to him for as long as I could, putting off what I knew was the inevitable, sad goodbye.

Mourners filed into Mount Carmel Church on the corner of Havemeyer and North 8th Street, as limousines sat parked outside and more limos pulled up. They came from all over to pay their final respects to Jimmy Nap. He was a man of great respect, who had no enemies and a sterling reputation with those who knew him. That's just how he wanted it to be. Everybody loved Jimmy Nap and they all wanted to say goodbye.

There was an empty parking space in front of the church. Big Mike, a 400 lb, six-foot tall guy, who wore dark glasses, a black raincoat and fedora hat, stood at the curb beside the space. A car pulled up and parked in it. Four Hispanic men got out.

Big Mike confronted them. "Hey guys, you can't park here."

The Hispanics cursed at him in Spanish as they walked away.

Big Mike didn't let people curse at him. "What did you just say to me? Do you know whose funeral this is?" Mike charged after them.

From the steps of the church, I saw the scuffle and rushed over to intervene. "Mike, it's okay, it's okay." Then I addressed the Hispanics. "Listen, this is my father's funeral. Jimmy Nap. Please move the car. We need the space for the hearse."

The Hispanics looked at each other and then one of them, in broken English, looked at me and spoke. "Jimmy Nap?"

"Yeah, my father, Jimmy Nap," I said.

"*Si*, he's good man."

Then one Hispanic said something to the other three in Spanish. He moved the car out from the spot in front of the church. The other three Hispanics then began to help Big Mike save spots in front of the church for the other limousines that were pulling up. "We help...we help..." said one of them as they offered their services.

"*Grazias*," I said to them, and then I turned to Big Mike.

"Everybody loved him, TN," Mike said to me.

I smiled and went back into the church.

It was a beautiful but very emotional funeral service for Jimmy Nap. Everybody who was anybody in the mob, boxing, and show business was there. The place was packed. Laura and me and the kids sat in the front pew as the priest gave his blessings over the coffin.

My daughter Helen, who was nine, ran from the pew to the coffin. She threw herself onto it and then turned to me in the front row. "Daddy...Daddy...Grandpa's pill box is in the casket. But he won't know when to take his pills, because he doesn't have his watch on his wrist."

Everyone in the church wept. There wasn't a dry eye in the house. I escorted little Helen back to her seat and sat down beside her. The priest continued with his blessing.

We buried Jimmy Nap in St. John's Cemetery in Middle Village, Queens.

After my father died, I became a complete and total alcoholic. I started drinking every day, all the time, day and night. Before my father's death, I was a heavy drinker, but I always had reason to be sober around him. I would drink fancy things, like martinis, or Manhattans. Never with Scotch or anything like that. Unless it was mixed with a martini. Or gin mixed with vermouth. But when my father died, I became a Dewars on the rocks type of drinker. I drank hard and fast. And constantly. I became an out and out drunk. I would sleep for 17 to 20 hours, then go out and drink for 72 hours. Then I would start all over again.

When you do this to yourself, day in and day out, for years and years, you begin to lose touch with things—like your family and what's going on at home. And sometimes you need a good swift kick in your ass to bring you back to reality.

Chapter 29

Sentenced to The VA Hospital

AFTER WHAT I DID TO THAT punk who touched my daughter in the college bathroom, I was arrested and brought to the Queens House of Detention. I lay flat on my back on a bunk in a small cell with a handful of other guys—all different types—from accountants to cold-blooded murderers. I passed the time by staring up at a cockroach crawling across the ceiling. The roach, who was doing a good job clinging on and defying gravity, suddenly lost its grip and fell on my bed. I stood and tried to locate him, not wanting him crawling on me, or worse, in me. I had heard of those things getting into people's ears and having to be surgically removed. So I lifted the mattress, shook it and turned it over.

"Don't turn that over," a voice called out to me from the other side of the cell. He was a skinny black guy with a turban on his head.

I shot him a "Don't fuck with me" stare.

"Don't you understand?" he continued, "That's where they're buried, man. In the mattress. The roaches. And if you feel any lumps, don't smash 'em. They come out after you."

The other guys in the cell laughed. The guy in the turban wasn't kidding. "I'm serious. Just leave your mattress the way it is. Trust me."

I looked at the guy for a moment and then put the mattress back down. "Thanks, guy," I said, and lay back down.

"Listen," he came closer to me. "What's your name?"

"Tony."

He extended his hand to me. "Tupac," he said.

"Two packs of what?"

The guys in the cell laughed again. I wasn't joking.

"Tupac Shakur."

"Two packs of Coors? Are you outta your mind? I don't have any beer in here, ya nut."

The guys all stopped laughing and it got tense in the cell. They thought I was making fun of him. I wasn't. Another guy called out to me, trying to keep the peace, "Don't you know who he is, man? That's Tupac Shakur, the rapper."

I looked at Tupac, who looked more surprised than angry, wondering if I was really making fun of his name of if I had never heard of him. "When you take me away from Sinatra, I don't know who the hell anybody is."

He came closer to me and he smiled. "I like you, Tony; like you, man. And since you don't know who I am or what I do, maybe I should show you a little sample."

Then Tupac started rapping. Right there in the cell. He made up all kinds of crazy rhymes with lyrics about the different guys in the cell. Voices called out and echoed down the corridor from the other cells, "Tu-pac! Tu-pac! Tu-pac!"

Then Tupac asked me to join in. "C'mon, Tony, now sing me an Italian rap song."

I refused at first but he kept it up. That Tupac was pretty damn persistent and a heck of a performer. High energy and high spirited. So I thought for a second, and said what the heck. Where was I, Carnegie Hall? How picky could these guys be? I began to sing "Strangers in the Night."

Cellmates from down the hall, who had moments ago been calling out cheers to Tupac, now shouted out boos. I turned to Tupac and said, "See, I told you..."

He laughed and put his hand out to me. I grabbed it and we put our arms around each other. I didn't know who he was before that night, or why he was there. That's one thing you never do in the tank. You never ask anybody why they're in there. I found out later he was there for allegedly raping his girlfriend. I also found out they had deliberately put us in the same cell, hoping we'd get into a brawl. I guess they underestimated how much we had in common.

Three years later Tupac was killed in a drive-by shooting in Las Vegas. I didn't listen to his type of music and only the most unusual circumstances could have ever brought us together. But life is funny that way. I remember feeling bad when I heard about Tupac's death. Whatever he was and whatever he was involved in, I will always remember him as a nice young man with a warm face who helped me pass one difficult night in a jail cell.

They set my bail at two hundred fifty thousand dollars. I had to wait seven months for the case to go to court. In those months, I drank the life right out of my body. Literally. By the time I got to the courtroom, I had more alcohol in my body than blood.

I stood beside my attorney in the court room of Judge Joan O'Dwyer. Just as she began to speak, I collapsed to the ground. The court officers and Laura rushed to me. I was dead. I thought for sure I was dead. But I could hear voices. They seemed distant, but they were there. Paramedics rushed in. He has no potassium. He has no blood. He has no this. No that. I could make out the voices. But I wasn't there. I was somewhere else. Far away.

I woke up in a bed in the VA hospital. Laura, Tanya, Veronica, and Helen were at my bed side. Laura was stroking my face.

An alcoholic coma. That's what they called it. Poisoned by the booze. This is what I did to myself. For nine long days I stayed like this. Somewhere between worlds. Heaven. Hell. Tucumcari. Who knows? But on the ninth day, I returned to purgatory.

The first thing I saw was my beautiful family. Right there beside me. Laura smiled through weepy eyes.

"Tony, you're back!"

I made a pact right then and there. No more hurting. No more drinking. No more. I would get clean. I was determined. I was ordered to stay in treatment at the VA Hospital as a recovering alcoholic.

After six months, the doctors sent word to Judge Joan O' Dwyer that I was fit to stand trial and defend myself against six counts of attempted murder. I was facing eight-and-a-half to 15 years in prison.

In Judge O'Dwyer's courtroom, the trial continued. "Mr. Napoli," she said to me, "I understand you would like to talk to the jury and tell them your side of the story."

I stood before the Judge, now clear of eye for the first time in a long time. I was well dressed and made for a sharp, credible appearance. I had a legal aide attorney because I was supposedly of low income and an outpatient assigned to the VA Hospital. But super attorney Barry Slotnick, known for handling high-profile criminal cases, was pulling the strings behind the scenes. At the time he was defending Vincent "The Chin" Gigante, boss of the Genovese family, against racketeering charges.

He was at the courthouse to sit as a spectator and school my court-appointed attorney between recesses. That appointed attorney, a total waste, followed Slotnick's instructions. Half the time he was asleep during the trial. He complained that he had to drive in from Westchester to the courthouse in Long Island City and that the traffic was unbearable. My courthouse was located in Court Square, Long Island City, so his commute was a short one. No wonder poor people go to jail: they have disinterested lawyers like this guy defending them! God bless Slotnick. He whispered in my ear during recesses, telling me that The Chin sent his love and that I can take the witness stand if I wanted to defend myself in my own words. So I did.

"Yes, Your Honor," I said, "I don't want to answer yes or no questions. I would like to give them my scenario. If it pleases the court."

Judge O' Dwyer, slim with light brown hair down to her shoulders, replied sternly, "It does." She allowed me to speak directly to the jury, uninterrupted by the DA. I turned to them. I looked across their faces. The jury was made up of six men and six women, and three alternates. Two of the jurors were black. The rest were white. They all looked like middle-aged, family oriented people. I wanted them to see me as a person, as a father who had snapped in defending his daughter's dignity. I appealed to their sense of family and decency. I made it all very personal.

"I'll tell you why I did what I did. You're looking at me today. I made a deal so that you would only look at me. See, you aren't going to look at my daughter in here. You're not going to meet her at all. I wouldn't put her on this stand. I wouldn't have her go through what she went through all over again. It's my job to protect her. That's what a parent does. What I did to that boy, I did because I went crazy."

I looked over to the punk, now dressed up in a suit, looking like a choir boy, and much younger than before, as he sat beside the prosecutor.

"I blacked out. I lost it. A father's love can be crazy sometimes. I was crazy. So no, you won't be meeting my daughter. But when you go home, whoever here has a daughter, or a granddaughter, of their own, who goes to school. Whatever school it is…college, high school, grammar school. When you see her leaving in the morning, with a big smile on her face, maybe a bow in her hair…looking as beautiful and innocent as the day she was born…that's when you'll meet my daughter. When you see your own child, and you think about somebody violating her, touching her in places no one should ever touch her in, that's when you'll see my daughter's face, in your own daughter's face. And maybe you'll see me in you too. Think, what would you do if somebody did to yours what he did to mine? I'm a father. It's my job to protect. That's what father's do. They protect their children. If that's a crime, then I'm guilty."

I eyeballed the jurors one last time. A few of them wiped away tears, and those who weren't crying were holding them back. Then I stepped down from the witness stand.

The jury took just twenty minutes to come back with five 'not guilty' verdicts. They found me guilty of only one count of misdemeanor assault. My personal plea, combined with a defense strategy, designed by Slotnick, to portray me as a veteran who had been damaged psychologically from the stress and agony of combat training, worked wonders with the jury. I was sentenced to 39 more months in the VA Hospital for psychiatric treatment and alcohol detox. It was just what I needed and a long time coming. I would enter that hospital a free man. I would leave a new man.

It wasn't just the court verdict. It was also the dream I had when I first entered that VA hospital. My father said, "It's time to do good, TN. I died rich. And ya know why? It wasn't because of the money or the power or anything like that. It was because I helped people. Some people are going to remember me for who I was, the company I kept, the rap sheet, all the bad. But for the people I touched...the ones whose rent I paid, whose kids I put through school, whose neighborhood I kept safe...they're going to remember me for what I did. For how I made their lives better. I protected my family. How many times did somebody come to me and say, "That TN, he did this or he did that, we're going to have to do something about it?"

"Too many times to count," I acknowledged.

"And I'd say, if you think you could take care of him, you go ahead and try. Meanwhile, they knew they could never touch you, or else they had to deal with me. I protected you. That's what a father does. He protects his child. But those days are over now, TN. You did a lot of bad. Now it's time to do some good. It's not too late. There's still time. Ya hear me? There's still time..."

Chapter 30

The Road To Sobriety

"My name is Anthony Napoli and I am an alcoholic."

This was the hardest sentence in the world for me to say.

At first, as I stood before a group of my fellow veterans in an Alcoholics Anonymous meeting at the VA Hospital in the Fort Hamilton section of Brooklyn, I could not get these words to come out of my mouth. The court told me I had to be there. Common sense told me I needed to be there. But fighting that little voice inside me, the voice of denial, was the hardest thing to get past. That voice didn't want me to be there and kept telling me so. *You can handle this, TN. You can stop on your own. You are in control.* That voice was holding onto the past, onto all I was, and keeping me from becoming all I could be.

For as long as I could remember, everything I had done in my life—good and bad, mostly bad, but everything to be sure—included drinking. I drank through it all. Through the laughter and the tears, the triumphs and the tragedies, there was always a drink in my hand. Births, deaths, sentencings, beatings, sit-downs, trips, crimes, all of it. The one constant was the drink. It was so habitual, so much a part of who I was, that to cut it out of my life felt like cutting off a limb. I didn't feel whole without a drink in me. As much as I knew I had to let go of it, if I wanted to save my life, I didn't want to let go—not too easily anyway.

The voice inside told me to wear my fedora hat and used my rough demeanor as a defense. The AA counselor told me to introduce myself to the group of about 15 other guys. So I started with the first part of the sentence.

"My name is Anthony Napo—"

The counselor cut me off. "Anthony, please, no need for last names. So if you would...please re-introduce yourself to the group."

"Oh...okay. Reintroduce myself. Yeah...sure." I tried again. "My name is Anthony. Just Anthony. But my friends, they call me Tony...Tony Nap. Or TN."

"Yes, okay, Tony. And...?"

"And what?" I asked in a huff. The voice kept telling me not to take no shit from nobody, especially this guy who was trying to take my right hand from me.

"Is there anything else you would like to add?"

"Like what?" He was starting to aggravate me. *Break his jaw*, said the voice.

"Anything else that might be relevant as you introduce yourself to this particular group."

"Not that I can think of, no."

Bust his head open. Teach him not to mess with you.

"Something everyone in the group has in common."

I shrugged. I wasn't taking his hint. Or I didn't want to. I knew what he wanted me to say. Admission is the first step toward healing. *Fuck him*, said the voice.

"The reason we're all here."

"Oh. Okay. Yeah. Yeah, I gotcha. My name is Anthony. My friends call me Tony...Tony Nap. And I am a...*professional drinker.*"

"Tony, excuse me for asking, but what exactly is a professional drinker?"

"A dressed-up bum."

The vets laughed. They knew that I was having fun with the guy.

"Tony, we prefer using the term 'alcoholic' in here."

"Alcoholic! Maybe you prefer it, not me. I'm no alcoholic."

"We all have to come to terms with our disease."

"Disease? Watch your mouth, Popcorn!"

"Yes, Tony, it's a disease you have. We all have it. So if you could, for the sake of the group, and yourself, please reintroduce yourself."

The voice said to belt him in the mouth and head down to the local pub. We don't need this shit!

I just looked at him and said, "Fine."

The voice suddenly went silent.

"My name is Anthony. My friends call me Tony. Tony Nap." Then I sucked in a deep breath, took a long pause and I said it. Once. Fast. No delay. "And I'm an alcoholic." I turned to the counselor. "There. Happy now?"

The counselor smiled and then he and the group spoke in unison, "Hi Tony!"

"We're happy to have you here, Tony," said the counselor.

Yeah, well, I wish I could have said I was happy to be there. I mean, I wanted to get better. I wanted to *be* better. For my own sake. For my family's sake. The whole thing. But having to come to grips with who you are, or rather, what you are, is the hardest step. It also happens to be the first and most important step. Call yourself a drunk, a professional drinker, a dressed up bum. An alcoholic. Call yourself whatever you want. The reality is that you drink too much alcohol and you have to stop. You have to find the strength inside yourself to recognize what it's doing to your life and stop.

"Is there anything else you would like the group to know about you? Anything about your life. Where you're from? Your favorite color?"

"Are you being smart with me again, Popcorn?"

"I mean no disrespect, Tony. I assure you. I just want you to feel free to share your thoughts and feelings openly in this room."

Thoughts and feelings? Where was the voice now when I needed it most? Somebody get me out of here before I turn into a fag!

"Tell us who you are, Tony."

What did he want, my whole friggin' life story?

"Only if you want to tell it," he said.

"How much time you got, guy?"

The vets laughed again.

"We have as long as it takes. In your case, I think we have 39 months," said the counselor, not letting me off the hook and not laughing.

I stood there in silence. *Shit. Where do I even start?*

"Start at the beginning," encouraged the counselor.

The beginning? Christ. The beginning was so long ago, I don't even know if I remember it anymore.

"How about someplace in the middle then?"

The middle's a little fuzzy too.

"The end?"

Well, we're not at the end yet, are we?

"Start wherever you want, Tony. And I mean that with all due respect. We're all ears."

All ears? I have to talk and they're all going to listen too? What kind of a place is this? "Well, I'm my father's son. That's probably the first thing you should know about me."

"What exactly does that mean?"

It means it was my blessing and my curse in life, being the son of a powerful and influential father.

"Could you please tell us more about your father?"

More? *Minchia!* He was worse than the feds. This guy really did want my whole life story. And I ended up telling it to him, and to the whole group too. Nobody fell asleep. When I was done I said, "So that's how I ended up here."

The group sat and stared at me, momentarily speechless. Maybe it was a little too much for them all at once. I'll tell you, for a guy who spent most of his life not talking, when I finally did, I had an awful lot to say.

"That is...uh...quite a story, Tony," said the counselor.

"I told you it would be."

He turned to the group. "Would anybody like to go next?"

No one responded. I guess I was a tough act to follow.

Then, suddenly, a veteran with a cowboy hat, stood and threw a chair across the room. He shouted, "I have a burning desire to kill my son! I had a dream last night that I shot him right in his fucking head!"

The group just looked at him in stunned silence.

Then the counselor spoke to the guy. "But you don't have any children, Fred."

"Oh...yeah...that's right," said the veteran and he sat back down calmly.

It was nice not being the craziest one in the room for once.

Well, the therapy I received at the VA Hospital in Fort Hamilton each day for five days a week, six hours a day was not just an AA meeting that you attend a few times a week. I was in a very strenuous program, and one of the finest in the country. And the government paid for it. Because, I'm a veteran who served and defended this great country of ours. I told my counselors that I want the whole world to know about that program.

To attend classes, I took trains and buses every day to study psychology; medical knowledge of the damage alcohol and drugs can do to the brain and other parts of the body; health and hygiene, and science. I also attended AA meetings one hour each day to listen to a speaker who had been dedicated to sobriety for five years or more.

After a little more than three years of therapy, the drinking stopped for good. The rest of my life started. It was time to make amends.

Chapter 31

Wiseguy Turns Nice Guy

God grant me the serenity to accept the things I cannot change, the courage to change the things I can, and wisdom to know the difference.

AT THE END OF EVERY AA meeting, the group recited the serenity prayer. It was brought to the attention of Alcoholics Anonymous in 1939 by William Griffith Wilson, known better as Bill W, co-founder of AA. Bill W liked the prayer and handed it out at a meeting one day and it has been part of AA ever since. It has also been used in Narcotocs Anonymous and other Twelve Step programs. I still recite it to this day.

After years of serenity prayers and therapy, I was on my way. The road to sobriety was bumpy at first, but I was managing to stay on course. My family me and were beginning to heal. Laura had taken Helen, my youngest, to therapy for a year as well, so she could learn how to live with an alcoholic father. Now I found out what everyone else had known for so long: that I was, indeed, an alcoholic. God bless these strong women I had in my life for their love and support.

AA was my first step toward a new life of "doing good," as my father had instructed me while in my dream, of making amends.

My next step was helping veterans who were confined to VA hospitals in completing their service-connected injury forms. This was not something I was ordered to do. It's something I wanted to do. I visited all the VA hospitals in the New York City area, using my own money to pay for expenses. So many of these men were entitled to money that they didn't even know was coming to them from the government. The government is good at taking money from people, not so good at giving it back.

I did my own research by reading VA regulations from a book called *Annual VA Benefits for Veterans and Their Dependants*. I also learned a lot from my own practical experience, while spending time doing my court-ordered therapy with other veterans at the VA hospital. I learned that Jimmy Carter, the worst president we ever had in this country, might actually have done something good. When he gave amnesty to all those draft dodgers who deserted their country during the Vietnam War, he also made it so that most of our other veterans from previous wars, who had undesirable discharges, could be upgraded to a general discharge. That would allow them to use the VA facilities and hospitals. And it would also allow them to apply for other benefits that would not have been available to them previously under an undesirable discharge.

I was also surprised to find out was how many wiseguys had served in the Armed Forces but didn't know they were entitled to benefits for their service. Just because they had a criminal record, many of them thought they had forfeited their right to their benefits. Not so. They still served their county and were entitled. In fact, on behalf of several guys, I argued that their service may have even led to their life of crime. It may have done something to their heads—damaged them in a way that made them violent and drawn to dangerous, illegal activities. Some of them said to me, "No, Tony, I was crazy way before I joined the service." But the government didn't need to know that.

Many of them were shocked to learn that the same government that had spent countless years and untold dollars trying to convict them would now be sending them a check every month for their service to their country.

When the guys found out that in some cases they were getting an extra $800 to $2,000 a month from Uncle Sam, they were thrilled. Even the ones who didn't need it were thrilled. I never met a wiseguy who didn't like making more money. Come to think of it, I never met *any guy* who didn't.

But some of these guys really did need the money. They weren't all bosses and capos. Some were lower level associates and guys who were barely eking out a living when they went away. Now they come out of jail and they have nothing left. In many cases, the government had confiscated their money and possessions when they were convicted. Now the guy just wants to collect a check so he can live and put food on his table every night. He probably never had a real job and no social security or any other form of income. Some of these guys were close friends of my father, so when they come to me for help, I'm happy to do it, at no charge.

Call it what you want. Hustlers hustling hustlers. Maybe some things never change. But this is my way of doing something good. Of making amends for all the bad I did.

I feel like I've gone from a bad guy to a good guy, from "a wiseguy to a nice guy." That's what a *New York Daily News* article said about me. Nobody ever called me a nice guy before. I like the sound of that. That *New York Daily News* article hangs on the bulletin boards in jailhouses and in most of the VA hospitals across the country to encourage fellow veterans and to alert them to the fact that whether they are wiseguys, recovering alcoholics, drug addicts, or all of the above, that they can follow my lead into the world of sobriety and that their country will pay them back for the sacrifices they made years earlier.

These veterans know they can contact me and I will do their paperwork as well as appeal their cases as a volunteer. Those veterans who are living in other states often contact me by e-mail and I direct them to the right department in their area for the help they need. Most days I am on the phone for a good part of the day helping recovering alcoholics to stop drinking.

Doing this kind of work makes me feel complete. It makes me feel that all the bad I did for all those years led to something good. It makes the journey seem purposeful. Like there was a reason for it all. If I knew doing good felt this good I would have done it years earlier.

And I certainly wasn't expecting to be honored. I have awards from the Military Order of the Purple Heart for the volunteer work I do for them. I have helped over 200 veterans receive compensation for their service-connected injuries. I belong to the commanders club of the service organization called Disabled American Veterans. Also, I have received awards from a service organization called "Rolling Thunder." They are a group of over a thousand Vietnam veterans who ride motorcycles to Washington, DC a few times a year to protest against various government policies that they believe are harmful to military men and women.

I have also helped the widows and dependent children of 100 % disabled veterans. I help to do the paperwork for them so that they can collect the proper compensation they are entitled to. I help the dependent children of veterans with the paperwork required for them to receive benefits while they continue their schooling until they reach the age of 26. Few widows know that they are also entitled to further schooling, and I advise them too. I have even help spouses and dependent children get their benefits while the veteran is still alive. I also assist disabled veterans as they get older and must be admitted to a VA residence because they have no one else to take care of them.

For me, this is all about giving back. I've spent plenty of time taking in my life. Now I am *giving*. My father always said that it was better to give than to receive. I never could see that. Now I see it. As usual, he was right.

Thanks to the AA program and its teachings, I am still sober. Fifteen years and counting. It is a far better and healthier way of life. If only I had known then what I know now. But at least I found out before it was too late.

Chapter 32

The Pen is Mightier Than The Sword

YOU'RE NEVER TOO OLD TO learn something in life and you're never too old to change. Part of that change involves an acknowledgement of the past, of where you have been, so you can appraise where you are now and where you are going.

Some people have asked, how the hell could he write this book? They haven't said that to my face, of course, but they've said it to others. I've heard it through the grapevine. My response: How could I *not?*

I never pretend that this book is anything but my point of view. It's how I saw it and heard it; how it was told to me and how I interpreted it. Another person, standing right next to me, could have seen it all a little different. But this is how it looked through my eyes, standing in my shoes.

For a guy who spent most of his life dousing his feelings in whiskey and using his fists to solve every problem that came his way, it is a revelation to now understand the value of *talking* about things. In the case of this book, in *writing* about things. When Edward Bulwer-Lytton wrote, in 1839, "The pen is mightier than the sword," I'm not sure he was thinking about lives like mine. But that old and clichéd adage really holds true here. Getting it all out of my system and onto the page has made all the difference. It beats drinking it away, or using brute force to push it away. I can see it all now, and so clearly too. All the faces, and names, all the beatings and bailouts, and bottles. I see the life I lived in a way that I never could have if I had not written this book.

I know how difficult that is for people in my old business to understand. We were raised on the notion that you never talk about the life. That you die with certain things. You take them to your grave. And I will take many things to my grave, believe me. But the things that I know can benefit others—addressing addiction, avoiding a life of crime, enhancing a relationship between a parent and child—these are issues that I want to share. My hope is that purging myself of my own flaws, shortcomings and in some cases, my out-and-out demons, can only help others.

When I have spoken of the life, I have only described how it related to me and my father. I have not told a rat's tale. I've told a son's tale. I have spoken only about *my* business, my life and world, not others. Where names have been mentioned, it has only been to display a historical context for the story. Those who know me know that I was not in this to glorify myself or to vilify anyone else. I was in it to search for the truth.

But let the critics do what they do, whether they be family members, old associates, whoever. Let them talk. I know why I wrote this book. I wrote it because I needed to write it. Because it's healthier to let certain things out than to try and bury them. I wrote it as an ode to my father. To explore what my relationship with him was, where it all went wrong and how I put it all back together again.

In 1961, in the middle of it all, my father was opposed to me writing a book. Now I understand why. Back then I was crazy to even consider it, and he told me so. In 2008, with all of it behind us, I think he would support my decision to write it and my reasons for writing it.

The best thing that has come out of this book is how often I have thought about my father since I started writing it. It's been like seeing him and talking to him all over again, every day for two years. All those memories came rushing back in, both good and bad. So many people spoke to me about my father, and they all spoke so lovingly. Their thoughts and memories of him were so warm, I couldn't help but feel good when I heard their words. But I never sugar coated the bad. The truth requires seeing and saying it all. Not just how you wish things were, but how they actually were.

Sometimes when I see some of the old fighters at the Ring 8 meetings, I think of my father and how proud he'd be of what became of the organization that he loved and helped found. I also think of another young fighter who stood in the ring so many years ago. One who could have been a contender, who could've gone to the Olympics. Now that kid was a fighter. He didn't know he would become a tough guy, a soldier, a fugitive, a hustler, a survivor. He took it on the chin more than a few times, that's for sure. But he always got back up from the canvas. In the end, he was his father's son, and his father was his don. In the end, that's all it ever could be.